HISTORY OF THE INDIAN WARS

HISTORY
OF THE
INDIAN WARS

HENRY CLAY TRUMBULL

GYAN

Published by

Gyan Publishing House
5, Ansari Road
Daryaganj, New Delhi-110002
Phone: 011-47034999, 9811692060
E-mail: books@gyanbooks.com

Distribution Network
gyanbooks.com
India, USA, Canada, UK, Australia

ISBN: 978-93-7014-690-7 (PB)
First Published, 1846

2nd Impression 2025

Printed at: Gyan Press, Delhi.

HISTORY OF THE INDIAN WARS
Author: HENRY CLAY TRUMBULL

History of the Indian wars

Henry Trumbull, Eleazer G. House

A View of Col. Johnson's Engagement with the Savages (commanded by Tecumseh) near the Moravian Town, October 5th, 1812.

1 Col. Johnson heroically defending himself against the attack of an Indian Chief.
2 The American Infantry firing upon a body of the enemy on the left.
3 A dismounted Dragoon personally engaged with one of the enemy.
4 The cavalry pursuing the retreating savages across the hills.
5 Tecumseh rallying his men, and encouraging them to return to the attack.
6 A savage in the act of scalping a wounded drummer of the American Infantry.
7 The savages, pursued by the cavalry, retreating to a swamp on the left.
8 The enemy (rallied by their commander Tecumseh) returning to the attack.

HISTORY

OF THE

INDIAN WARS:

TO WHICH IS PREFIXED A SHORT ACCOUNT OF THE

DISCOVERY OF AMERICA BY COLUMBUS,

AND OF THE

LANDING OF OUR FOREFATHERS AT PLYMOUTH,

WITH THEIR MOST REMARKABLE

ENGAGEMENTS WITH THE INDIANS

IN NEW ENGLAND,

FROM THEIR FIRST LANDING, IN 1620, UNTIL THE DEATH OF KING PHILIP, IN 1679.

BY HENRY TRUMBULL.

TO WHICH IS NOW ADDED

A HISTORICAL ACCOUNT OF THE SUFFERINGS OF THE INHABITANTS OF THE FRONTIER SETTLEMENTS BY THE SAVAGES, DURING THE FRENCH AND REVOLUTIONARY WARS;

AND ALSO THE

PARTICULARS OF EVERY IMPORTANT ENGAGEMENT WITH THE INDIANS, IN THE SOUTHERN AND WESTERN STATES AND TERRITORIES, TO THE PRESENT TIME.

A NEW EDITION,

WITH AN ENTIRE NEW ARRANGEMENT, ESSENTIAL CORRECTIONS, AND LARGE ADDITIONS.

"My countrymen, these things ought not to be forgotten; for the benefit of our children, and those that follow them, they should be recorded in History."—*Franklin.*

BOSTON:

PUBLISHED BY GEORGE CLARK.

1841.

TABLE OF CONTENTS.

Page.

CHAPTER XVII.

CHAPTER XVIII.

CHAPTER XIX.

CHAPTER XX.

CHAPTER XXI.

CHAPTER XXII.

TO THE PUBLIC.

There can be no subject more interesting, and more important to be preserved, than what relates to the settlement of this country, with the hardships suffered and perils encountered by our forefathers. They had not only to contend against all the evils attendant upon subduing a wilderness and guarding against starvation, but to defend themselves against a numerous savage foe, who were naturally jealous of the English, and opposed to their getting possession of their country. Though they at first seemed disposed to treat them as friends, yet most of the tribes in New England afterwards became their most inveterate enemies, and a bloody war continued till they were destroyed or driven from the country. For a period of something like a century and a half, these wars continued, and formed the most important subjects of discussion both in private circles and in legislative proceedings; during which time a great many extraordinary events took place, that were the subjects of narrative, which were published in pamphlets, or handed down from one generation to another by tradition. To preserve all that is worthy of being recorded, will be found not only interesting to the reader at the present time, but will be of the utmost importance to the forming a correct history of our country.

The following work is a compilation from various sources, and, as now published, forms a pretty correct account of the Indian wars, from the first settlement of the country to the present time. Mr. Trumbull prepared, as it is understood, from papers left by his ancestors, a history of these wars, from the landing of the pilgrims to the death of King Philip; with some account of the savage barbarities committed on our eastern and western frontiers. This, as far as it goes, is probably as correct and authentic an account of these events as can be expected to be obtained at the present day. He printed several large editions, which were sold throughout the country, and became universally known as "Trumbull's Indian Wars." The popularity of the work induced its enlargement, and additions were made from such materials as could be easily found, which swelled the bulk without much improving its value. Subsequently the copyright passed into the hands of Mr. George Clark, who, as a publisher, made the most of his bargain, by printing and supplying the market with a cheap and popular book. Still to increase the size, additions were made, from time to time, of such materials as could be easily obtained to enlarge the volume, by inserting public documents, private letters, and official returns, with all their details, which were of little interest to the common reader, and of no value as to history.

It was thought to be too important a work to be continued to be printed in such an irregular and imperfect manner; and the subscriber was solicited by the proprietor to make such alterations and additions as should be deemed necessary to render it more worthy the public patronage; which was undertaken more as a printer and corrector of the press, than as an author. The task has been attended with considerable labor, and whether well or ill done, must be left to the public to judge. Many things have been omitted, and others condensed, so as to make the language more uniform, and the narrative of events more intelligible to the reader. Nearly one hundred pages have been added, in which are given the most important cases of suffering by the inhabitants of the frontier settlements, from Indian hostilities, during the French wars, till the conquest of Canada, as also that of the Revolutionary war; to which has also been added the more recent Indian hostilities on our western and southern frontiers, with such particulars of the war with the Seminoles, or Florida Indians, as could be obtained.

The whole has been chronologically arranged and divided into chapters, with suitable heading to each, and a table of contents prefixed, for the convenience of reference; and it is confidently believed that it will be found to be a tolerably correct and faithful historical narrative of the wars with the aborigines of this continent, from the first discovery by Columbus to the present time.

It will not be improper here to remark, that all the accounts of Indian hostilities, horrid barbarities, and savage cruelties, are given on one side; for the poor Indian has no advocate, or any one to tell his story. No one comes forward to plead in his behalf, and state the causes that might perhaps justify him for committing these acts. Horrid acts of cruelty have been committed by civilized nations, when at war, but these are little thought of, and are suffered to pass off without notice. That the Indians have received great wrongs from the hands of the white man, cannot be denied; and that they should be actuated by a spirit of revenge, and retaliate for these wrongs, is perfectly natural; for they had no other means of getting any redress for their grievances. By appealing to the white man for justice, they only courted insult and greater wrongs. Dr. Franklin says, "We call them savages because their manners differ from ours, which we think the perfection of civility; they think the same of theirs. Perhaps, if we could examine the manners of different nations with impartiality, we should find no people so rude as to be without any rules of politeness, nor any so polite as not to have some remains of rudeness."

When this continent was discovered, it was found to be peopled by many millions of rational and intelligent beings, who were divided into nations or tribes, and had their forms of government and their laws, suitable to their condition; and many of them had made considerable advances in what is termed civilization. They no doubt enjoyed as much happiness as falls to the lot of the inhabitants of any other part of the world. But now where are they? It is true a few remnants of them still remain; but it is probable, ere another century passes away, nothing will be known of them except what may be recorded in history. These things seem mysterious; but it would be impious to murmur at the decrees of fate. There are changes constantly going on, not only in the human family, but in the natural world. The injustice done to the original inhabitants of this country, by driving them from where the Great Spirit had placed them and given them an inheritance, cannot be atoned for by man, but must be left to the decision of a higher tribunal than can be found on earth. Much has been said, and many plans have been proposed, to better their condition, by endeavoring to induce them to adopt some more certain plan of getting a living than by hunting; but in general this has only tended to make their condition worse; for it seems evident that they must exist in their natural state, or dwindle and waste away, becoming miserable and degraded outcasts.

The present policy of our government is to locate all that remain of the Indian tribes in our neighborhood beyond the Mississippi. But how long will they be suffered to remain there unmolested? The current of emigration to the West will soon come in contact with them. Their lands will be wanted by the white man; and the same difficulties will again take place, and the same tragic scenes be again enacted as heretofore. Besides, they will have numerous tribes between them and the Pacific Ocean, who will naturally join with them in defending themselves against the encroachments of the white people. This will form a sort of new era in the history of Indian warfare; and no permanent peace can be looked for until the whole Indian race shall be exterminated.

It cannot be expected that an impartial history of the aborigines of America can be written during the present age. Our prejudices are so firmly fixed by the relations we have heard from our childhood of savage cruelties, that it is difficult to divest ourselves of them. The popular feeling is averse to doing them justice. But it is to be hoped that when time shall have worn away these prejudices, some future historian will rise up and do them ample justice, by giving to the world a correct and impartial history of their rise and fall. The subject is a noble one, and the materials abundant for such an undertaking. They have produced many great men and heroes, who would not suffer in comparison with those of other times who have been celebrated in history. Their perceptions in regard to moral principle, their strict regard to truth, and freedom from hypocrisy and dissimulation, place them in many respects above those nations who possess the advantages of civilization. For the present, all we can do is to record the passing events of the day, and preserve whatever is worthy of being handed down to posterity as characteristic of this peculiar people.

E. G. House.

Boston, May 15, 1841.

DISCOVERY BY COLUMBUS.

To the avarice of mankind, and the enterprise of the Portuguese, we owe the present abundance of the gold, the silver, the precious stones, the silks and the rich manufactures. To that same avarice we owe the discovery of the New World, the idea of whose very existence was for a long while held so absurd, that the love of gain itself could not prompt men to the undertaking, though the boldest navigator of all ages offered to risk his life and reputation in the attempt.

Christoval Colon, or, as he is commonly called, Christopher Columbus, to whom the high honor of this most important of discoveries is due, is generally held to have been a Genoese, though this has been disputed, and it has been alleged, on very plausible grounds, that he was an Englishman. Be that as it may, he was a navigator skilful and enterprising beyond his age, and a brave commander. Yet, at the age of forty, he was very little known to his compatriots. The idea of finding a new terrestrial hemisphere does not appear to have occurred to him, but, judging from the spherical form of the earth, he thought it practicable to reach the East-Indies by sailing directly west from Europe, an opinion that is evidently correct, supposing that our continent did not bar his progress. It seems singular that this idea never occurred to any one before him, and still more so that the most enlightened men of the age treated his proposals with contempt. As his means were small and the expenses of his enterprise must necessarily be great, he first submitted his views to the government of Genoa, in hope to obtain the requisite aid, but they were rejected as altogether chimerical. He next offered his service as an explorer of unknown regions to the court of Portugal;

but though that nation was then distinguished above all others by its spirit of enterprise, and the reigning king, John the second, was a wise and sagacious prince, the prejudice of his counsellors, to whom the project of Columbus was referred, defeated his views in that quarter also. His next application was to Ferdinand and Isabella, reigning sovereigns of Castile and Arragon, but they were too much occupied in wresting the kingdom of Grenada from the Moors, to give his plans the consideration due to their importance. About the same time, he sent his brother Bartholomew to England, to solicit the assistance of Henry the seventh. That mean prince, though he rejected the proposals of the Genoese, determined to profit by them, and despatched an expedition on his own sole account, on the track Columbus had marked out. The courage of its commanders failed them, and they returned to England as they went.

Columbus passed many years in fruitless applications to the Court of Ferdinand and Isabella, but at last, Grenada being conquered and the war with the Moors at an end, Isabella had leisure to attend to Columbus. Possessed of a mind of no common order, she was not slow to see that his project was at once reasonable and of the highest importance, and she openly avowed herself his patroness. Her husband, a cautious and narrow minded, though sagacious prince, would not commit himself. All the aid he lent the adventurer was the sanction of his name. It is with a woman, therefore, that the world finder must divide the fame of his discovery.

Three vessels, two of them not larger than our ordinary fishing smacks, were thought sufficient for this important expedition. Expense, had long been the sole obstacle to the success of the adventurer's solicitations, yet the whole cost of his armament when equipped, and furnished with a twelvemonth's provision, was no more than 17,600 dollars. It must be remembered, however, that the value of the dollar was much greater then than it is now.

Columbus sailed from Palos, in Andalusia, on the 3d of August, 1492. He made the Canary Islands, and then stretched boldly westward into an unknown ocean, in latitude 28° north. From various causes, and among others a violent tempest, he made slow progress. His men were not free from the ignorance of the age, and a spirit of discontent arose among them which it required all his courage and prudence to restrain. Their terrors at last rose to the height of mutiny, and they talked of throwing their admiral overboard, so that he was compelled to compromise with them. He promised to abandon his enterprise and return home if they did not discover land within three days. He could now make this promise without much danger of frustrating his main object, for from the quantities of wood and weeds on the surface of the sea, from flocks of land birds, from a carved piece of wood that was picked up and from other appearances, he was assured that the shore was at hand.

On the night of the 23d of October a light was discovered from the mast head of the foremost vessel. The despondence of the crew was now changed to rapture. In the morning they landed at an island of surpassing beauty and abounding with inhabitants of a race wholly unknown to them. Both sexes went entirely naked, their manners were kind and gentle, and they received the Spaniards with joy and homage, taking them for celestial visitants. Alas! had they believed the white race fiends from hell, the treatment they afterwards received from them would almost have justified the supposition.

Columbus named the island San Salvador. It was one of the cluster since generally called the Bahamas, and is 3° 30′ more southerly of Gommorra, that one of the Canaries at which he took leave of Europe. Columbus did not tarry long—he had not come in quest of islands, and he was not satisfied. His discovery only served to confirm him in his original opinion, and he firmly believed that the land before him was one of the East-India islands. Sailing southward, he soon discovered the islands of St. Mary of the conception, Ferdinand and Isabella. He next made out Cuba and another large island, which he called Espagnola, and it is still known as Hispaniola, St. Domingo and Hayti. Here he built a fort and left a small colony, after which he returned to Spain, taking with him several of the natives of the newly found islands. On his course he discovered the Carribee Islands.

After having been seven months and eleven days absent, Columbus arrived at the port of Palos on the 15th of March, 1493. Great rejoicings were had on his arrival, for, from the sight of a few articles of gold he had brought from America the most extravagant ideas of the wealth of the new lands were entertained. The highest honors were paid to the intrepid mariner. The king and queen issued letters patent confirming to him and his heirs all the high privileges which had been agreed on, in case of his success before his departure, and his family were enrolled among the proudest nobility of Spain.

Still neither the Spaniards nor any other European nation entertained the least doubt that the lands Columbus had found were parts of India, for at that time the extent of India was unknown. For this reason it was that Ferdinand and Isabella gave them the name of "Indies" in the instrument by which they ratified their agreement with Columbus, and on this account they still erroneously bear that name, and all the aborigines of the new world are called Indians.

The success of Columbus had its natural effect. The whole enterprise of Spain was roused. No time was lost, no expense was spared, in equipping a fleet to accompany the great mariner back to the lands he had made known. A fleet of seventeen vessels was fitted out within six months and manned with fifteen hundred men, among whom many of the noble and the distinguished of Spain did not disdain to enroll themselves. It was one of the popular opinions of the day that the new found land was either the Ophir of Solomon or the Cipango of Marco Polo. Ferdinand himself caught the prevailing enthusiasm of the day and was desirous of securing his part of the golden harvest expected to be reaped in the new world. He applied to the Pope to be invested with a right in the lands discovered, or to be discovered. A shew of a religious motive was necessary, and he made his zeal to convert the natives to the Catholic faith the basis of his hypocritical plea; not without the desired effect.

The reigning pope, Alexander the fourth, was one of the vilest of men and cared as little for the conversion of the heathen as Ferdinand. But he had the interest of his own family at heart and the friendship of the Spanish monarch was of no little importance to him. He was himself a native of Arragon. His favor and pontifical sanction only were asked, and these involved neither expense nor risk. He therefore made no difficulty in bestowing upon Ferdinand and Isabella "all the countries inhabited by infidels which they had discovered." Yet it was necessary to prevent this grant from interfering with one of the same character that he had made not long before to the crown of Portugal. He therefore decreed that an imaginary meridian line one hundred miles to the westward of the Azores should be the boundary between the parties. All lands eastward of this notable boundary he conferred on the Portuguese; all westward upon the Spaniards.

Columbus sailed on his second voyage of discovery from Cadiz, on the 25th of September 1493. On his arrival at Hispaniola he had the mortification to learn that all the colonists he had left there had been put to death by the natives, a just punishment for their lawless ravages, tyranny and cruelties. Nevertheless, he was not discouraged. He laid out the plan of a large city on a plain near a capacious bay, to which he gave the name of Isabella his royal patroness and appointed his brother Diego to preside over it, as deputy Governor. He then, on the 24th of April 1494, set sail with a ship and two other small vessels in quest of new discoveries. He touched at many small islands on the coast of Cuba, and also at the great and fertile island Jamaica, which he found inhabited by a bold, warlike and ferocious race, since called the Caraibs, or Caribees, radically distinct from the natives of Hispaniola, of whom they were the terror and the scourge. He then returned to Hispaniola.

During his absence the Spaniards, insolent and exulting in the consciousness of superior power, had oppressed and abused the innocent and gentle natives in the most wanton manner. Scarcely an injury can be conceived that was not inflicted on them. These abuses, as freely bestowed as they were little deserved, had at last roused the timid natives to insubordination and vengeance. It was now a question whether the foreigners or the rightful owners of the soil should be masters of the island. Columbus determined on war. He attacked the natives in the night, while they were assembled in the middle of an extensive plain, and completely routed them, without the loss of a man. It has before been hinted that this race of savages were not warlike by disposition or habit. The thunder of the Spanish cannon, being strange was also appalling to them, and the charge of the cavalry was still more so. It is common for all nations who are unacquainted with the horse to suppose him to be a rational creature, or at least that he and his rider are parts of one and the same animal. It was so with the natives of Hispaniola. Their undisciplined masses could ill withstand the real shock and the superstitious terror of the charge of a mounted squadron sheathed in steel from top to toe on whom their lances and arrows made not the least impression. The Spaniards had yet other and no less dreadful allies. These were bloodhounds whose ferocity nothing could quell, who fastened upon and tore them limb from limb. Under such circumstances it is not wonderful that a vast multitude of Indians were defeated by a small band of trained soldiers. They fled ; great numbers were slain and many more were consigned to galling and hopeless slavery.

The character of Columbus stands very high and we think deservedly so in the estimation of mankind. He is justly venerated as a man whose courage, fortitude and perseverance no dangers, obstacles or sufferings could shake, and was undoubtedly a sincere and pious Christian after the manner of his sect and times. Nor was he less distinguished for his private virtues and amiability of character. His severity to the natives of the New World admits of much extenuation. The Indians were not christians, and to the unchristian christian world of the fifteenth century it seemed of little consequence what sufferings might be inflicted on any men without the pale of the church. The distressed state of the Spanish colony, too, pleads in favor of Columbus. Unaccustomed to labour, and strangers to the deadly climate of the West-Indies, great numbers of the colonists fell victims to disease, hardship and exposure. The rest were rapidly declining, and such had been the injuries inflicted by them on the natives, that no kindness on their part could have re-established confidence and friendship. It may be said, too, that Columbus treated the unhappy savages with less inhumanity than his successors in the career of discovery and conquest. Still, these matters are but extenuation, not justification of his conduct, which ought ever to be viewed with abhorrence. It is painful to detract from the character of acknowledged and surpassing merit, yet it is the duty of the annalist to make truth the guiding star of his course, no matter who suffers. If Columbus had not formed a specific design to wage an offensive war against the natives previous to his second departure from Spain, and consequently before he was aware of the destruction of his people whom he had left in Hispaniola, it is yet certain that the idea of being involved in hostilities with the simple Indians had entered his mind. The fact, that he carried a large number of fierce and powerful bloodhounds with him proves it.

He had found the natives peaceable and friendly, and had, therefore no reason to apprehend that they would commence hostilities. The cavalry he took with him, as they were feared and reverenced by the Indians, were quite sufficient for the security of the colony, supposing that friendship with them had been an object. But it was inconsistent with the views of the Spaniards to treat them as a free people. Lust of gold was the grand incentive of the settlers, and as some of the natives were decorated with golden ornaments, and it was supposed that the mountains of the island abounded with the precious metals, great expectations had been formed by the patrons of Columbus and the nation at large. His interest and his ambition urged him to fulfil those expectations as far as possible. Gold could not be obtained without the aid of the Indians, who were so indolent from constitution, habit and climate that nothing but actual compulsion could induce them to labour. To avoid the mortification of failure, therefore, and to secure farther support, Columbus deliberately devoted a harmless race of men to slaughter and slavery. Such as survived the massacre of their first dreadful defeat, and retained their liberty, fled to the mountains and inaccessible fastnesses of the island, which not affording them an adequate maintenance, they were obliged to purchase food of their cruel invaders with gold. The tribute imposed on them was rigorously exacted. The wretched remains of this once free and happy people reduced from plenty to starvation, from freedom to miserable, laborious and hopeless slavery, gave themselves up to despair and perished miserably. Such was their invincible repugnance to labour, that thousands hung and otherwise destroyed themselves to avoid it. In less than half a century, a population of three millions had dwindled to a mere handful. These are historical facts, and yet Columbus is extolled for his humanity!

Columbus and his companions seem to have discovered two distinct races of men in the West-Indies. The natives of Hispaniola, Cuba, the Bahamas, &c. are described as having been black, small of stature, feeble of body and mind, kind, humane, hospitable, excessively indolent, averse to exertion, whether physical or mental and in no wise addicted to, or fitted for war. Their scourge and terror, the other race, since called the Caraibs or Carribees inhabited Jamaica, the Carribee and many other islands. They were a cruel, fierce and warlike people, and carried death and desolation wherever they went. They were by no means indolent: their canoes visited all parts of the West-Indian Archipelago and they were no strangers to the main land of North and South America. They did not submit tamely to the aggressions of their invaders, but met them boldly and struck them blow for blow, till they became nearly extinct. A small remnant of them still survives on the island of St. Vincent, but so amalgamated with the negroes that their national character and physiognomy are almost entirely obliterated. Yet they have not lost the spirit and bravery of their ancestors. It is not a century since they maintained themselves against all the forces that could be detached from the other British West India islands against them. Their cause was just, for they fought for the lands of their inheritance, and after a protracted struggle, the authorities made peace with them.

Many tales are told of the ferocity of the Caraibs, which, as they come from their enemies must be received with due allowance. Still no doubt remains but that they were a cruel people, much like our North American Indians, from whom no doubt they sprung. In one remarkable particular they differed from the other aborigines. They flattened the heads of their infants, while the skull was yet soft and plastic, between two boards, so that in manhood the forehead was flattened and depressed to an extraordinary degree. It is related of some of them that they could look perpendicularly upwards without throwing their heads back in the least. The same absurd practice prevails among the Flat Heads and other tribes on the Columbia River to this day.

THE CONQUEST OF MEXICO.

We presume only to give a brief abstract of the most important Indian war that ever took place. The facts attending the subversion of the powerful empire of Mexico, are too many and two well known to need that we should dwell upon them.

Diego Velasquez conquered Cuba in the year 1511, and, as well as others of the Spaniards subject to his authority, entertained the idea of making further discoveries to the westward. With the aid of Francisco Hernandez Cordova, a wealthy planter, he fitted out three small vessels on board of which a hundred and ten men embarked and sailed from St. Jago de Cuba on the 8th of February 1517. Standing directly west, they made land in twenty-one days, which proved to be the coast of Yucatan. They found the natives dressed in cotton garments, dwelling in houses of stone and otherwise exhibiting tokens of (for the age) high civilization.

They attacked the Spaniards with great bravery and wounded fifteen of them by the first flight of their arrows, but were in their turn so astounded by the fire arms, that they fled in the utmost dismay.

Cordova took two prisoners and continued along the coast to Campeachy, where, stopping to water at the mouth of a river at Potonchan, he was again furiously attacked by the natives and forty seven of his party were killed and only one of the whole body escaped unhurt. After this fatal repulse nothing remained for them but to return to Cuba.

But they had discovered a populous and rich country, which was sufficient to re-awaken the cupidity of the Spaniards. Velasquez fitted out four ships, with two hundred and forty men and gave the command to Juan de Grijalva. They landed at Potonchan and defeated the Indians, who, however, fought with desperate valour. As the Spaniards sailed along the coast they had ample leisure to admire the beauty of the country, the villages and the cities. They gave the land the name of New Spain. Landing at Tabasco, they learned through the captives taken in the former expedition that they were in the dominion of a powerful prince named Montezuma. They made a very satisfactory survey of the coast, and then returned to Cuba after an absence of about six months.

On his return Grijalva found an expedition fitted out for the conquest of Mexico, the command of which was ultimately given to Hernando Cortez, a Castilian of noble blood and unquestionable military abilities. They soon set sail. The fleet consisted of eleven small vessels, on board of which were six hundred and seventeen men, thirteen of whom only were armed with musquets, Thirty-two others carried cross-bows and the rest were armed with swords and spears. They had also sixteen horses, fourteen small field pieces. With this small force Cortez set out to make war on the monarch of dominions more extended than Spain itself. Religious fanaticism urged his soldiers on. " Let us follow the cross," said they, " for under that sign we shall conquer."

At Tabasco the Natives gave Cortez battle, but were beaten in several engagements with great slaughter. These disasters, together with the terror of the horses and fire arms, broke their spirit. They sued for peace, paid tribute to Cortez and acknowledged the king of Spain as their sovereign.

At Tabasco, deputies from the governors (under Montezuma) of two provinces waited on Cortez to know his intentions and to offer him assistance. The wily Spaniard assured them that he came in perfect friendship, as an ambassador from a powerful monarch, upon business of such importance as could only be entrusted to Montezuma himself. He therefore desired to be conducted to his presence. The Mexicans were much embarrassed, neither daring to offend Cortez by refusal, nor conduct the Spaniards to their king who had a sovereign dread of them. They endeavored to temporize with the invaders and to conciliate them with rich gifts, which, however, only inflamed their cupidity.

In eight days an answer was received from the Indian King, accompanied by presents of great value to render it palateable. The purport of Montezuma's message was, that though he sent the Spaniards these tokens of his regard, he would not allow them to approach his capital, or even to remain in his dominions. But Cortez adhered to his original views, and a second message was despatched to Montezuma, reiterating his proposal. This prince, though the fiercest and most warlike who ever sat on the Mexican throne, with a vast extent of territory, millions of hardy subjects and very considerable revenues, was seized with a fit of irresolution, in which his people participated. It arose from an ancient tradition that the empire was to be ruined by a race of men from the east. Nevertheless Montezuma finally made up his mind to order the strangers to leave his dominions immediately.

In the meanwhile mutiny broke out in the Spanish camp. After raising Cortez to the command, Velasquez had become jealous of him, and had used all endeavors to make him unpopular in the army. His adherents, on receiving the final orders of Montezuma;

made choice of Diego de Ordaz to remonstrate with Cortez on the imprudence of attempting the conquest of a mighty empire with so small a force. Accordingly he gave orders to his troops to re-embark, which was so little to the liking of the majority of his troops, who were not in the interests of Velasquez, that they revolted. The chief, therefore, feigning to yield to their wishes, which were in fact his own, rescinded his orders, and prepared for his career of conquest. To this effect he established a form of government, and magistrates and officers were appointed without any regard to the authority of Velasquez. Cortez himself resigned his command, and was reinvested with it, by the suffrage of the troops, so that he no longer looked up to the governor of Cuba as the source of his authority. His next step was to arrest the most factious of the partizans of Velasquez and to throw them into irons. He was afterwards reconciled to them and they proved faithful to his interest.

Soon after the inhabitants of the province of Zampoalla offered to rebel against Montezuma, of whose tyranny and cruelty they were weary, and to assist Cortez. The cacique of Quibislan followed their example, as did also the Totonaques, a fierce tribe of mountaineers. This advantage was counterbalanced by discontents and conspiracies in the Spanish camp, to which Cortez put an end in a most desperate manner. He caused his ships to be broken up, and thus left his followers no choice but to conquer or die.

Cortez marched from Zampoalla on the 16th of August, with five hundred men, fifteen horse and six field pieces. The cacique of Zampoalla furnished him with provisions and with two hundred men to carry them. On his arrival at Tlascala, the fierce inhabitants of that province, who had long maintained their independence against the sovereigns of Mexico, attacked him, but being worsted with great loss in several battles, they treated for peace and agreed to assist the Spaniards against Mexico. They joined the ranks of Cortez to the number of six thousand, and the united forces advanced to Cholula, a place considered holy by the Mexicans and the sanctuary of their gods. Here Montezuma had given orders that the invaders should be well received, with what object the reader will presently see.

It was presently discovered that the inhabitants had entered into a conspiracy to cut the Spaniards off; upon which Cortez drew up his forces and attacked them sword in hand, while the Tlascalans pressed them in the rear. The massacre lasted two days, during which every enormity was committed. Six thousand of the Cholulans perished, before Cortez agreed to pardon the remainder.

From Cholula, Cortez marched directly to Mexico, where he was received with great distinction. First came out a thousand men in garments of cotton and wearing plumes to salute him and announce the approach of Montezuma. Then appeared two hundred more, clad in uniform. After these approached an assemblage of richly dressed nobles, in the midst of whom was the king borne in a litter on the shoulders of four of his principal subjects, with all the paraphernalia of regal splendour. Before him marched three officers with golden rods, which when they lifted, the people bowed their heads and hid their faces, as unworthy to look at so great a monarch. Cortez dismounted, and Montezuma alighted to greet him, while his attendants spread cotton cloths in the street that his feet might not touch the ground. However, nothing material passed. The king conducted Cortez and his allies to the quarters destined for them, which was a large building surrounded by a stone wall; a very defensible position, which the Spaniards lost no time in fortifying.

Mexico is situated in a large plain surrounded by mountains, and built on the shore and some small islands in a lake. The access to the city was by artificial causeways or streets, which were of great length. One was a mile and a half long, another three miles and a third six miles. In each of these causeways there were openings through which the water flowed, and covered with timber which could easily be removed. The temples of the gods and the houses of the nobility were of great magnitude, but the common people lived in mere huts, regularly ranged on the banks of the canals which passed through the city. The market was so spacious that forty or fifty thousand people carried on traffic in it. The whole city was estimated to contain sixty thousand inhabitants. Every thing gave token of a high state of civilization, and yet, strange to relate, all this splendour was achieved by a people who were strangers to the use of iron and who had no domestic animals.

In the mean while a Mexican army had marched to subdue the Indians, who had thrown off the yoke of Montezuma and the Spanish garrison which Cortez had left behind him had sallied out to the assistance of their allies. Though the Mexicans were defeated, Escalante, the Spanish commander, and seven of his men were killed. Another was taken alive and beheaded and his head was sent round to the different cities to shew the Mexicans that their invaders were not immortal, as they had believed. From this and other causes, Cortez resolved to get Montezuma into his power as a hostage for the peaceable behaviour of his subjects. At his usual hour of visiting the king, he took with him ten of his soldiers, and thirty more followed, as if by mere carelessness. On meeting, he reproached Montezuma bitterly with the late conduct of his army, and finally, compelled him to go with them to their quarters. A tumult broke out among the people at this flagrant insult, and the king was obliged to appease them by declaring that he went with his captors by his own free will and consent.

Though he was received and treated with respect, the king was closely watched. The general and seven of the officers of his army were given up to the Spaniards to appease their resentment, who tried them by a court-martial and sentenced them to be burnt alive, for doing their duty as brave men and loyal subjects. The Mexicans looked on and saw them die without attempting to rescue them. Cortez took other measures to insure his safety, and built two brigantines which gave him the command of the lake. All this was done in the name and with the enforced sanction of Montezuma.

Encouraged by the king's tame submission, Cortez urged him to declare himself a vassal of the king of Castile, and he was base enough to comply. The chief men of the empire were assembled, and in a set speech, but with tears and groans, he declared his submission. But to allay the indignation of the people, Cortez proclaimed that his master had no intention to dethrone the king, or to alter the laws of the empire. The present made by Montezuma on this occasion, together with all the gold and silver the invaders had received from him and his subjects at other times, was melted down and amounted to six hundred pesos, exclusive of jewels and ornaments of gold and silver. About half of this treasure was divided among the soldiery.

The spirit of resistance among the Mexicans was at last roused by an attempt on the part of Cortez to convert them forcibly to the christian faith. From that moment they harbored the idea of revenge. An event occurred which seemed for a time to favor their designs. Velasquez fitted out an expedition to supplant Cortez. He despatched Pamphilo de Narvaez to Mexico with eighty horse, eight hundred foot, of whom eighty were musketeers, a hundred and twenty cross-bow men and 12 pieces of cannon. He landed in safety, interested the natives in his favor and even contrived to establish a secret correspondence with Montezuma, who regarded him as a deliverer. Cortez proposed terms of compromise, but they were rejected with scorn. Cortez then marched against Narvaez with two hundred and fifty men. He attacked the position of Narvaez in the dead of the night, obtained a complete victory and in the morning the new comers laid down their arms. Narvaez himself was taken and thrown into fetters. The prisoners, however, were treated with kindness, and such was the address of Cortez that almost all of them were induced to join his standard.

But during the absence of Cortez, the Mexicans rose upon the Spanish garrison in the capital, killed and wounded several of them, destroyed their magazine of provisions and burned the two brigantines. The danger of their monarch no longer restrained them, for their fury was roused to the utmost pitch by an unprovoked massacre of

3

a great number of their people, perpetrated by the Spaniards at a religious festival. All cried aloud for vengeance. Cortez immediately made haste towards the city with his troops and two thousand Tlascalans and arrived just in time to save the garrison from destruction. Nevertheless, the natives attacked a considerable body of the Spaniards in the market-place and defeated them with some loss. The next day they assaulted the Spanish quarters in great numbers, in the most heroic manner. Though the artillery mowed them down like grass, though every blow of sword and lance fell with deadly effect on their naked bodies, the utmost efforts of the invaders were scarcely sufficient to withstand them, and they only retired when it was too dark to fight any longer. The next day Cortez made a rally, and the whole day was spent in mortal combat in the streets. Vast numbers of the natives fell and a part of the city was burned. On the other hand the Spaniards were dreadfully annoyed by showers of stones and arrows from the house tops, and were finally compelled to retire with a loss of twelve killed and sixty wounded. Another sally met with the same success and the general himself was slightly wounded.

Finding that he had underrated the Mexicans, and that he could no longer maintain himself in their capital, Cortez bethought himself that he might make use of Montezuma to overawe his subjects. On the morrow, when the Indians advanced to renew the attack, he produced the captive king, clad in the robes of royalty, upon the battlements. At the sight of their sovereign, the weapons dropped from the hands of the Indians. But the discourse he addressed to them, though intended to sooth and persuade them to peace, only served to exasperate. They poured in such a volley of stones and arrows in the transport of their indignation, that before the Spaniards had time to withdraw or defend the unhappy prince, he was struck by two darts, and by a stone in the temple. Then, struck with horror at their own violence, they fled. The wounds of the king proved mortal.

Cortez now saw that a retreat was necessary, but this was not easy. The Indians seized a high tower that overlooked the Spanish quarters and thence so annoyed the Spaniards, that it was found necessary to storm it. Thrice were they repulsed, and it was only when Cortez headed his troops in person that the Mexicans were dislodged. A dreadful carnage ensued, the natives defending themselves to the last with heroic valor. Two young nobles resolved to sacrifice themselves, so that they might rid their native land of its arch enemy. They approached Cortez in attitudes of submission, seized him and endeavored to drag him with themselves, from the summit. In the very act of falling, the Spanish leader shook them off, and the gallant youths were dashed to pieces. The tower being destroyed, the Spaniards prepared to retreat.

They marched out upon the shortest of the causeways before mentioned in the dead of the night. They had prepared a portable bridge, by which to cross the traverse cuts in it and placed it across the first interstice. While they were crossing, the Mexicans hemmed them in and attacked them on every side. The bridge by some means became fast wedged where it was placed. All Mexico swarmed to the slaughter. Fresh warriors instantly filled the place of the fallen. Weary of carnage, the Spaniards gave way before the multitude, and the confusion was soon universal. Horse and foot officers and soldiers, friends and enemies were intermingled in mortal struggle.

Cortez, with a few followers, forced his way over the two remaining breaches in the causeway, for the bodies of the slain served him for a bridge. Having formed his men on the main land, he returned to the assistance of the main body, and finally succeeded in effecting their retreat and his own. But less than half of his army survived the horrors of that dreadful night. Velasquez de Leon, the second in command, perished. All the artillery ammunition and baggage and the greater part of the horses were lost. Two thousand of the Tlascalan allies were also slain.

As the Spaniards retreated toward Tlascala, swarms of the natives hung upon them and harrassed them at every step, and thirst and famine threatened to finish what the sword had begun. At the pass of Otumba they came upon the grand Mexican army drawn up in countless myriads to oppose their passage. Cortez alone of the whole Spanish army did not despair at the sight. He recollected that the great banner of the empire was always carried by the general, and that its fall was considered by the Mexicans decisive of the fate of the day. Without hesitation he led his men to the charge, aiming wholly at the sacred flag. After a desperate conflict he slew the Indian general with his own hand, the banner fell and the countless host of natives fled in dismay. On the next day the Spaniards entered the Tlascalan territories, where they were received with the greatest kindness, for hatred of Mexico was deeply rooted in the hearts of the Tlascalans.

It is inconsistent with the plan of this volume to relate how Cortez quelled mutinies among his own troops, punished some disaffected native tribes and won the love and confidence of others, or how he received reinforcements from the Spanish West-Indies. Those who would have a minute detail of his proceedings must seek it in histories of greater pretensions than this. Suffice it that six months after his disastrous retreat he again set out for Mexico with five hundred and fifty infantry, forty horse and ten thousand Tlascalans.

Guatimozin, nephew of Montezuma, now filled the throne. He took every measure that wisdom and courage could suggest to avert the storm that threatened him, but all in vain. Cortez did not venture directly to the capital, but spent three months in reducing the neighboring towns and in building vessels upon the lake of Mexico. The inhabitants of many of them threw off their allegiance and joined him. What was of more importance a reinforcement reached him from Hispaniola, consisting of two hundred men, eighty horses, two heavy cannon and a considerable supply of arms and ammunition. He now laid siege to Mexico, cut off the supplies of fresh water, and by means of his fleet so straitened the Mexicans that the emperor gave orders to attack it. The natives attempted to board the vessels in canoes, but were repulsed with immense loss. They were more fortunate in repelling the direct attacks of the invaders. The natives defended themselves with the most desperate bravery. For more than a month by night and by day, by land and by water, one furious conflict succeeded another. Several of the Spaniards were slain, all were worn out by hardship and privation. Disconcerted at the obstinacy of the natives, Cortez resolved to set the fortune of the war on the hazard of one furious assault. It was unsuccessful. His troops forced their way into the city indeed, but it was only to be driven out again by the infuriated multitude. The rout was complete. Cortez himself was dangerously wounded and nigh being taken. Twenty Spaniards perished in the conflict and twenty more who were taken prisoners were sacrificed to the Mexican god of war within sight of their defeated companions.

Nevertheless Cortez persevered, but in a more cautious manner. He advanced slowly upon the Mexicans, continually gaining ground and keeping what he gained. Still they defended every inch of the ground, though great numbers of them fell daily and the survivors suffered sorely from hunger. To fill up the cup of their misery a contagious distemper broke out among them. Guatimozin still scorned all terms of capitulation.

At last the invaders had laid three fourths of the city in ruins and effected a secure lodgment in the centre of it. The remaining quarter was hard pressed. Guatimozin was taken in an attempt to escape by water. He appeared before Cortez with great dignity. "I have done what became a king," said he. "I have defended my people to the last. Nothing now remains but to die. Take this dagger (touching the one the Spaniard wore) plant it in my breast and end a life that can no longer be of use."

Resistance was now over, and Mexico was fallen, after a siege of seventy-five days. The Spaniards, however, were disappointed of the spoil for which they had contended so fiercely. When his downfall became inevitable, the Indian emperor had ordered his treasures to be thrown into the lake. The Tlascalans carried off the greater part of the remaining spoil. The sum divided by the soldiers was so small that they became highly exasperated against Guatimozin, who still refused to discover where he had hidden his treasure. Entreaties and threats were alike wasted upon him. To pacify his brutal followers the miscreant Cortez put the unhappy sovereign and his chief favorite to the torture, which they bore with inflexible fortitude, and finally stretched them upon a bed of living coals. Overcome by the extreme agony his fellow-sufferer turned an imploring eye upon the monarch, as if to ask permission to reveal all he knew. The royal sufferer understood it and scornfully asked " Am *I* on a bed of roses ?" The reproach was enough—the favorite was silent and expired. The monarch himself was released and reserved for other indignities and sufferings.

We have now done with the greatest of Indian wars. It presents the melancholy spectacle of a powerful empire subverted, a whole nation decimated and thrown back from a high state of civilization into barbarism, and a paradise changed into a den of blight, blood and desolation—a hell upon earth and for what ? To gratify the lust, avarice, bigotry and ferocity of a handful of vagabonds, miscreants and bloodhounds. Have mankind been the gainers by the event. O no !

" Freedom shrieked when Guatimozin fell."

May that bloodiest page in the book of History, the conquest of Mexico be forever blotted out. Or if man must still be benefitted by the accursed record, let it remain. Let the modern Spaniard blush as he reads the crimes of his countrymen. Let Cortez live in story, let his name be remembered, but only to be mentioned with abhorrence. The vagabond cut-throat who knew no law but that of the strongest, who acknowledged no right, who respected no tie, who possessed no virtue or kindly feeling, the invader, the robber, the murderer by wholesale, the hypocrite, the monster, may well serve as a beacon of everlasting infamy to future ages. All his talents, all his fortitude, all his valor are insufficient to wipe out the shame of the least of his actions.

Turn we to a brighter picture; to the heathen and barbarian Guatimozin, who was all that Cortez was not. A wise statesman, a true patriot, a skilful general and a heroic warrior. He slew none unjustly, he robbed none, he invaded none, he oppressed none. Called to the helm at a stormy crisis, he did not shrink from it, or spare to oppose his naked breast to the mail clad Spaniards. His spirit never failed him, not even in tortures at which humanity shudders. The warrior and patriot king is forgotten, and his atrocious oppressor is remembered with admiration. Such is human perversity.

THE CONQUEST OF PERU.

In 1524, three extraordinary men lived in Panama, in New Spain, viz: Francisco Pizarro, Diego de Almagro and Hernando Luque. Pizarro was a bastard, and in early life a swine herd, after which he became a soldier. He was a very brave man, but so ignorant that he could neither write nor read. Almagro was a foundling, and a soldier also. He was a man of intrepid valor, great activity and likewise of an open and generous character; but he lacked the craft and cunning of Pizarro. Luque was a priest and school-master, and very rich withal. All of them had heard of a great and rich country on the shore of the South Sea, and they agreed to attempt the conquest of it. Pizarro engaged to command the armament, Almagro offered to conduct the supplies and reinforcements, and Luque contributed his gold. The agreement was ratified by a solemn mass, and they entered into a contract to commit rapine and murder in the name of the Prince of Peace.

Small were the means with which this great enterprize was undertaken. Pizarro set sail in a small vessel, with only a hundred and twelve men. Contrary winds kept him beating about seventy-two days, during which his scanty band suffered much from hunger, fatigue and frequent rencontres with the natives. He was at last obliged to retire to Chuchama, where he was overtaken by Almagro, with seventy men, who had suffered as much, and from the same causes, as the followers of Pizarro. Almagro himself had lost an eye, in a contest with the natives. After the meeting, Almagro returned to Panama to recruit, but with all his exertions, he could only raise eighty men. With this small reinforcement the adventurers landed at Tacamez, on the coast of Quito, where they found the natives clad in cotton, and adorned with trinkets of gold and silver. They dared not, however, with their small force, invade so populous a country, and retired to the island of Gallo. Here an order from the governor of Panama reached them ; commanding the expedition to return. So much had the private men suffered, that they were very willing to obey. Pizarro drew a line in the sand with his sword, and having declared that all who wished to leave him were permitted to do so, found himself left with only thirteen soldiers.

This small band established themselves in the island of Gorgona, till at last they were joined by a small reinforcement from Panama. They then stood to the south east, and in twenty days touched on the coast of Peru. At Tumbez, a place of some note, they first obtained an idea of the magnificence of the Peruvian empire. They beheld a thickly peopled country, well cultivated, the natives decently clothed, and farther advanced in civilization than the inhabitants of Mexico. They had even domestic animals. But what chiefly attracted their eyes, was the profusion of gold and silver. Not only were the people decorated with these metals, but even their common culinary utensils were formed of them.

Pizarro ranged along the coast, keeping up a peaceable intercourse with the natives, for he was not strong enough to attack them. He procured some of their *Lamas*, or tame cattle, some vessels of gold and silver and two young men, who, he intended should serve him as interpreters, and so returned to Panama, after an absence of about three years. Hence he repaired to Spain, where he had the address to secure the favor of the court Luque was nominated bishop of the country to be conquered, Almagro only obtained the command of Tumbez, and Pizarro was appointed Governor and Captain-General, with supreme civil and military authority. In return, he engaged to raise two hundred and fifty men, and to provide ships, arms and all things necessary for the conquest of Peru.

Small as the number of men he had engaged to raise and supply was, it was with great difficulty that Pizarro got together the half of them; and that only by the aid of Cortez. With these, however, he landed at Nombre de Dios and marched to Panama, accompanied by his three brothers. On his arrival, he found Almagro so exasperated at his conduct, that he refused to act longer in concert with him, and was endeavoring to get a new enterprize on foot, to thwart and rival him, for he justly considered that Pizarro had engrossed to himself all the honors, and had left him but a very humble part to play. Thus will thieves quarrel for their booty, even before it is won. The cunning of Pizarro, however, soon brought about a reconciliation. Nevertheless, their united endeavors could only equip three small vessels and a hundred and eighty soldiers, thirty six of whom were horsemen. Leaving Almagro at Panama, Pizarro landed his handful of troops in the north of Peru in thirteen days, and immediately marched southward. It would be of little avail to recount the wanton outrages committed by him and his followers on the harmless Peruvians. At length, after much suffering, they reached the province of Coaque, and, having taken the principal settlement of the natives by surprise, they found themselves in possession of gold and silver to the value of thirty thousand pesos and other booty of great value.

Pizarro hardly met with resistance till he reached the island of Puna, in the bay of Guyaquil; where the inhabitants defended themselves so bravely, that it cost him six months' exertion to reduce them. Thence he proceeded to Tumbez, where the sickness of his troops compelled him to remain three months.

In the mean while two reinforcements, amounting together to thirty men, under two leaders of great experience and reputation, joined him from Nicaragua. With this accession of strength, he proceeded to the river Piura and there founded St. Michael, the first Spanish settlement in Peru. As he advanced toward the centre of the empire, he became better informed concerning its affairs. At this time the dominions of the Incas extended fifteen hundred miles along the coast of the Pacific; while its breadth was much less considerable. The sovereigns, called Incas, were revered as persons of divine origin, and ruled with despotic sway. Their blood was deemed too pure to be mingled with that of any other race and others were treated with respect almost amounting to adoration. Nevertheless, they were of a gentle and benevolent disposition and ruled for the good of their subjects. At the first coming of the Spaniards, Huara Capoc sat upon the throne. He was distinguished no less for military talent than for the pacific virtues of his race. He had subdued the kingdom of Quito, by force of arms, resided in its capital, and contrary to the customs of his country, married the daughter of the vanquished monarch. Atahualpa, his son, succeeded to his throne and his authority; soon to be despoiled of both by Pizarro.

Nevertheless, his title was disputed by his elder brother Huascar, who solicited the aid of the Spaniards, to whom this civil broil gave a manifest advantage. Pizarro left a small garrison in St. Michael, and marched against Atahualpa with sixty-two horsemen and a hundred and two infantry, of whom twenty were armed with cross-bows and three with muskets. To an envoy of Atahualpa, who met him with a valuable present, and an offer of the Inca's friendship, he pretended that he came as an ambassador from a powerful monarch, to offer the Peruvian prince aid against the enemies who disputed his title. These professions, probably, induced the Peruvians to suffer the invaders to advance without molestation to Caxamalca; where they took possession of a fort and intrenched themselves. Here too, the Inca sent them new presents, and renewed his proffers of friendship.

In Caxamalca Pizarro tookpossession of a large court, on one side of which was a palace of the Inca, and on the other a temple of the god of the Peruvians, the Sun. The whole was surrounded by a strong rampart of earth. Thus posted, he despatched Hernando Soto and his brother Ferdinand to the Inca's camp. Their embassy brought on a visit from Atahualpa to the messengers of his wicked invaders. It was an unhappy courtesy: the splendour of the Inca, and the riches displayed by his attendants served greatly to inflame the worst passions of the ravenous thieves to whom he designed to do honor. From the moment when, on their return to Caxamalca, they related what they had seen, Pizarro resolved to get possession of the person of the unhappy monarch.

He availed himself of a promised visit from Atahualpa to execute this treacherous design. He divided his cavalry into three squadrons, and formed his infantry in one body, excepting twenty picked men whom he kept about his own person. The artillery and the cross-bow men were stationed opposite the avenue by which the Inca was to approach.

Early on that fatal morning the Peruvian camp was in motion; but as the Inca wished to appear in all his splendor, it was late in the day before he began his march. At last, he approached. First appeared four hundred men, and then the monarch, upon a throne adorned with plumes, and almost covered with plates of gold and silver and precious stones, carried on the shoulders of his attendants. Then came the principal officers of his court and several bands of singers and dancers, and the whole plain was covered with the Peruvian troops, amounting to upwards of thirty thousand men.

As the Inca drew nigh, the Spanish chaplain, Valverde, stepped forward with a crucifix and a breviary, and explained to him, as well as he was able, the fall of Adam, the atonement of Christ and the right of the king of Castile to the New World. In consequence of all this, he desired Atahualpa to embrace Christianity, and to acknowledge the spiritual and temporal jurisdiction of the Pope and the king of Castile, promising him the protection of the Spanish Monarch if he complied, and threatening him with war in case of a refusal.

Of course, this strange harrangue was incomprehensible to the Inca, but its arrogance he understood, and was indignant at it. He replied that his authority was his by inheritance, and that he could not conceive how a foreign priest could dispose of what did not belong to him. He had no inclination, he said, to renounce the religion of his fathers in order to worship the god of the Spaniards who was subject to death ; and as to the other particulars of the priest's discourse, he desired to know where he had learned such extraordinary things. " In this book," said Valverde, offering him his breviary. The Inca put it to his ear, and then threw it disdainfully on the ground. " It is silent," said he ; " it tells me nothing." " To arms, Christians, to arms !" cried the enraged priest. " The word of God is insulted. Avenge the profanation on these impious dogs." Pizarro instantly gave the signal of assault. The music struck up, the cannon and musketry began to play, and the horse and infantry charged the Peruvians sword in hand. The natives fled in the utmost consternation, without attempting either to annoy the enemy or to defend themselves, so much were they surprised and amazed. Pizarro, with his chosen band, made directly toward the Inca ; and notwithstanding the resistance of his nobles, who fell in heaps around him, made him a prisoner. Dire was the carnage then : it did not cease till the close of day. More than four thousand Peruvians were slain ; but not a single Spaniard fell. The plunder was immense.

At first the captive monarch could scarcely realize the misery of his condition, but despair was not long in coming and he sunk into profound dejection. He had however, discovered the ruling passion of the Spaniards, the lust of gold. He attempted to bribe them. The apartment in which he was confined was twenty-two feet long and sixteen broad. He undertook to fill it as high as he could reach with vessels of gold, as a ransom. Pizarro eagerly accepted this tempting proposal.

The Inca's subjects obeyed his orders with the utmost alacrity. The gold was obtained and shared, and each individual Spaniard was rich. The Inca having fulfilled his part of the agreement, insisted on having his freedom; but nothing was farther from the thoughts of Pizarro. The followers of Almagro insisted upon putting the captive king to death, and the tidings of Peruvian armies assembling in the borders of the empire aroused his fears and suspicions, and rendered him more willing to comply with their wishes. Atahualpa inadvertently contributed to hasten his own fate. He justly admired the arts of reading aud writing, and long deliberated with himself whether it was a natural or an acquired ability. To solve this doubt, he desired one of the Spanish soldiers to write the name of God on his thumb nail. This he shewed to several Spaniards, and, to his amazement, they all returned the same answer, without hesitation. When he shewed it to Pizarro, however, the marauding leader was obliged, with blushes and confusion, to acknowledge his ignorance. From that moment Atahualpa despised him, and could not conceal his contempt. This scorn stung Pizarro to the quick, and the Inca's fate was sealed.

But to give his abominable proceedings the colour of justice, Pizarro determined to try the Inca with all the formalities of the courts of Spain. He himself and Almagro, with two assistants, were the judges. Before this unrighteous tribunal the unhappy Inca was charged with being a bastard and an idolater, with having usurped the regal power, with having commanded human sacrifices, with having many concubines, with having embezzled the royal treasures, and with having incited his subjects to take up arms against the Spaniards. On these absurd charges the Court found the Inca guilty, and sentenced him to be burned alive. His tears and entreaties were alike unavailing; pity never touched the heart of Pizarro. He ordered the prince to immediate execution, and what added to the bitterness of his last moments, Valverde offered to console and to convert him. The most powerful argument he could advance, however, was a mitigation of punishment; but that was effectual. The unhappy monarch consented to receive Christian baptism, and instead of being burned, was strangled at the stake.

On the death of Atahualpa, Pizarro invested one of his sons with the ensigns of royalty. The people of Cuzco, however, acknowledged a brother of the deceased Inca as their sovereign. But neither of them, possessed much authority. Commotions arose in every quarter, and all Peru became a scene of bloodshed, insurrection and disorder, all of which the Spaniards beheld with pleasure, as it favored their designs. Ambitious men in different parts of the empire aspired to independent authority, and usurped jurisdiction. The general who commanded for Atahualpa in Quito seized his master's brother and children, put them to death and endeavored to establish a kingdom for himself.

The report of the riches won by Pizarro drew flocks of adventurers to his standard from the different Spanish colonies, so that he was able to march upon Cuzco at the head of five hundred men, after leaving garrisons behind him. Large bodies of Peruvians had assembled to oppose him; but, as usual, they were defeated with great loss, while but very few of the Spaniards were killed and wounded. Pizarro gained possession of Cuzco, and of an immense spoil.

In the mean while Benalcazar, governor of St. Michael, led a body of Spaniards against the city of Quito, where, as report said, an unheard of treasure was deposited. Notwithstanding the great distance of that place from St. Michael, and the difficulty of traversing a mountainous and woody country, where he was continually exposed to the attacks of the bravest of the Peruvians, his valor and good conduct surmounted every difficulty, and he entered Quito with his troops—only to meet with a disappointment. The Indians had now learned the ruling passion of their invaders, and had carried off their treasures with them.

Dissensions, now that the conquest of Peru was achieved, broke out among the invaders. Almagro had been appointed governor, with jurisdiction over two hundred leagues of territory, stretching beyond the southern limits of the province allotted to Pizarro. He now pretended that Cuzco, the residence of the Incas, was within his boundaries, and attempted to become master of it. Juan and Gonzalo Pizarro opposed him. The dispute was about to be decided by the sword when Francisco Pizarro arrived and an arrangement took place. It was agreed that Almagro should attempt the conquest of Chili, and in case he did not find an establishment agreeable to his wishes in that province, a suitable provision was to be made for him in Peru on his return. The history of the conquest of that unhappy empire is now complete—but perhaps a brief account of the fate of its ruthless invaders may not be unacceptable to the reader.

The hardy natives of Chili resisted Almagro successfully, and besides, many of his followers perished of the fatigues of the march. In the meanwhile new swarms of Spaniards poured into Peru, and in full confidence of security, scattered themselves over the empire. A small force only remained in Cuzco, under Juan and Gonzalez Pizarro and their brother, which the Inca observing, conceived that the time for vengeance was come. He set up the banner of war, and all Peru was instantly in arms. Many Spanish settlers were massacred, and several detachments were cut off. Two hundred thousand Indians invested Cuzco, which was feebly defended by its garrison, during nine months. Another army attacked Lima, and the extinction of the Spanish name in Peru seemed at hand. While these things were going on, and just after Juan Pizarro had been slain, Almagro suddenly returned from Chili and entered into negociations with both parties. These were interrupted by a sudden attack made on him by the Inca, who was however defeated, and Almagro reached the gates of Cuzco, which he entered by surprize, seized the two Pizarros and established his jurisdiction.

Shortly after the Pizarro party again made head against him, and were defeated. Had he now put his enemies to death, as he was advised to do, the contest would have been ended, but this he had not the heart to do, and gave Francis Pizarro time to raise forces anew.

He was also weak enough again to enter into negotiations with this arch enemy. While these were in process one of the brother prisoners managed to corrupt sixty of his guards and made his escape with them. The other was soon after set at liberty by Almagro, and as soon as this was done, Francis Pizarro threw off all disguise. Treaties were held in scorn and Pizarro marched upon Cuzco with seven hundred men. Battle was joined. Almagro, being at the time sick, was obliged to depute the command to a subordinate officer, and defeat was the consequence. A large proportion of Almagro's followers were butchered in cold blood, when the battle was over. The chief himself was taken, and rigorously guarded. Cuzco itself was sacked.

Almagro remaining several months in close custody, his spirit was at last broken. When a sentence of death was pronounced upon him, he had recourse to the most abject entreaties to save himself. He reminded the Pizarros of their former friendship, of his having spared their lives under great provocation, and conjured them to spare his age and infirmity. All was unavailing—he was strangled in prison, a fate he well deserved for his outrages upon Peru, but not at the hands of the Pizarros. He left a natural son, by an Indian woman.

The first intelligence of these transactions was carried to Spain by some of Almagro's officers, and created a strong sensation, which Francis Pizarro, who shortly followed them, could not remove. It was determined to send a person to Peru, who should settle the distracted state of affairs, and the royal choice fell upon Christoval Vaca de Castro, an eminent, learned and wise civilian. If he found Pizarro alive, he was to leave him in possession of his office of governor, taking on himself that of judge; if dead, he was to be his successor. Before he arrived however, the governor had parcelled out the empire among his followers, with small regard to the claims of the adherents of Almagro, who, therefore, meditated revenge. They gathered at Lima, under the auspices of the young Almagro, and conspired against the governor's life. Pizarro gave little heed to their cabals. "As long as every man in Peru knows that his life is entirely in my power," said he, "my life is in no danger." He was mistaken. At noon-day, on the 26th of June, nineteen of the most determined conspirators sallied out of Almagro's house in complete armour shouting "Long live the king, and let the tyrant die!" They gained Pizarro's palace without being observed, and were mounting the stairs leading to his apartment before the alarm was given. But no danger could appal the savage governor. He called for arms and commanded an officer in attendance to make fast the door. Instead of doing this, the bewildered functionary ran out and asked the conspirators where they were going. They stabbed him to the heart and burst in. Some of those present sprang from the windows, others attempted to fly, and a few drew their swords and followed Pizarro into another apartment. The governor himself defended the entrance with his sword and target and fought with the utmost desperation, but in vain. His defenders fell one after another, and after having fought till he was so weary that he could scarce wield his sword, Pizarro snared their fate. The assassins then ran into the street, and waving their bloody weapons, proclaimed his death. Two hundred of their associates conducted Almagro in solemn procession through the streets and compelled the magistrates to acknowledge him as governor. The palace of Pizarro and the houses of his adherents were pillaged.

Such was the death of the conqueror of Peru, a man in whose character the most partial eye can discern no one good quality, unless the most savage ferocity be so considered, and whose leading points were lust of blood, gold and ambition. The history of the world, probably, cannot shew a man so utterly wicked and detestable, not even Hernando Cortez, who had at least religious fanaticism to palliate his atrocities. As he lived so he died, a memento of depravity to the very last.

Of the inferior actors in this bloody drama few words need be said. In a long series of rebellions and turmoils, which merit as little attention, but for their results, as the quarrels of wolves, they perished. Almagro fell in battle against Vaca de Castro. Gonzalo Piz-

5

arro, being in likewise defeated and taken in the act of open rebellion by Gasca, the royal governor who succeeded to the authority of De Castro, died by the hand of the executioner, together with his principal followers. These co-workers in iniquity being swept off, the no less unjust authority of Spain was firmly established, and the rightful lords of the soil, the feeble bodied and minded aborigines of Peru, have ever since groaned under the yoke of the stranger, as they probably will do for centuries to come.

THE NATCHES.

Litte is known of this interesting people. In tne early part of the eighteenth century their principal settlement was near Natches on the Mississippi, then a French military post, and commanded by Monsieur de Chopart. Their chief was called the Grand Sun. His brother, called the Stung Serpent, was a famous warrior, and both were very friendly disposed toward the whites till the cruel injustice and oppression of De Chopart forced the tribe into a war. The affair happened in 1729.

The French commander had determined to build a village, and no spot appeared to him so fit for his purpose, as the principal seat of the Natches, called by them White Apple, which he peremptorily required them to vacate. Grand Sun answered that it was their inheritance, and he therefore thought it but reasonable that they should still retain it. The fiery Frenchman assured him that, unless he complied, he should have cause for repentance; upon which the chief retired, saying that he would take the advice of his counsellors.

The council resolved to lay before De Chopart a representation of the hardship of the case, should they lose the harvests on which they mainly relied for subsistence. Vehement abuse and a reiterated command to depart instantly was the answer they received. The Natches, justly indignant at such treatment, then entered into a conspiracy to destroy their invaders and to temporize in order to gain time. To this end they offered to pay tribute to the commandant, on condition that he would suffer them to remain till they could gather their harvest, which offer was readily accepted. In the mean while, messages were sent to the Suns, or chiefs of the other branches of the tribe, inviting them to assist in the massacre of the French, and appointing a day. Accordingly, the slaughter took place and the French perished, to the number of seven hundred, though not for want of sufficient warning.

A woman who was much attached to the whites, and had learned the secret of the conspiracy, gave timely information to the commandant, who was, however, so engrossed by his own arrogance and folly that he paid no regard to her. He even threatened to punish any of his own people if they gave credit to such reports, and actually put seven of them in irons. To fill the measure of his presumption, he sent a messenger to the Grand Sun himself, to ask at what time he intended to make the attack. Of course, the chief denied having any hostile intention, and thereby confirmed De Chopart in his stupid disbelief.

The 30th of November, being the Eve of the fete of St. Andrew and a season of festivity, afforded the Natches a favourable opportunity to attack. The whites at Natches were cut off to a man. De Chopart himself was slain with a wooden weapon, by a person considered the meanest in the tribe, according to the direction of the chiefs, who despised him so much for his military incapacity that they held him unworthy to die a warrior's death or by a warrior's hand.

It had been the intention of the chiefs to drive the French entirely out of Louisiana; but the refusal of several of the tribes to join in the conspiracy hindered the accomplishment of their design. They were even unable to secure themselves against a terrible retaliation. The people of New-Orleans, together with about fifteen hundred Choctaws, took the field against them, and encamped before the fort at Natches, then in possession of the Grand Sun. A treaty of peace was concluded between the parties, of which the terms were very honorable to the Natches; but these, being probably apprehensive of some intended treachery, broke up their camp in the night, crossed the Mississippi, and settled about a hundred and eighty miles above the Red River, where they built a fort and remained unmolested nearly a year, the colony not having force sufficient to attack them. However, troops were sent over from France and they were invested in their fort. In two desperate sallies which they made, they were signally repulsed and most of them slain. The French then opened a mortar battery upon them. The third shell fired bursting in the midst of the fort occasioned great consternation among the survivors, and they capitulated. They were taken to New-Orleans, where an infection broke out among them. What became of the men is not known! they were probably put to death. The women and children were employed as slaves on the royal plantations till it was found convenient to send them to St. Domingo, where they were sold, and thus the Natches became extinct.

In regarding the fate of this unfortunate tribe but one cause for satisfaction presents itself, namely, that our pilgrim fathers cannot justly be reproached for maltreatment of the aborigines by either Spaniard or Frenchmen. If they warred on and oppressed the natives on slight pretences, and sold prisoners of war into slavery, we have at least the poor consolation, that others have practised the same enormities, on a larger scale.

Little more can be said of the Natches but that they are supposed to have been much farther advanced in civilization than any tribe north of Mexico. They had permanent dwellings, an organized priesthood and government, some idea of the rights of property and depended mainly on agriculture for subsistence. When this is said all is said.

LANDING OF OUR FOREFATHERS

It is a singular fact, that a search for gold was one if not the chief of the motives of all the early adventurers who persued carreer of discovery in both North and South America, with almost the only exception of the pilgrims, as they are called. We have it on record that the precious metal was supposed to exist on the ice-bound shore of Davis' Straits, and that a cargo of yellow sand was carried to England for chemical analyzation. Exploration was, however, carried on with by no means so much zeal in the climes which presented little hope of a golden reward, as in the more inviting regions of the South. A nobler motive than lust of gain was required to people the comparatively sterile shores of New-England. From the time that Cabot found the way to North America (in 1497) till a century after, few attempts were made to explore, much less to colonize. Sir Francis Drake, indeed,(knighted for deeds for which he ought to have been hanged) gained some knowledge of the west and eastern shores of the Northern half of the New World; but his object was plunder not knowledge. Sir Walter Raleigh was the first navigator who made a decided attempt at exploration, who gave the land a name and settled a colony.

Colonization, as a system, was at that time no part of the concern of the English government. The lands which only, it was held, the English had a right to settle, afforded no prospect of great and immediate gain. An incentive for emigration was found, however in the then existing political state of things. England had just thrown off the yoke of Rome; but the discipline of the Roman Church was not at the same time abandoned. The spirit of religion and of fanaticism were both wide awake. A dissent from the Anglican church was held as great an offence as an adherence to that of Rome, and was punishable by law. This,of course, was a very serious annoyance; nay, an intolerable oppression, by various sects then called into existence by the awakened spirit of inquiry.

Among these sects was one which differed less from the Episcopal Church than the others, and were accordingly persecuted more as we uniformly find that a slight difference between friends kindleth a greater fire than a total difference between strangers. These were the Puritan, who refused to comply with the forms of Episcopacy, though they professed its spirit.

In the year of our Lord 1610, a small congregation of these harmless, but persecuted sectaries, being the flock of a Mr. Robinson, emigrated to Holland and settled at Leyden, in order that they might worship God according to the dictates of their own consciences. Here they continued to dwell about 10 years ; but did not find their expectations wholly realized. The ecclesiastical laws of the land, indeed, neither sanctioned nor condemned them, or any other Christian sect, but then they made no converts. The Dutch gave them a hospitable reception and treated them with much kindness and respect, but could by no means be prevailed on to conform to their mode of worship or renounce their own principles, which the English conceived to be incompatible with the Christian character. The little sect, therefore, fell fast into decay. Within the ten years of their residence in Holland, they lost half their number from deaths and returns to England. Their worldly affairs, too, did not prosper; for all of which reason the remaining few determined to seek a country where their own belief should be paramount, and where the prospect of their children would be better. New-England was the Canaan they proposed to settle themselves in, and they found no difficulty in procuring a royal grant of a large tract of land.

Here, whatever their descendants may have done after them, they did not expect to amass wealth or intend to drive out the natives ; but to live unmolested, by honest industry, and to cultivate justice and friendship with the Indians. After a day or two set apart for solemn humiliation before God and religious exercises, it was resolved that a part of the congregation should sail to America, whither, if they found the prospect favorable, the rest should soon follow them.

They purchased two small ships and repaired to Plymouth, in England, whence it was proposed to set forth. On the fifth of August 1620, they were affectionately commended to the holy protection of Divine Providence by their pious pastor, and took leave of the Old World forever.

For twenty days their voyaging was as favorable as could be expected; but on the twenty-first a tremendous gale threatened them with destruction. It lasted three days, every moment of which they looked for instant death. Nevertheless the vessels did not part company, but when the tempest was over, one of them was so shattered as to be deemed incapable of making the voyage. She was therefore abandoned by her passengers, who were received on board the other

After a passage of more than three months, on the memorable 10th of Nov. 1620, they, to their great joy made Cape Cod, where they landed without difficulty the next day. Although, if it may be said without profanity, the prospect before them presented little to be thankful for, they did not fail to return thanks for their safe arrival. Their situation was nevertheless deplorable. Winter was sitting in: they were on a bleak, inhospitable and perhaps hostile shore, and howling wilderness before them, and no friend to receive, or house to shelter them.

Having found a harbour where their ship might ride in safety, ten of the most resolute of the party set out to explore the country, and discover, if they could, a suitable spot for a settlement. They had not proceeded more than a league into the woods when they met a party of five Indians, the first of any the company had ever looked upon. They were clad in skins and armed with bows and arrows. Though the English made signs of friendship, the natives fled in the utmost consternation as soon as they perceived them. They had good reason for their fears: the crew of an English ship had carried two of their fellows forcibly into slavery two or three years before.

On the approach of night the little party encamped, or rather bivouacked; not forgetting to set a strict watch. In the morning they resumed their march, following the tracts of the Indians aforesaid, in hopes of coming to their village and of procuring a supply of fresh provisions, which the party much needed, after so long a voyage. They did not succeed in this, but about noon they arrived at a space of cleared ground with several little hillocks, which they supposed to be graves, which, however were not. There was also a great quantity of stubble, several planks and a small earthen pot, all of which appeared to be signs of recent habitation. A little farther on they found more of the abovesaid hillocks, and, opening them, found that they contained something more savory than dead bodies, namely, considerable quantities of maize, or Indian corn. It was the first they had ever seen, and appeared to them a curiosity. Some of them, after tasting were for leaving it as it was, as worthless, but on the whole they concluded to take it to their ship.

On finding their way back, which they had some difficulty in doing, they were received with much satisfaction. They shewed the grain and recommended the place where they had found it, as suitable for a winter habitation. In pursuance of this advice, the whole company proceeded to the spot on the twenty-fifth. They called it New Plymouth, in remembrance of the port from which they had sailed, and concluded to abide there for the winter. The first care, being a matter of necessity, was to erect a few temporary huts; the next was to erect themselves into a body politic, by a solemn combination. This took place on the tenth of December. They prescribed to themselves such a government and laws as they judged right and equitable, and bound themselves to it by the following instrument.

"In the name of God, amen. We, whose names are underwritten, the loyal subjects of our dread sovereign, King James, by the grace of God, King of Great Britain, France and Ireland, and defender of the faith, &c. having undertaken for the glory of God, advancement of the Christian faith, and the honor of our king and country, a voyage to plant the first colony in the north parts of America, do by these presents solemnly and mutually, in the presence of God, and one another, covenant and combine ourselves together into a civil body politic, for our own convenience and the preservation and support of the ends aforesaid; and by virtue hereof, do enact, constitute and frame such just and equal laws, ordinances, acts, constitutions and officers, from time to time, as shall be thought most meet and convenient for the general good of the colony, unto which we promise all due submission and obedience. In witness whereof we have hereunto subscribed our names, at New Plymouth, on the 10th day of December, A. D. 1620."

John Carver,	John Alden,
William Bradford,	John Turner,
Edward Winslow,	Francis Eaton,
William Brewster,	James Chilton,
Isaac Allerton,	John Craxton,
Miles Standish,	John Billington,
Joseph Fletcher,	Richard Bitteridge,
John Goodman,	George Soule,
Samuel Fuller,	Edward Tilley,
Christopher Martin,	John Tilley,
William White,	Thomas Rogers,
Richard Warren,	Thomas Tinker,
John Howland,	John Ridgdale,
Stephen Hopkins,	Edward Fuller,
Digery Priest,	Richard Clarke,
Thomas Williams,	Richard Gardiner,
Gilbert Winslow,	John Allerton,
Edmund Morgeson,	Thomas English,
Peter Brown,	Edward Leister.

John Carver was then elected governor for one year by ballot.

On the nineteenth of December, Mrs. Susannah, wife of Mr. William White, was delivered of the first child ever born of white parents in New-England. These small matters have been considered of some importance on account of the circumstances in which they happened; and therefore it is that they are mentioned.

On the twenty-third of the same month a second party of thirteen persons was despatched in quest of discoveries.

As they were making the circuit of the deep bay of Cape Cod, they discovered a large party of natives on shore, employed in cutting up a fish like a grampus.

They immediately put on shore, but were no sooner discovered by the Indians than the latter fled, with precipitation and alarm. The English took possession of the fish, and resolved to encamp near it for the night. They had hardly discovered that their acquisition was excellent food and set about erecting a temporary shelter, when they were saluted with a shower of arrows. Receiving so unceremonious an attack they were about to flee to their boat when their leader, Governor Carver, a man of much courage and experience exhorted them to shew a firm front, and maintain their ground, as a precipitate flight was almost certain to be their destruction. He also despatched two or three for the arms, which had imprudently been left in the boat, and the whole body then moved slowly toward the shore, in close order. If too hard pushed, the governor directed them to face about and fire upon the savages. Perceiving the English retiring, the Indians took courage and vigorously assailed them with clubs, stones, hatchets, &c. upon which the former obeyed their orders and three or four of the Indians fell. Utterly disconcerted by so (to them) amazing a repulse, and at the extraordinary wounds of their brethren, they gave a yell that might have been heard three miles and fled in every direction. This was perhaps the first time the report of a gun had been heard in New-England.

The English immediately returned to Plymouth without having made any important discoveries, and as it was not thought probable that any would be made during that season, the whole company concluded to remain where they were till spring. The winter proved uncommonly long and severe, and the hardships and sufferings of the pilgrims were great. The clams and shell fish they picked up on the sea shore were their staple article of subsistence. Little accustomed to such a mode of life, many of them perished, and it would have gone hard with the few survivors had the natives attacked them. Two circumstances prevented this. A year or two before an epidemic, supposed to have been the small pox, had fearfully thinned their numbers, and besides they had had terrible proof of the efficacy of fire arms. Though they were daily seen, not one of them ventured within gun-shot of the settlement, till, on the twentieth day of March following, the English were not a little surprised at seeing a single native walk boldly into the middle of their village and at hearing him address them in broken English. They learned from him that he came from the eastern shore, where he had had intercourse with certain fishermen, from whom he had acquired some words of English. He gave them other information of more importance, concerning the state of the country, the number of the natives, &c. They now learned that they were living on the lands of a chief named Massasoit, whose village was at a great distance.

Samoset, for so was this Indian named, was dismissed with presents and friendly assurances. The next day he returned with his chief Massasoit and a number of his followers. He was a very robust middle aged man, of grave countenance and spare of speech. He wore beads around his neck and smoked tobacco and his head and his face were painted and oiled. During his visit he evinced much fear and trembling, but no lack of good faith. Nevertheless a treaty was concluded with him, and it was agreed that the English and Indians should live amicably together. Whatever provisions the Indians were willing to part with, were to be fairly paid for by the whites, and as long as Massasoit lived, the conditions were faithfully fulfilled on both sides. The chief seems to have been a most estimable man. Though he had been brave and successful in war he was ever the advocate of peace. He was just, humane and beneficent; true to his word and in every respect an honest man. His territories were large and his power and influence great. His death was regretted alike by whites and Indians.

In the spring of 1621, the English made their first plantations. About two months after Governor Carver died; a great loss to the colony. His wife followed him to the grave in a few weeks. Mr. William Bradford was appointed to fulfil the vacancy occasioned by the death of Governor Carver.

New-England from this time began to be rapidly peopled by the Europeans. So great was the emigration from the mother country, that in less than six years from the time that the first adventurers landed at New Plymouth, there were seven considerable towns built and settled in Massachusetts.

In the summer of 1627, Mr. Endicott, one of the original planters, was sent over to begin the plantation at Naumkeag, (now Salem.) The June following about 200 persons, furnished with four ministers, now came over and joined Mr. Endicott's colony; and the next year they formed themselves into a regular church. This was the first church gathered in Massachusetts, and the second in New-England. The church at Plymouth had been gathered eight years before. In 1629, a large embarkation was projected by the company in England. At the request of a number of respectable gentlemen, most of whom afterwards came over to New-England, the general consent of the company was obtained, that the government should be transferred and settled in Massachusetts.

In 1630, seventeen ships from different ports in England, arrived at Massachusetts, with more than 1500 passengers, among whom were many persons of distinction. Incredible were the hardships they endured. Reduced to a scanty pittance of provisions, and that of a kind to which they had not been accustomed, numbers sickened and died, so that before the end of the year they had lost 200 of their number. About this time settlements were made at Charlestown, Medford, Boston, Dorchester, Cambridge and Roxbury.

In the years 1632 and 1633, great additions were made to the colony. Such was the rage for emigration to New-England, that the King and counsel thought fit to issue an order February 7, 1633, to prevent it. The order, however was not strictly obeyed.

In 1635, the foundation of a new colony was laid in Connecticut, adjoining this state. Of this river and the country adjacent Lord Say and Lord Brook were the proprietors; and at the mouth of it a fort by their direction was built, which in honor to them was called

Saybrook fort. New-Haven was settled soon after the building of this fort, as was a number of other towns of considerable note in Connecticut. Some difficulty arising among those who first settled at New Plymouth, a part of the inhabitants, to prevent any serious consequences, removed to a pleasant and fertile island to the south west of Cape Cod, now called Rhode Island, while others settled at Providence, Warwick, Taunton, &c. Thus it was that in the course of a few years a great part of N. England, which so late was an uncultivated forest, resounding with yells of savages and beasts of prey, became the place of abode of our persecuted forefathers.

But this newly settled country was not to be acquired without bloodshed. The natives, although they at first appeared harmless and well disposed toward the new settlers, from the rapid increase and two frequent aggression of the latter, jealousy of the former was excited, which they soon began more openly to manifest as will appear by what follows.

INDIAN WARS IN NEW ENGLAND.

CHAP. I.

COMMENCEMENT OF HOSTILITIES WITH THE NATIVES.—DESTRUCTION OF THE PEQUOTS, AND DEATH OF SASACUS, THEIR CHIEF.—BATTLE BETWEEN THE MOHEGANS, UNDER UNCAS, AND THE NARRAGANSETS, UNDER MIANTINOMI, IN WHICH THE LATTER IS SLAIN.—PEACE BETWEEN THE NARRAGANSETS AND THE ENGLISH.

THERE was a tribe of Indians, inhabiting the borders of Connecticut river from its mouth to within a few miles of Hartford, called Pequots, fierce, cruel, and warlike, and the inveterate enemies of the whites; never failing to improve every opportunity to exercise toward them the most wanton acts of barbarity. In June, 1634, they treacherously murdered Capt. Stone and Capt. Norton, who had been long in the habit of visiting them occasionally to trade. In August, 1635, they inhumanly murdered a Mr. Weeks and his whole family, consisting of a wife and six children, and soon after murdered the wife and children of a Mr. Williams, residing near Hartford. Finding, however, that, by their unprovoked acts of barbarity, they had enkindled the resentment of the English, who, aroused to a sense of their danger, were making preparations to exterminate this cruel tribe, the Pequots despatched messengers with gifts to the governor of the colonies, the Hon. Josiah Winslow. He being, however, inflexible in his determination to revenge the death of his friends, dismissed these messengers without any answer. The Pequots, finding the English resolute and determined, and fearing the consequences of their resentment, the second time despatched messengers with a large quantity of wampum as a present to the governor and council; with whom the latter had a considerable conference, and at length concluded a peace on the following terms.

ARTICLES.

I. The Pequots shall deliver up to the English those of their tribe guilty of the death of their countrymen.

II. The Pequots shall relinquish to the English all their right and title to lands lying within the colony of Connecticut.

III. The English, if disposed to trade with the Pequots, shall be treated as friends.

To these articles the Pequots readily agreed, and promised faithfully to adhere, and at the same time expressed a desire to make peace with the Narragansett Indians, with whom they were then at war.

Soon after the conclusion of peace with the Pequots, the English, to put their fair promises to the test, sent a small boat into the river, on the borders of which they resided, with the pretence of trade; but so great was the treachery of the natives, that, after succeeding by fair promises in enticing the crew of the boat on shore, they were inhumanly murdered.

The Pequots, despairing of again deceiving the English in the manner they had lately done, now threw off the mask of friendship, and avowing themselves the natural enemies of the English, commenced open hostilities, and barbarously murdering all that were so unfortunate as to fall into their hands. A few families were at this time settled at or near Weathersfield, Ct. the whole of whom were carried away captives. Two girls, daughters of Mr. Gibbons of Hartford, were in the most brutal manner put to death. After gashing their flesh with their knives, the Indians filled their wounds with hot embers, in the mean time mimicking their dying groans.

The Pequots, encouraged by the trifling resistance made by the English to their wanton acts of barbarity, on the 20th of June, 1636, besieged fort Saybrook, in which there were about twenty men stationed. The Indians numbered about one hundred and fifty. They surrounded and furiously attacked the fort at midnight, yelling and mimicking the dying groans of such as had fallen victims to their barbarity, but the English, being fortunately provided with a piece or two of cannon, caused their savage enemies to groan in reality, who, after receiving two or three deadly fires from the besieged, retreated, leaving behind them dead, or mortally wounded, about twenty of their number. The English sustained no loss in the attack.

The governor and council of Massachusetts colony, alarmed at the bold and daring conduct of the Pequots, on the 20th of August despatched Capt. Endicot of Salem with ninety men to avenge these murders, unless they should consent to deliver up the murderers, and make reparation for the injuries the English had sustained. Capt. Endicot was directed to proceed first to Block Island, then inhabited by the Pequots, put the men to the sword, and take possession of the island; the women and children to be spared. Thence he was to proceed to the Pequot country, demand the murderers of the English, a thousand fathom of wampum, and a number of their children as hostages.

Capt. Endicot sailed from Boston on the morning of the 20th. When he arrived at Block Island, about sixty Indians appeared on the shore, and opposed his landing. His men soon, however, effected a landing, and after a little skirmishing drove the Indians into the wood, where they could not be found.

The English continued two or three days on the island, in which time they destroyed one hundred wigwams and about fifty canoes, when they proceeded to the Pequot country. When they arrived in Pequot harbor, Capt. Endicot acquainted the enemy with his designs and determination to avenge the cruelties practised upon his countrymen. In a few moments, nearly five hundred of the enemy collected on the shores; but as soon as they were made acquainted with the hostile views of the English, they hastily withdrew, and secreted themselves in the swamps and ledges inaccessible to the troops. Capt. Endicot landed his men on both sides the harbor, burnt their wigwams and destroyed their canoes, killed an Indian or two, and returned to Boston. Enough, indeed, had been done to exasperate, but nothing to subdue a warlike enemy.

Sasacus, chief of the Pequots, and his captains, were men of great and independent spirits. They had con-

7

quered and governed the nations around them without control. They viewed the English as strangers and mere intruders, who had no right to the country, nor to control its original proprietors; as independent princes and sovereigns, they had made settlements in Connecticut without their consent, and brought home the Indian kings whom they had conquered, and restored them their authority and lands. They had built a fort, and were making a settlement without their approbation, in their very neighborhood. Indeed, they had now proceeded to attack and ravage the country. The Pequots in consequence breathed nothing but war and revenge: they were determined to extirpate or drive all the English from New England. For this purpose they conceived the plan of uniting the Indians generally against them. They spared no art nor pains to make peace with the Narragansets, and to engage them in the war against the English; to whom they represented that they were bad men, and the natural enemies of the natives, and who also were foreigners, overspreading the country, and depriving the original inhabitants of their ancient rights and possessions; that unless effectual means were immediately provided to prevent it, they would soon dispossess the original proprietors, and become the lords of the continent. They insisted that by a general combination they could either destroy or drive them from the country; that there would be no necessity to come to open battle; that by killing their cattle, firing their houses, laying ambushes on their roads, in their fields, and wherever they could surprise and destroy them, they might accomplish their object. they represented that if the English should effect the destruction of the Pequots, they would soon destroy the Narragansets. So just and politic were these representations, that nothing but that thirst for revenge which inflames the savage heart could have resisted their influence; indeed it is said that for some time the Narragansets hesitated.

The governor of the colonies, to prevent a union between these savage nations, and to strengthen the peace between the Narraganset Indians and the colonies, despatched a messenger to invite Miantinomi, their chief sachem, to Boston. The invitation was accepted, and while at Boston, with the governor and council, he entered into a treaty, the substance of which was as follows: That there should be a firm peace maintained between the English and Narragansets; and that the latter should not harbor the enemies of the English, but deliver up to them such fugitives as should resort to them for safety. The English were to give them notice when they went out against the Pequots, and the Narragansets were to furnish them with guides.

In February, 1637, the English in Connecticut colony represented to the governor their desire to prosecute more effectually the war with the Pequots, who yet continued to exercise towards them the most wanton acts of barbarity. They represented that on the 10th January a boat containing three of their countrymen was attacked by the enemy when proceeding down the river; that the English for some time bravely defended themselves, but were overpowered by numbers; that the Indians, when they had succeeded in capturing the boat's crew, ripped them up from the bottom of their bellies to their throats, and in like manner split them down their backs, and, thus mangled, hung them upon the trees by the river-side. They represented that the affairs of Connecticut colony at this moment wore a most gloomy aspect; that they had sustained great losses in cattle and goods the preceding year, but were still more unfortunate the present; that they could neither hunt, fish, or cultivate their fields, nor travel at home or abroad, but at the peril of their lives; that they were obliged to keep a constant watch by night and day—to go armed to their daily labors and to the houses of public worship. And although desirous to prosecute the war more effectually with the common enemy, they were not in a situation to do it, and therefore humbly prayed for assistance.

The report of the horrid and unprovoked cruelties

of the Pequots, practised upon the defenceless inhabitants of Connecticut colony, roused the other colonies to the most spirited exertions. Massachusetts determined to send two hundred and Plymouth forty men to assist their unfortunate brethren in prosecuting the war. Capt. Patrick with forty men was sent before the other troops, in order that he might be enabled seasonably to form a junction with those in Connecticut, who, notwithstanding their weak and distressed state, engaged to furnish ninety men.

On Wednesday, the 10th of May, the Connecticut troops proceeded to fort Saybrook. These consisted of ninety Englishmen and seventy Mohegans and river Indians, the latter commanded by Uncas, sachem of the Mohegans, and the former by Capt. John Mason, who was accompanied by the Rev. Mr. Stone of Hartford, as chaplain. The Mohegans, being detached from the English, on their way to Saybrook, fell in with a considerable body of the enemy, whom they defeated. They killed twenty-two, and took eighteen of them prisoners.

Among the prisoners there was one who was recognised as a perfidious villain; he had lived in the fort some time before, and well understood their language. He remained attached to their interest until the commencement of hostilities with the Pequots, when he deserted from the fort and joined the enemy, whom he served as a guide, and through whose instigation many of the English had been captured and put to death. Uncas and his men insisted upon executing him according to the custom of their ancestors, and the English, in the circumstances in which they were, did not judge it prudent to interfere. The Indians enkindled a fire, near which they confined the prisoner to a stake, in which situation he remained until his skin became parched with the heat: The Mohegans then violently tore him limb from limb, and barbarously cutting his flesh in pieces, handed it round from one to another, eating it, while they sung and danced round the fire in a manner peculiar to savages. The bones, and such parts of the unfortunate captive as were not consumed in this dreadful repast, were committed to the flames and consumed to ashes.

On the 19th, Capt. Mason and his men proceeded to Narraganset Bay, where they safely arrived on the 21st. He marched immediately to the plantation of Canonicus, a Narraganset sachem, and acquainted him with his designs, despatching a messenger to Miantinomi, to inform him likewise of their expedition. The next day Miantinomi, with his chief counsellors, met the English. Capt. Mason informed him that the cause of his entering his country with an armed force was to revenge the injuries which the Pequots had done to the English, and desired a free passage to their forts, which they intended to attack. After a solemn consultation, in the Indian manner, Miantinomi observed, "that he highly approved of the expedition, and would send men to assist the English, but that they were too few in number to fight the enemy; that the Pequots were great warriors, and rather slighted the English."

Capt. Mason landed his men and marched to the plantation of Miantinomi, which, by previous agreement, was to be the place of general rendezvous. In the evening, an Indian runner arrived with information that Capt. Patrick, with the men under his command, had arrived at the plantation of Roger Williams, in Providence, and was desirous that Capt. Mason should postpone his march until such time as he could join him. Capt. Mason, after mature deliberation, determined, however, not to wait his arrival, although a junction was considered important. His men had been detained much longer than was agreeable to their wishes, and the Mohegans, apparently, were impatient for battle. The little army, therefore, consisting of ninety Englishmen, sixty Mohegan and river Indians, and about two hundred Narragansets, commenced their march on the 24th, and in the evening of that day reached Nihantick, which bounded on the country of the Pequots. Nihantick was the seat of a Narraganset sachem, who seemed displeased with the expedition, and would not suffer the

English to enter his fort. Capt. Mason, suspecting the treachery of this fellow, placed a sentinel at night at the entrance of the fort, determined that, as he could not be permitted to enter, no one should come out to advise the enemy of his approach.

On the morning of the 25th, Capt. Mason was joined by an additional number of Narragansets and a few Nihanticks. They formed a circle, and brandishing their scalping-knives, made protestations how gallantly they would fight, and what numbers they would kill. Capt. Mason had now under his command near five hundred Indians, in addition to his former force, with whom he early resumed his march for the head-quarters of his enemy. The day proved uncommonly warm, and the men, through excessive heat and want of provisions, were only enabled by night to reach Paucatuck river; where the Narragansets began to manifest great fear, and to inquire of Capt. Mason his real design. He assured them it was to attack the Pequots in their fort; at which they appeared greatly surprised, and exhibited a disposition to quit the English and return home.

Wequash, a Pequot sachem, who had revolted from Sasacus, was the principal guide of the English, and he proved faithful. He gave such information respecting the distance of the forts of the enemy from each other, and the distance they were then from that of the chief sachem, as induced Capt. Mason to determine to attack the latter, which his guide represented as situated at the head of Mistick river. He found his men so much fatigued by their march through a pathless wilderness, with their provisions, arms, and ammunition, that his resolution appeared absolutely necessary. The little army, accordingly, on the morning of the 26th, proceeded directly for Mistick, and at sundown penetrated a thick swamp, and, imagining that they could not be far distant from the fort, they pitched their little camp between two large rocks, now known by the name of Porter's Rocks, situated in Groton. The sentinels, who were considerably advanced in front of the main body of the English, distinctly heard the enemy singing and dancing through the night at their fort.

The important day was approaching when the existence of Connecticut was to be determined by the sword, in a single action; and to be decided by the valor of less than a hundred brave men. About two hours before day, the men were aroused from their slumbers by their officers, and after commending themselves and their cause to the Almighty, proceeded with all possible despatch for the enemy's fort. When within a few rods of it, Capt. Mason sent for Uncas and Wequash, desiring them in their Indian manner to harangue and prepare their men for combat. They replied, that their men were much afraid, and could not be prevailed on to advance any farther. "Go, then," said Capt. Mason, "and request them not to retire, but to surround the fort at any distance they please, and see what courage Englishmen can display!" The day was now dawning, and no time was to be lost. The fort was soon in view. The soldiers pressed forward, animated by the reflection that it was not for themselves alone that they were to fight, but for their parents, wives, children, and countrymen! As they approached the fort within a short distance, they were discovered by a Pequot sentinel, who roared out, Owanux! Owanux! (Englishmen, Englishmen.) The troops pressed on, and as the Indians were rallying, poured in upon them the contents of their muskets, and instantly hastening to the principal entrance of the fort, rushed in, sword in hand. An important moment this; for, notwithstanding the blaze and thunder of the fire-arms, the Pequots made a powerful resistance. Sheltered by their wigwams, and rallied by their sachems and squaws, they defended themselves, and, in some instances, attacked the English with a resolution that would have done honor to the Romans. After a bloody and desperate conflict of near two hours, in which hundreds of the Indians were slain, and many of the English killed and wounded, victory still hung in suspense. In this critical state of the action, Capt. Mason had recourse to a successful expedient. Rushing into a wigwam within the fort, he seized a brand of fire, and in the mean time crying out to his men, "We must burn them!" communicated it to the mats with which the wigwams were covered, by which means the whole fort was soon wrapt in flames. As the fire increased, the English retired and formed a circle round the fort. The Mohegans and Narragansets, who remained idle spectators to the bloody carnage, mustered courage sufficient to form another circle in the rear of them. The enemy were now in a deplorable situation. Death inevitably was their portion. Sallying forth from their burning cells, they were shot or cut in pieces by the English; many, perceiving it impossible to escape the vigilance of the troops, threw themselves voluntarily into the flames.

The violence of the flames, the reflection of the light, the clashing and roar of arms, the shrieks and yells of the savages in the fort, and the shouting of the friendly Indians without, produced an awful scene. In less than two hours from the commencement of the bloody action, the English completed their work. Eighty wigwams were burnt, and upwards of eight hundred Indians destroyed. Parents and children, the sanup and squaw, the aged and the young, perished in promiscuous ruin! The loss of the English was comparatively small, not exceeding twenty-five killed and wounded.

After the termination of this severe engagement, as the English were proceeding to embark on board their vessels, which, fortunately for them, at this moment arrived in the harbor, they were attacked in the rear by about three hundred of the enemy, who had been despatched from a neighboring fort to assist their brethren. The English gave them so warm a reception that they soon gave way and fell back to the field of action; where, viewing for a few moments with apparent marks of surprise and horror the shocking scene which it presented, they stamped, bellowed, and with savage rage tore their hair from their heads; and then with a hideous yell pursued the English, as if with determination to avenge the deaths of their friends, even at the expense of their lives. They pursued them nearly six miles, sometimes shooting at a distance from behind the rocks and trees, and sometimes pressed hard upon them, hazarding themselves in open field. The English killed numbers of them, but sustained no loss on their part. When a Pequot fell, the Mohegans would cry out, run and fetch his head. The enemy, finding at length that they discharged arrows in vain, and that the English appeared to be well stocked with ammunition, gave over the pursuit.

In less than three weeks from the time the English embarked at Saybrook, they returned, with the exception of the few killed and wounded, in safety to their respective habitations. Few enterprises were ever, perhaps, achieved with more personal bravery; in few have so great a proportion of the effective men of a whole colony or nation been put to so great and immediate danger; in few have a people been so deeply and immediately interested as were the English inhabitants of Connecticut at this important crisis. In these respects, even the great armaments and battles of Europe are comparatively of little importance; and it ought never to be forgotten, that through the bravery and unconquerable resolution of less than one hundred men, Connecticut was once saved, and the most warlike tribe of Indians in New England completely exterminated.

The few Pequots who now remained alive, conceiving it unsafe to inhabit a country so exposed to invasion, removed far to the westward, among whom was Sasacus, their principal sachem. On the 25th June, the Connecticut troops, under Capt. Mason, together with a company from Massachusetts, commanded by Capt. Stoughton, were sent in pursuit of them. They proceeded westward, and on the 27th fell in with and defeated a considerable body, and took about fifty of them prisoners, among whom were two sachems, whose lives were offered them on condition of their serving as guides.

8

The English on their march frequently fell in with small detached parties of the enemy, whom they captured or destroyed; but could not obtain any information relative to the main body, commanded by Sasacus. Finding that the two sachem prisoners would not give them the information required, on the 29th they beheaded them at a place called Menunkatuck, (now Guilford,) from which circumstance the place still bears the name of Sachem's Head. The English on the 30th arrived at Quinnipaik, (now New Haven,) where they were informed by a friendly Pequot that the enemy were encamped in a swamp, a few miles to the westward. The troops pushed forward, and on the succeeding day arrived at the border of the swamp, where they found a thicket so extremely boggy as to render it inaccessible to any one but the natives. The English, therefore, thought it most advisable to surround the swamp, and annoy the enemy as opportunity presented. The Indians, after a few skirmishes, requested a parley, which being granted, Thomas Stanton, interpreter to the English, was sent to treat with them. He was authorized to offer life to such as had not shed the blood of the English; upon which, the sachem of the place, together with about three hundred of his tribe, came out, and producing satisfactory proof of their innocence, were permitted to retire; but the Pequots boldly declared, that they had both shed and drank the blood of Englishmen, and would not upon such terms accept of life, but would fight it out. The English, unwilling to brook the threats and insulting language of the Pequots, attempted to devise means of attacking the whole body of them without further delay. The officers were, however, divided in opinion as to the mode. Some were for setting fire to the swamp; others for cutting their way through with hatchets; and others for surrounding it with a palisado. Neither of these plans were, however, adopted. As night approached, the English cut through a part of the swamp, by which means its circumference was considerably lessened, and they enabled so completely to surround the enemy as to prevent their escaping during the night. Early the ensuing morning, the Indians, perceiving themselves completely hemmed in by the English, made a violent attempt to break through their lines; they were, however, driven back with great loss. They next attempted to force the line formed by the Connecticut troops, but here they met with a much warmer reception. The contest now became close and severe. The Indians, who were about six hundred in number, appeared determined not to yield but at the expense of their lives. One of the most resolute of them walked boldly up to Capt. Mason with an uplifted tomahawk, and, when about to give the fatal stroke, received a blow from the cutlass of the latter, which severed the head of the savage from his body. The enemy soon after made another attempt to break through the lines of the English, in which, after a violent struggle, they finally succeeded. About sixty of their bravest warriors escaped; the remainder were killed or taken prisoners. The loss of the English was eleven killed and twenty wounded.

The prisoners taken were divided among the troops, some of whom were retained by them as servants, and the remainder were sent to the West Indies and sold to planters. The prisoners reported that the whole tribe of Pequots was now nearly exterminated; that in different engagements there had been upwards of two thousand of them killed, and one thousand captured, among whom were thirteen sachems; and that six yet survived, of whom one was Sasacus, who had fled, with a fragment of his tribe, to a country bordering on the Hudson river, inhabited by the Mohawks.

After the swamp fight, the Pequots became so weak and scattered, that the Mohegans and Narragansets daily destroyed them, and presented their scalps to the English. The few that fled with Sasacus to the westward were totally destroyed by the Mohawks. The scalp of Sasacus was in the fall of 1638 presented to the governor and council of Massachusetts.

Soon after the extermination of the Pequots, the

Narragansets, the most numerous tribe in New England, being displeased with the small power with which they were vested, and the respect which the English uniformly manifested for Uncas, appeared disposed to break their treaty of friendship. Miantinomi, without consulting the English according to agreement, without proclaiming war, or giving Uncas the least information, raised an army of one thousand men, and marched against him. The spies of Uncas discovered the army at some distance, and gave him intelligence. He was unprepared, but rallying about five hundred of his bravest men, he told them they must by no means suffer Miantinomi to enter their town, but must go and give him battle on his way. The Mohegans, having marched three or four miles, met the enemy upon an extensive plain. When the armies had advanced within fair bowshot of each other, Uncas had recourse to stratagem, with which he had previously acquainted his warriors. He desired a parley, which being granted, both armies halted in the face of each other. Uncas, gallantly advancing in front of his men, addressed Miantinomi to this effect: "You have a number of stout men with you, so have I with me. It is a great pity that so many brave warriors should be killed in consequence of a misunderstanding between us two. Come, like a brave man, as you profess to be, and let us decide the dispute alone. If you kill me, my men shall be yours; but if I kill you, your men shall be mine." "No," replied Miantinomi; "my men came to fight, and they shall fight." Upon which, Uncas falling instantly to the ground, his men discharged a shower of arrows, and rushing upon them in the most furious manner, with a hideous yell, put them to flight.

The Mohegans pursued the enemy with the same fury and eagerness with which they commenced the action. The Narragansets were driven down rocks and precipices, and chased like a doe by the huntsman. Many of them, to escape from their pursuers, plunged into a river from rocks of near sixty feet in height. Among others, Miantinomi was hard pushed; some of the most forward of the Mohegans, coming up with him, twirled him about, and so impeded his flight, that Uncas, their sachem, might alone have the honor of taking him. Uncas was a man of great bodily strength, —he rushed forward like a lion greedy of his prey, seized Miantinomi by the shoulder, and, giving the Indian whoop, called up his men who were behind to his assistance. The victory was complete. About fifty of the Narragansets were killed, and a much greater number wounded and taken prisoners. Among the latter was a brother of Miantinomi, and two of the sons of Canonicus, whom Uncas conducted in triumph to Mohegan. A few days after, Uncas conducted Miantinomi back to the spot where he was taken, for the purpose of putting him to death. At the instant they arrived on the ground, an Indian, who was ordered to march in the rear for the purpose, sunk a hatchet in his head, and despatched him at a single stroke. He was probably unacquainted with his fate, nor knew by what means he fell. Uncas cut out a large piece of his shoulder, which he devoured with savage triumph, declaring, in the mean time, that it was the sweetest meat he ever eat,—it made his heart strong. The Mohegans buried Miantinomi at the place of his execution, and erected upon his grave a pillar of stones. This memorable event gave the place the name of Sachem's Plains, which are situated in the eastern corner of Norwich.

The Narragansets became greatly enraged at the death of their sachem, and sought means to destroy Uncas, whose country they in small parties frequently invaded, and, by lying in umbush, cut off a number of his most valuable warriors. As Uncas was the avowed friend of the English, and had in many instances signalized himself as such, they conceived it their duty to afford him all the protection possible. They despatched messengers to acquaint the Narragansets with their determination, should they continue to molest and disturb the repose of the Mohegans. The messengers of the English met with quite an unfavorable reception; to whom one of the Narraganset sachems declared, that he would kill every Englishman or Mohegan that came within his reach; that whoever began the war, he would continue it; and that nothing should satisfy him but the head of Uncas.

The English, irritated at the provoking language of the Narragansets, now determined not only to protect Uncas, but to invade their country with an army of three hundred men; first to propose a peace on their own terms, but if rejected, to attack and destroy them. For this purpose Massachusetts was to furnish one hundred and ninety, and Plymouth and Connecticut fifty-five men each.

The Narragansets, learning that an army was about to enter the heart of their country, and fearful of the consequences, despatched several of their men to sue for peace on such terms as the English should be pleased to grant. The governor and council demanded that they should restore to Uncas all the captives and canoes which they had taken from him, and pledge themselves to maintain perpetual peace with the English and their allies, and to the former to pay an annual tribute of two thousand fathoms of wampum. These indeed were hard terms, against which the Narragansets strongly remonstrated; but, aware that the English had already a considerable force collected for the purpose of invading their country, they at length thought it most prudent to acquiesce.

During the war between the Narragansets and Uncas, the former once besieged the fort of the latter, until his provisions were nearly exhausted, and he found that his men must soon perish, either by famine or the tomahawk, unless speedily relieved. In this crisis, he found means of communicating an account of his situation to the English scouts, who had been despatched from the fort in Saybrook to reconnoitre the enemy. Uncas represented the danger to which the English would be exposed, if the Narragansets should succeed in destroying the Mohegans. It was at this critical juncture that the greatest portion of the

English troops in Connecticut were employed on an expedition abroad. A Mr. Thomas Leffingwell, however, a bold and enterprising man, on learning the situation of Uncas, loaded a canoe with provisions, and under cover of the night paddled from Saybrook into the river Thames, and had the address to get the whole into the fort. The enemy soon after, discovering that Uncas had received supplies, raised the siege. For this piece of service, Uncas presented Mr. Leffingwell with a deed of a very large tract of land, now comprising the whole town of Norwich.

CHAP. II.

TREATY OF PEACE WITH PHILIP, THE CELEBRATED CHIEF OF THE NIPNET TRIBE.—TREACHEROUS CONDUCT OF PHILIP, AND WAR WITH HIM AND THE NARRAGANSETS.—GREAT BATTLE NEAR MOUNT HOPE, IN WHICH THE INDIANS ARE DEFEATED.

THE English in New England now enjoyed a peace until the year 1671, when they again took up arms to revenge the death of one of their countrymen, who had been inhumanly murdered by an Indian belonging to the Nipnet tribe, of which the celebrated Philip, of Mount Hope, now Bristol, Rhode Island, was sachem. It was thought the most prudent step by the governor and council, first to send to Philip and acquaint him with the cause of their resentment, and the course which they were determined to pursue in case he refused to deliver into their hands the murderer. Philip, being sent for and appearing before the court, affected to be much dissatisfied with the conduct of the accused, ussuring them that no pains should be spared to bring him to justice; and more fully to confirm his friendship for the English, expressed a wish that what he was about to make might be committed to paper, that he and his council might thereunto affix their signatures. The governor and council, in compliance with the request, drew up the following, which, after being signed by Philip and his chief men, was presented to the governor by Philip, in confirmation of his friendly assurances.

"Whereas my father, my brother, and myself have uniformly submitted to the good and wholesome laws of his majesty the king of England, and have ever respected his faithful subjects, the English, as our friends and brothers, and being still anxious to brighten the chain of friendship between us, we do now embrace this opportunity to pledge ourselves that we will spare no pains in seeking out and bringing to justice such of our tribe as shall hereafter commit any outrage against them; and to remove all suspicion, we voluntarily agree to deliver up to them all the fire-arms which they have heretofore kindly presented us with, until such time as they can safely repose confidence in us; and for the true performance of these our sacred promises, we have hereunto set our hands.

Chief sachem.
Philip's X mark
Chief men.
Porkanoket's X mark.
Uncombo's X mark.
Samkama's X mark.
Wocokom's X mark."

In the presence of the Governor and Council.

Notwithstanding the fair promises of Philip, it was soon discovered by the English that he was playing a deep game—that he was artfully enticing his red brethren throughout the whole of New England to rise en masse against them, and drive them out of the country. The Narragansets, for this purpose, had engaged to raise four thousand fighting men. The spring of 1672 was the time agreed upon, on which the grand blow was to be given. The evil intentions of Philip were first discovered and communicated to the English by a friendly Indian of the Narraganset tribe.

KING PHILIP.

Fortunately for them, this Indian had been taken into favor by the Rev. Mr. Elliot, by whom he had been taught to read and write, and became much attached to the English. The governor, upon receiving the important information relative to the hostile views of Philip, ordered a military watch to be kept up in all the English settlements within the three colonies; by some of whom it was soon discovered that the report of their Indian friend was too well founded, as the Indians of different tribes were daily seen flocking in great numbers to the head-quarters of Philip; previously sending their wives and children to the Narraganset country, which they had ever done previous to the commencement of hostilities.

The inhabitants of Swanzey, a small settlement adjoining Mount Hope, the head-quarters of Philip, were the first who felt the effects of this war. Philip, encouraged by the numbers who were daily enlisting under his banners, and despairing to discover a cause that could justify him in commencing hostilities against his "friends and brothers," as he had termed them, resolved to provoke them to a war, by killing their cattle, firing their barns, &c. This plan had the desired effect, as the inhabitants, determined to save their property or perish in the attempt, fired upon the Indians; this was deemed cause sufficient by the latter to commence their bloody work. The war-whoop was immediately sounded, and the Indians commenced an indiscriminate murder of the defenceless inhabitants of Swanzey, sparing not infants at the breast; but three of seventy-eight persons which the town contained made their escape. Messengers were despatched with the melancholy tidings of this bloody affair to the governor, who, by and with the advice and consent of the council, despatched a company of militia, with all possible speed, to the relief of the distressed inhabitants residing near the head-quarters of Philip. As soon as they could be raised, three companies were despatched, under the command of Captains Henchman, Prentice, and Church, who arrived in the neighborhood of Swanzey on the 28th June, where they were joined by four more companies from Plymouth colony. It was found that the Indians had pillaged and set fire to the village, and with their booty had retired to Mount Hope. A company of cavalry were sent, under the command of Capt. Prentice, to reconnoitre them; but before they arrived at a convenient place for this purpose, they were ambushed and fired upon by the enemy, who killed six of their number and wounded ten. The report of their guns alarming the remaining companies of the English, they hastened to the relief of the cavalry, who, at this moment, were completely surrounded by about six hundred Indians, between whom and the English a warm contest now ensued. The savages fought desperately, and more than once nearly succeeded in overpowering the English; but, very fortunately for the latter, when nearly despairing of victory, a fresh company of militia from Boston arrived. They flanked the enemy on the right and left, and, exposing them to two fires, soon overpowered and drove them to seek shelter in an adjoining wood, inaccessible to the English. In this severe engagement, the English had forty-two killed, and seventy-three wounded, many of them mortally. The loss of the enemy was supposed to be much greater.

On the 30th, Maj. Savage, who had been appointed commander in chief of the combined English forces, arrived with an additional company of cavalry, who, with the remaining companies, the following day commenced their march for Mount Hope, the head-quarters of Philip. On their way, the English were affected with a scene truly distressing. The savages, not content with bathing their tomahawks in the blood of the defenceless inhabitants of Swanzey, had, it was discovered, in many instances, detached their limbs from their mangled bodies, and, affixing them to poles, they were extended in the air! among which were discovered the heads of several infant children; the whole of which, by order of Maj. Savage, were collected and buried.

The English arrived at Mount Hope about sunset; but the enemy, receiving information of their approach, had deserted their wigwams and retired into a neighboring wood. Maj. Savage, to pursue the enemy with success, divided his men into companies, which he ordered to march in different directions, stationing forty at Mount Hope. On the 4th of July, those under the command of Capts. Church and Henchman fell in with a body of the enemy, to the number of two hundred, whom they attacked. Victory for a considerable length of time appeared in favor of the savages; but, very fortunately for the former, being commanded by bold and resolute officers, they defended themselves in a heroic manner until relieved by a company of cavalry, commanded by Capt. Prentice. The Indians now, finding the fire of the English too warm for them, fled in every direction, leaving thirty of their number dead, and about sixty severely wounded on the field of action. In this engagement, the English had seven killed and thirty-two wounded, five of whom survived the action but a few hours.

This action, so far from daunting the bold and resolute Capt. Church, seemed to inspire him with additional bravery. Unwilling that any of the enemy should escape, he boldly led his men into an almost impenetrable forest, into which those who had survived the action had fled. The Indians, perceiving the English approaching, concealed themselves from their view by lying flat on their bellies, in which situation they remained concealed until the English had advanced within a few rods of them, when each, unperceived, fixing upon his man, discharged a shower of arrows among them. This unexpected check threw the English into confusion, which the Indians perceiving, they rushed furiously upon them with their knives and tomahawks, shouting horribly. Their cavalry being unable to afford them assistance, the English were now in a very disagreeable situation; the trees being so very large as to render it difficult to use their fire-arms with any effect, and they were soon so encompassed by the savages as to render almost every effort to defend themselves useless. Of sixty-four who entered the swamp only seventeen escaped, among whom, fortunately, was their valuable leader, Capt. Church.

The English, finding that they could neither bring the enemy to action in open field, or engage with any chance of success in the forest where they were lodged, returned home, with the exception of three companies, who were stationed by Maj. Savage near the borders of the swamp into which it was suspected that Philip with a number of his tribe had fled. This swamp was two miles in length, and to the English inaccessible. Philip had been watching the motion of his enemies, and seeing a great part march off, conjectured that their object was to obtain reinforcement. Impressed with this belief, he resolved to improve the opportunity to escape with a few chosen men by water, which he with little difficulty effected the succeeding night, taking advantage of a low tide. The enemy were, soon after their escape, discovered and pursued by the inhabitants of Rehobeth, accompanied by a party of the Mohegans, who had volunteered their services against Philip.

The Rehobeth militia came up with the rear of the enemy about sunset, and killed twelve of them, without sustaining any loss on their part; night preventing their engaging the whole force of Philip; but early the next morning they continued the pursuit. The Indians had, however, fled with such precipitancy that it was found impossible to overtake them. They bent their course to the westward, exhorting those tribes through which they passed to take up arms against the English.

The united colonies now became greatly alarmed at the hostile views and rapid strides of Philip. The general court was constantly in session, and endeavoring to plan means to cut him off before he should have an opportunity to corrupt the minds of too many of his countrymen.

While the court was thus deliberating, information

was received that Philip had arrived in the neighborhood of Brookfield, about sixty-five miles from Boston, and a number of its inhabitants had been inhumanly butchered by his adherents. Orders were immediately issued for the raising of ten companies of foot and horse, to be despatched to the relief of the unfortunate inhabitants of Brookfield; but before they could reach that place, Philip and his party had entered the town and put to death almost every inhabitant which it contained; the few that escaped having taken the precaution to assemble together in one house, which they strongly fortified. This was furiously attacked by the savages, and several times set on fire, and the besieged were on the point of surrendering, when Maj. Willard happily arrived to their relief. Between the English and Indians a desperate engagement ensued; the former, by the express command of their officers, gave no quarter, but in a very heroic manner rushed upon the savages with clubbed muskets. The action continued until near sunset, when the Indians that remained alive sought shelter in the neighboring woods. In this engagement the English had twenty-three killed and seventy-two wounded. The enemy's loss was two hundred and seventeen killed, and between two and three hundred wounded; who, by way of retaliation for their barbarity exercised towards the defenceless inhabitants of Brookfield, were immediately put to death.

The governor and council, on learning the fate of the unfortunate inhabitants of Brookfield, despatched a reinforcement of three companies of cavalry to Maj. Willard, and ordered the like number to be sent him from Hartford, in Connecticut colony; with which he was directed to pursue Philip with fire and sword to whatever part of the country he should resort.

It being discovered that a part of Philip's forces had fled to Hatfield, two companies of English, under the command of Capts. Lathrop and Beers, were sent in pursuit of them, and within about three miles of Hatfield, overtook and attacked them; but the force of the English being greatly inferior to that of the enemy, the former were defeated and driven back to the main body; which enabled the enemy, who had in the late engagement been detached from their main body, to join Philip. On the 13th September, information was received by Maj. Willard, that the enemy had successfully attacked and defeated the troops under the command of Capt. Lathrop; that they were ambushed and unexpectedly surrounded by a thousand of the enemy, to whom they all fell a sacrifice except three. The defeat of Capt. Lathrop took place in the neighborhood of Deerfield; for the defence of which there was an English garrison, whom the Indians were about to attack, when Maj. Willard happily arrived; at his approach they fled.

On the 10th October following, a party of Philip's Indians successfully assaulted the town of Springfield, which they pillaged and set fire to, killing about forty of the inhabitants. On the 14th, they assaulted the town of Hatfield, in which two companies, under the command of Capts. Mosley and Appleton, were stationed. The enemy continued the attack about two hours, when, finding the fire of the English too warm for them, they fled, leaving a number of their party dead behind them.

Philip, now finding himself closely pursued by a large and formidable body of the English, deemed it prudent to bend his course towards his old place of residence; there to remain till the ensuing spring. But the commissioners of the united colonies, duly reflecting on the deplorable situation of their defenceless brethren throughout the country; aware that there were then a much greater number of their savage enemies embodied than at any former period, who, if suffered peaceably to retire into winter quarters, might prove too powerful for them the spring ensuing, resolved to attack the whole force under Philip in their winter encampment; for which purpose every Englishman capable of bearing arms was commanded by proclamation of the governor to hold himself in readiness to march at the shortest notice. The 10th of December was the day appointed by the commissioners on which the decisive blow was to be given. Six companies were immediately to be raised in Massachusetts, consisting in the whole of five hundred and twenty-seven men, to the command of which were appointed Capts. Mosely, Gardner, Davenport, Oliver, and Johnson. Five companies were raised in Connecticut, consisting of four hundred and fifty men, to the command of which were appointed Capts. Seely, Mason, Gallop, Watts, and Marshall; two companies in Plymouth, of one hundred and fifty men, who were commanded by Capts. Rice and Gorham. Three majors, of the three respective divisions, were also appointed, to wit: Maj. Appleton, of Massachusetts; Maj. Treat, of Connecticut; and Maj. Bradford, of Plymouth. The whole force, consisting of one thousand one hundred and twenty-seven men, was commanded by Maj. Gen. Winslow, late governor of the colonies.

On the 7th of December, the combined forces commenced their march for the head-quarters of the enemy. At this inclement season, it was with the utmost difficulty that the troops were enabled to penetrate through a wild and pathless wood. On the morning of the 9th, having travelled all the preceding night, they arrived at the border of an extensive swamp, in which they were informed by their guides the enemy was encamped to the number of four thousand. The English, after partaking of a little refreshment, formed for battle. Capt. Mosely and Capt. Davenport led the van, and Maj. Appleton and Capt. Oliver brought up the rear of the Massachusetts forces; Gen. Winslow, with the Plymouth troops, formed the centre; the Connecticut troops, under the command of their respective captains, together with about two hundred of the Mohegans, commanded by Oneco, the son of Uncas, brought up the rear.

It was soon discovered by an Indian, sent for the purpose, that in the centre of the swamp they had built a very strong fort, of so wise a construction, that it was with difficulty more than one person could enter it at a time. About ten o'clock, A. M., the English, with the sound of trumpet, entered the swamp, and when within about fifty rods of the fort were met and attacked by the enemy. The Indians, in the usual manner, shouting and howling like beasts of prey, commenced with savage fury; but with a hideous noise the English were not intimidated; charging them with unequalled bravery, the enemy were soon glad to seek shelter within the walls of their fort. The English, having closely pressed upon the enemy as they retreated, found themselves in a very disagreeable situation; exposed to the fire of the Indians, who were covered by a high breastwork, they were not even enabled to act on the defensive. At this critical juncture, the lion-hearted Oneco, with the assent of Gen. Winslow, offered to scale the walls of the fort, which being approved of by the English commanders, Oneco, with about sixty picked men, in an instant ascended to the top of the fort, where, having a fair chance of the enemy, they hurled their tomahawks and discharged their arrows with such success among them, as in a very short time to throw them into the utmost confusion. Those who attempted to escape from the fort were instantly cut in pieces by the troops without. The enemy, finding themselves thus hemmed in and attacked on all sides, in the most abject terms begged for quarter, which was denied them by the English. A great proportion of the troops being now mounted on the walls of the fort, they had nothing to do but load and fire, the enemy being penned up and huddled together in such a manner that there was scarcely a shot lost. This bloody contest was of near six hours' continuance, when the English, perceiving the fort filled with nought but dead or such as were mortally wounded, closed the bloody conflict.

The scene of action at this instant was indeed such as could not fail to shock the stoutest heart. The huge logs of which the fort was constructed were completely crimsoned with the blood of the enemy, while the surrounding woods resounded with the dying groans of the wounded. The number of slain of the enemy in this severe engagement could not be ascertained ; it was, however, immense. Of four thousand, supposed to have been present at the commencement of the action, not two hundred escaped ! among whom, unfortunately, was the treacherous Philip.

After the close of this desperate action, the troops, having destroyed all in their power, left the enemy's ground, and carrying about three hundred wounded men, marched back to the distance of sixteen miles, to head-quarters. The night proved cold and stormy, the snow fell deep, and it was not until midnight or after that the troops were enabled to reach their place of destination. Many of the wounded, who probably otherwise might have recovered, perished with the cold and inconvenience of a march so fatiguing.

Although the destruction of so great a number of the enemy was considered of the greatest importance to the English, yet it proved a conquest dearly bought. It was obtained at the expense of the lives of a great number of privates, and a great proportion of their most valuable officers ; among whom were the Capts. Davenport, Gardner, Johnson, Seely, and Marshall.

The courage displayed during the action by every part of the army ; the invincible heroism of the officers ; the firmness and resolution of the soldiers when they saw their captains falling before them ; and the hardships endured before and after the engagement, are hardly credible, and rarely find a parallel in ancient or modern ages. The cold the day preceding the action was extreme, and in the night the snow fell so deep as to render it extremely difficult for the army to move the day succeeding. Four hundred of the soldiers were so completely frozen as to be unfit for duty ! The Connecticut troops were the most disabled, having endured a tedious march, without halting, from Stonington to the place of public rendezvous. They sustained, too, a much greater loss in the action, in proportion to their numbers, than the troops of the other

10

colonies The bold and intrepid Capt. Mason, who received a fatal wound in the action, of which he died in about three months after, was the first after the Mohegans to mount the walls of the fort, nor did the troops under his command fail to follow the noble example. On enumerating the number of slain and wounded, it was found as follows:

Of the Companies commanded by

Captains	Mosely,	10	killed,	40	wounded.
	Oliver,	20	"	48	"
	Gardner,	11	"	32	"
	Johnson,	18	"	38	"
	Davenport,	15	"	19	"
	Gallop,	28	"	43	"
	Seely,	32	"	50	"
	Watts,	19	"	33	"
	Mason,	40	"	50	"
	Marshall,	25	"	37	"
	Gorham,	30	"	41	"
Sachem	Oneco,	51	"	82	"
	Total,	299.		513	

The loss of the troops from Connecticut was so great that Maj. Treat considered it absolutely necessary to return immediately home. Such of the wounded as were not able to travel were put on board a vessel and conveyed to Stonington. The troops on their return killed and captured about thirty of the enemy.

The Massachusetts and Plymouth forces kept the field the greater part of the winter. They ranged the country, took a number of prisoners, destroyed about three thousand wigwams, but achieved nothing very brilliant or decisive.

CHAP. III.

PHILIP'S WAR CONT.NUED.—HOSTILITIES COMMENCED BY THE INDIANS BORDERING ON THE RIVER MERRIMACK.

THE Nipnet and Narraganset tribes being by the late action nearly exterminated, the few who survived, by the direction of Philip, fled in small parties to different parts of the country, improving every opportunity that presented to revenge the untimely fate of their brethren. On the 10th February, 1678, about one hundred of them surprised the inhabitants of Lancaster, a part of whom, as a place of greater safety, had the day previous resorted to the dwelling of the Rev. Mr. Rowland; this, however, being constructed of dry logs, was set on fire by the Indians, which the unfortunate English within being unable to extinguish, they fell victims to the devouring flames. On the 21st, the enemy attacked the inhabitants of Medfield, twelve of whom they killed, and the remainder made captive.

On the 3d March, the Indians still continuing their depredations, two companies of cavalry, under the command of Capts. Pierce and Watkins, were ordered out for the purpose of affording protection to the defenceless inhabitants of towns most exposed to their incursions. On the 5th, they marched to Patuxet, near where there was a considerable body of Indians encamped, whom, on the morning of the 6th, they fell in with and attacked. The enemy at first appeared but few in number, but these were only employed to decoy the English, who on a sudden found themselves surrounded by near five hundred Indians; they with their tomahawks and scalping-knives rushed furiously upon them, threatening them with instant destruction. The English acted on the defensive, and though surrounded by five times their number, fought with their usual spirit, and were resolved to sell their lives at as dear a rate as possible. They were very soon, however, compelled to yield to the superior force of their savage enemies. Only five escaped. Though this victory was of considerable importance to the savages, it cost a number of their bravest warriors, ninety-three of whom were the next day found dead on the field of action. There were in this engagement about twenty friendly Indians with the English, who fought like desperadoes. One of them, observing Capt. Pierce unable to stand, in consequence of the many wounds he had received, for nearly two hours bravely defended him; when, perceiving his own imminent danger, and that he could afford the captain no farther assistance, by blacking his face as the enemy had done, he escaped unnoticed.

On the 25th March, a party of Indians attacked and burnt the towns of Weymouth and Warwick, killing a great number of the inhabitants. On the 10th of April following, they pillaged and burnt Rehobeth and Providence.

On the 1st of May, a company of English and one hundred and fifty Mohegans, under the command of Capt. George Dennison, were sent in pursuit of a body of the enemy, commanded by a son of Miantinomi. On the 8th of May, they met with and attacked them near Groton. The Indians appeared determined on victory or death, displaying an unusual degree of courage, but the English and Mohegans proved too strong for them; after destroying a greater part with their muskets and tomahawks, they drove the remainder into a neighboring river, where they soon perished.

On the 23d, Cononchet, sachem of the few scattered remains of the Narragansets, proposed to his council that the lands bordering on Connecticut river, not inhabited by the English, should be planted by them with corn, for their future subsistence; which being approved of by the latter, two hundred of the Narragansets were despatched for that purpose. The governor, being apprized of their intentions, sent three companies of cavalry to intercept them. About one hun dred of the Mohegans, under the command of Oneco, accompanied the English. The enemy were commanded by Cononchet in person, who first proceeded to Seekonk to procure seed-corn. It was in the neighborhood of this place that they were first engaged by the English and Mohegans. With becoming bravery, the enemy for a long time withstood the attack; but, being poorly provided with weapons, were at length overpowered and compelled to yield to the superior force of their enemies. In the midst of the action, Cononchet, being fearful of the issue, deserted his men, and attempted to seek shelter in a neighboring wood; but being recognised by the Mohegans, they pursued him. Cononchet, perceiving himself nearly overtaken by his pursuers, to facilitate his flight, first threw away his blanket, then his silver-laced coat, with which he had been presented by the English a few weeks previous; but finding that he could not escape from his pursuers by flight, he plunged into a river, where he was even followed by half a dozen resolute Mohegans, who laid hold of him, forced him under water, and there held him until drowned. The loss of the English and Mohegans in this engagement was twelve killed and twenty-one wounded; that of the enemy was forty-three killed, and about eighty wounded.

The inhabitants of New London, Norwich, and Stonington, having frequently discovered a number of the enemy lurking about in small bodies in the adjacent woods, by joint agreement voluntarily enlisted themselves, to the number of three hundred, under the command of Maj. Palmer, and Capts. Dennison and Avery, who, with the assistance of the Mohegans and a few friendly Narragansets, in three expeditions destroyed nearly one thousand of the enemy.

On the 8th of June, the Indians assaulted and burnt Bridgewater, a small settlement in the colony of Massachusetts. Forty of its inhabitants fell victims to savage barbarity.

The governor and council of Massachusetts colony,

aware of the danger to which many of the inland settlements were exposed, by frequent incursions of the enemy, and finding it extremely difficult to raise a sufficient force to oppose them in the many parts to which the fragments of the broken tribes had resorted, adopted the policy of sending among them as spies such Indians as were friendly and could be depended upon; which plan had its desired effect. These Indians, representing the force of the English much greater than it really was, and warning the enemy of danger which did not exist, deterred them from acting in many instances on the offensive. One of the friendly Indians, returning to Boston on the 10th of July, reported that a large body of Indians were embodied in a wood near Lancaster, which village they intended to attack and burn in a few days; that they had been encouraged to continue the war with the English by Frenchmen from the great lake, who had supplied them with fire-arms and ammunition.

On the receipt of this important information, the governor despatched three companies of cavalry, under command of Maj. Savage, for the defence of Lancaster, who, by mistaking the road, unfortunately fell into an ambush of about three hundred and fifty Indians, by whom they were instantly surrounded. The English exhibited great presence of mind, and repelled the attack of the enemy in a very heroic manner. The savages, being, however, well provided with fire-arms, soon gained a complete victory over the English, whose loss in this unfortunate engagement was fifty-four. The number of killed and wounded of the enemy could not be ascertained, as they remained masters of the field of action.

On the 15th, a severe engagement took place between a company of English cavalry and about three hundred of the enemy near Groton. The latter were not perceived by the former until they were within a few paces of them, the Indians having concealed themselves in the bushes, when suddenly issuing forth with a hideous yell, the cavalry were thrown into confusion;

but instantly forming and charging the enemy with great spirit, they fled in every direction. The cavalry, in attempting to pursue them, were once more ambushed. The contest now became close and severe. The Indians, having succeeded in decoying the English into a thick wood, attacked them with fury and success. The commander of the English being killed, every man sought his own safety. Of ninety-five, of which the company was composed, but twelve escaped. The loss of the enemy was supposed to be much greater.

On the 12th of August, a party of Indians entered the town of Westfield, killed and took a number of the inhabitants prisoners, and burnt several houses. Three of them soon after made their appearance at a house near said town, and fired at a man at his door, who fell. They ran towards him, and one of them, stooping to scalp him, was assaulted by the man's wife with a stroke from a hatchet, which went so completely into his body that with three different efforts she could not disengage it, and the Indian made off with it sticking in him. A second also made an attempt, when she, by a well-directed blow with a stick she had found, laid him on the ground. The third then ran, and as soon as the other had recovered his feet, he followed the example; on which the woman took her husband in her arms and carried him into the house, when he soon recovered.

On the 17th, a party of Indians commenced an attack on Northampton, but there being a number of soldiers stationed there, the enemy was repulsed.

On the 20th, a number of the inhabitants of Springfield were attacked by a party of Indians, as they were returning from divine service. Although the former were provided with fire-arms, the enemy succeeded in making prisoners of two women and several children, whom they soon after tomahawked and scalped; in which situation they were the next day found by a party of English sent out in pursuit of the enemy. One of the unfortunate women, although shockingly mangled, was found still alive, and so far recovered as to be able to speak. She gave the following account of the fate of her unfortunate companions: that they were first severely bound with cords, and the Indians soon after built a fire, regaling themselves with what they had previously stolen from the English; that soon after a warm dispute arose between them relative to the prisoners, each claiming the women for their squaws; that they at length proceeded to blows, and after beating each other for some time with clubs, it was agreed by both parties, to prevent further altercation, that the women should be put to death, which, as she supposes, they immediately carried into execution. The unfortunate narrator received a severe blow on the head, which brought her senseless to the ground, and while in this situation was scalped and left for dead by her savage enemies.

The inhabitants of Sudbury, with a company of soldiers, commanded by Lieut. Jacobs, of Marlborough, alarmed at the near approach of the enemy, who to the number of about two hundred were encamped near that place, resolved to attack them at night; accordingly, on the 6th September, they marched within view of them, and at night, as they lay extended around a large fire, approached them unperceived within gunshot, when they gave them the contents of their muskets. Many of those that remained unhurt, being suddenly aroused from their slumbers by the yells of their wounded brethren, and imagining that they were completely surrounded by the English, whom the darkness of the night prevented their seeing, threw themselves into the fire which they had enkindled, and there perished; but few, if any, escaped. In this attack the English sustained no loss.

On the 25th, a considerable body of the enemy attacked the inhabitants of Marlborough, many of whom they killed. A company of English, which had been ordered from Concord for the defence of this place, was cut off by the savages and totally destroyed. Two other companies, despatched from Boston for the like purpose, met with the same fate. It appeared that the governor, on learning the situation of the unfortunate inhabitants of Marlborough, despatched to their relief two companies, under the command of Capts. Wadsworth and Smith, who, before they arrived at the place of destination, were informed that the savages had left Marlborough and proceeded to Sudbury, twelve miles distant, which induced the English to alter their course and proceed immediately for the latter place. Of this it appeared that the enemy had been apprized by their runners, and had laid a plan to cut them off ere they should reach Sudbury, which they in the following manner completely effected. Learning the course which the English would take, they, within a few rods thereof, stationed fifty or sixty of their number in an open field, who were ordered to retreat into a neighboring thicket as soon as discovered and pursued by the English. In this place the remainder of the Indians, to the number of about three hundred, concealed themselves by lying prostrate on their bellies. The English, on their arrival, espying the Indians in the field, and presuming them to be but few in number, pursued and attacked them, who very soon retreated to the fatal spot where their treacherous brethren lay concealed, and prepared to give their pursuers a warm, if not a fatal reception. Here they were closely pursued by the English, who too late discovered the fatal snare which had been laid for them. In an instant they were completely surrounded and attacked on all sides by the savages. The English for several hours bravely defended themselves, but at length were borne down by numbers far superior to their own. Thus fell the brave Capt. Wadsworth and Capt. Smith, as well as most of the troops under their command.

The Indians bordering on the river Merrimack, feeling themselves injured by the continued encroachments of the English, once more resumed the bloody tomahawk, which had been buried for a number of years. On the 1st of November, they, in a considerable body, entered the villages of Chelmsford and Wo-

11

burn, and, taking advantage of their weak state, indiscriminately put to death every inhabitant they contained, sparing not the infant at the breast. On the 9th, they burnt the house of a Mr. Ezra Eames, near Concord, killed his wife, threw her body into the flames, and made captives of his children. On the 15th, they took prisoner a young woman, sixteen years of age, who, by the family with whom she resided, had been placed on a hill in the neighborhood of their dwelling, to watch the motions of the enemy. The account which the young woman gave of her capture and escape was as follows: That on the morning of her capture, the family having been informed that a party of Indians had the day previous been discovered in a neighboring wood, she, by their request, ascended a hill near the house, to watch their motions, and alarm the family if seen approaching; that about noon she discovered a number of them ascending the hill in great haste. She immediately attempted to evade them by retiring into a thicket, but the Indians, who, it appeared, had before observed her, found her after a few moments' search, and compelled her to accompany them to their settlement, about forty miles distant. It was here they gave her to understand she must remain and become their squaw, and dress and cook their victuals. She remained with them about three weeks, during which time they made several expeditions against the English, and returned with a great number of human scalps. On the night of the 6th December, they returned with six horses, which they had stolen from the English, which having turned into a small enclosure, they set out on a new expedition. She viewed this as a favorable opportunity to escape; to effect which, she caught and mounted one of the horses, and making use of a strip of bark for a bridle, she penetrated a wild and pathless wood, and arrived at Concord at seven o'clock the morning succeeding, having travelled all the preceding night, to evade the pursuit of the enemy! In like manner did one of the children of Mr. Eames escape from the Indians, although but ten years of age; he travelled sixty miles through an uninhabited wood, subsisting on acorns.

On the 12th December, a party of Indians attacked and killed several of the inhabitants of Bradford. The governor of Massachusetts colony, for the protection of the defenceless inhabitants bordering on the Merrimack, ordered the raising and equipping of four companies of cavalry, to the command of which were appointed Capts. Sill, Holyoke, Cutler, and Prentice.

On the 23d, the troops proceeded for the borders of the Merrimack, and on the 26th fell in with a considerable body of the enemy, whom they engaged and completely defeated. On the 4th of January, 1679, Capt. Prentice, detached from the main body, fell in with and engaged about one hundred of the enemy in the neighborhood of Amherst, whom he likewise defeated, but with considerable loss on his part.

On the 6th, a son of the brave Capt. Holyoke, of Springfield, receiving information that a number of the enemy, in small bodies, were skulking about in the woods bordering on that town, with twenty resolute young men marched out to attack them. Falling in with a considerable body of them, an engagement ensued, which, though severe, terminated at length in favor of the English. The Indians, being furnished with muskets, were unwilling to give ground, and would probably have remained masters of the field of action, had not the English received a reinforcement, which put them to flight. The loss of the English in the engagement was five killed and nine wounded, and that of the enemy twenty-three killed, and between thirty and forty wounded.

The savages were no longer confined to any particular tribe or place, but in parties of from fifty to one hundred were scattered all over the thinly inhabited parts of New England. A considerable body of them were yet in the neighborhood of Hadley, Deerfield, and Northampton, where they were continually committing their wanton acts of barbarity. Several of the towns above mentioned, duly reflecting on the danger to which they and their families were exposed, formed themselves into several companies, and made choice of their commanders. On the 4th February, receiving information that there were near two hundred Indians embodied in a swamp in the neighborhood of Deerfield, the above force marched to attack them. Arriving within view about daybreak, they discovered them in a profound sleep, stretched out upon the ground around their fire. The cavalry immediately dismounted, and, after forming, approached within pistol-shot before they were discovered by the enemy; who, being suddenly aroused from sleep, and astonished at the unexpected appearance of so many of their enemies, fell an easy prey to the English, who, without the loss of a man, killed one hundred and twenty of them; the remainder, as the only means of escape, plunged into a river, where probably many of them perished.

Although the English achieved this action without any loss on their part, they were on their return unhappily ambushed by about four hundred of the enemy. The English, having expended all their ammunition in the late engagement, and being much fatigued, were now in turn likely to fall an easy prey to their enemies, who, with their bloody knives and tomahawks, for the space of an hour, attacked them with the greatest success. Not one of the English, it is probable, would have survived this bold and unexpected attack of the enemy, had it not been for the presence of mind of their brave commander, Capt. Holyoke, who, by a stratagem, succeeded in saving a party of them. Capt. Holyoke had his horse killed under him, and at one time was attacked by five of the enemy, whom he beat off with his cutlass. The loss of the English in this unfortunate action was fifty-one killed and eighty-four wounded; many of the latter survived the action but a few days. The defeat and destruction of the English in this engagement was much to be lamented, as among the slain were the heads of several families, who had volunteered their services in defence of their infant settlement.

On the 10th, several hundreds of the enemy, encouraged by their late success, appeared before Hatfield, and fired several dwelling-houses without the fortifications of the town. The inhabitants of Hadley being seasonably apprized of the situation of their brethren of Hatfield, a number of them volunteered their services and marched to their relief. The Indians, as they were accustomed to do on the approach of the English, lay flat on their bellies until the latter had advanced to within bowshot, when, partly rising, they discharged a shower of arrows among them, which wounded several of the English; but they, having wisely reserved their fire, now in turn levelled their pieces with the best effect, before the savages had time to recover their legs. About thirty of the enemy were instantly despatched, and the remainder were dispersed.

On the 15th February, the governor of Massachusetts colony receiving information that the Indians were collecting in great numbers, under the immediate direction of Philip, near Brookfield, he despatched Capt. Henchman with fifty men to dislodge them. He, proceeding to Hadley, was joined by a company of cavalry from Hartford. On the 20th, they discovered and attacked a party near Lancaster, of whom they killed fifty, and took between fifty and sixty of their squaws and children prisoners. Capt. Henchman, on his way to Brookfield, discovered the dead bodies of several of his countrymen, half consumed by fire, who, it appeared, had a few days previous fallen victims to the wanton barbarity of the savages.

As the scattered remains of the Indians were harassed and driven at the time from place to place by the English, a number of them resorted to the western country, then inhabited by the Mohawks; but the latter, being on friendly terms with the English and Dutch, who were settling among them, were unwilling to harbor their enemies, and consequently attacked a considerable body of them on the 5th March. The engagement was a severe one. The fugitive Indians, being provided with fire-arms, repelled the attack of the Mohawks with a becoming spirit, but were at length overpowered and completely defeated. The loss on both sides was very great.

On the 20th, the Indians took a Mr. Willet prisoner, near Swanzey, and after cutting off his nose and ears, set him at liberty. On the 22d, a negro man, who had been for several months a prisoner among the savages, escaped from them and returned to the English, to whom he gave the following information: That the enemy were concerting a plan to attack Taunton and the villages adjacent; that for this purpose there were then embodied near Worcester one thousand of them, at the head of whom was Philip, and near one hundred of them were furnished with fire-arms; that a few days previous to his escape, a scouting party arrived and brought in with them two prisoners of war and three human scalps. To frustrate the intention of the enemy, the governor of Massachusetts colony despatched three companies of cavalry for the defence of Taunton.

CHAP. IV.

CONTINUATION OF THE WAR WITH PHILIP.—BATTLE WITH THE NARRAGANSETS, UNDER THE COMMAND OF THEIR QUEEN, WHO WAS TAKEN PRISONER.—PHILIP SLAIN BY A SON OF UNCAS.—HOSTILITIES OF THE INDIANS ON THE RIVER KENNEBECK, IN WHICH A GREAT BATTLE IS FOUGHT AND THE INDIANS TOTALLY DEFEATED, WHICH WAS FOLLOWED BY A TREATY OF PEACE.

The English of Connecticut colony, although but little troubled with the enemy since the destruction of the Pequots, were not unwilling to afford their brethren all the assistance possible in a protracted and bloody war with the common enemy. They accordingly furnished three companies of cavalry, who, under the command of the experienced Maj. Talcott, on the 5th April, proceeded to the westward in search of the enemy. On the 11th, they fell in with and defeated a considerable body of them. Apparently by the special direction of Divine Providence, Maj. Talcott arrived in the neighborhood of Hadley in time to preserve the town, and save its inhabitants from total destruction. The savages, to the number of five hundred, were on the eve of commencing an attack, when they were met by the major with the troops under his command. This unexpected relief animating the few inhabitants which the town contained, they hastened to the assistance of the cavalry, who were at this moment seriously engaged with the whole body of the enemy. The savages having gained some signal advantages, victory, for a considerable time, appeared likely to decide in their favor. Fortunately for the inhabitants of Hadley, they had, for their defence, a few weeks previous, procured from Boston an eight-pound cannon, which, at this critical period, loaded by the women, and being mounted, was by them conveyed to the English, which, being charged with small shot, nails, &c., was by the latter discharged with the best effect upon the enemy, who immediately fled in every direction. Thus it was that the English, in a great measure, owed the preservation of their lives to the unexampled heroism of a few women.

The governor and council of the united colonies, taking under serious consideration the miraculous escape of the inhabitants of Hadley from total destruction, and the recent success of the arms of the English in various parts of the country, appointed the 27th day of August, 1697, to be observed throughout the colonies as a day of public Thanksgiving and Praise to Almighty God. It may be well to observe, that this was the commencement of an annual custom of our forefathers, which to the present day is so religiously observed by their descendants throughout the New England states.

On the 3d September, the Connecticut troops, under the command of Maj. Talcott and Capts. Dennison and Newbury, proceeded to Narraganset in quest of the enemy, who, to the number of about three hundred, had been discovered in a piece of wood. The English were accompanied by their faithful friend Oneco, with one hundred Mohegans under his command. In the evening of the 5th, they discovered the savages encamped at the foot of a steep hill, on which Maj. Talcott made arrangements for an attack. The Mohegans were ordered by a circuitous route to gain the summit, to prevent the flight of the enemy. Two companies of cavalry were ordered to flank them on the right and left, while Maj. Talcott, with a company of foot, stationed himself in the rear. Having thus disposed of his forces, a signal was given by him for the Mohegans to commence the attack, which they did with much spirit, accompanied with such savage yells, that, had the enemy been renowned for their valor, they must have been to the highest degree appalled at so unexpected an attack. After contending for a few moments with the Mohegans, the enemy were attacked on the right and left by the cavalry, who with their cutlasses made great havoc among them; they were, however, unwilling to give ground until they had lost nearly one half their number, when they attempted a flight to a swamp in their rear; but here they were met by Maj. Talcott, with the company of foot, who gave them such a warm reception that they once more fell back upon the Mohegans, by whom they were soon overpowered, and would have been totally destroyed had not Maj. Talcott humanely interfered in their behalf, and made prisoners the few that remained alive. Among the latter was the leader, a squaw, who was called the Queen of Narraganset; and also an active young fellow who begged to be delivered into the hands of the Mohegans, that they might put him to death in their own way, and sacrifice him to their cruel genius of revenge, in which they so much delighted.

The English, although naturally averse to acts of savage barbarity, were not in this instance unwilling to comply with the unnatural request of the prisoner, as it appeared that he had in the presence of the Mohegans exultingly boasted of having killed nineteen English with his gun since the commencement of the war, and after loading it for the twentieth, (there being no more of the latter within reach,) he levelled it at a Mohegan, whom he killed, which completing his number, he was willing to die by their hands. The Mohegans accordingly began to prepare for the tragical event. Forming themselves into a circle, admitting as many of the English as were disposed to witness their savage proceedings, the prisoner was placed in the centre; when one of the Mohegans, who in the late engagement had lost a son, with a knife cut off the prisoner's ears, then his nose, and then the fingers of each hand, and after the relapse of a few moments dug out his eyes and filled their sockets with hot embers! Although the few English present were overcome with a view of a scene so shocking to humanity, yet the prisoner, so far from bewailing his fate, seemed to surpass his tormentors in expressions of joy! When nearly exhausted with the loss of blood, and unable to stand, his executioner closed the tragical scene by beating out his brains with a tomahawk!

The few Indians that now remained in the neighborhood of Plymouth colony, being in a state of starvation, surrendered themselves prisoners to the English; one of whom, being recognised as the person who had, a few days previous, inhumanly murdered the daughter of a Mr. Clarke, was, by order of the governor, publicly executed. The remainder were retained and treated as prisoners, who served as guides. Twenty more of the enemy were on the succeeding day surprised and taken prisoners by the English.

The troops under the command of Maj. Bradford, and Capts. Mosely and Brattle, on the 15th September surprised and took one hundred and fifty of the enemy prisoners, near Pautuxet, among whom was the

12

squaw of the celebrated Philip; and on the day succeeding, learning that the enemy in considerable bodies were roving about in the woods near Dedham, Maj. Bradford despatched Capt. Brattle with fifty men to attack them; who, the day following, fell in with and engaged about one hundred of them. As hatchets were the only weapons with which they were provided, they made but a feeble defence, and were soon overpowered by the English, who took seventy-four of them prisoners; the remainder having fallen in the action. The above party was commanded by a blood-thirsty sachem, called Pompham, renowned for his bodily strength, which exceeded that of any of his countrymen ever met with. He bravely defended himself to the last. Being wounded in the breast, and unable to stand, he seized one of the soldiers while in the act of despatching him with the butt of his gun, whom he would have strangled, had he not been fortunately rescued by one of his comrades.

A general famine now prevailed among the enemy, in consequence of being deprived of an opportunity to plant their lands. Numbers were daily compelled by hunger to surrender themselves prisoners to the English, among whom was a Nipnet sachem, accompanied by one hundred and eighty of his tribe.

On the 12th of October, Capt. Church, with fifty soldiers and a few friendly Indians under his command, defeated a party of the enemy near Providence; and on the day following, conducted by Indian guides, discovered a considerable body of the enemy encamped in a swamp near Pomfret. A friendly Indian, at first espying them, commanded them to surrender; but the enemy did not appear disposed to obey. Being sheltered by large trees, they first discharged their arrows among the English, and then with a terrible yell attacked them with their long knives and tomahawks. The English, meeting with a much warmer reception than what they expected, gave ground, but being rallied by their old and experienced commander, Capt. Church, they rushed upon them with such impetuosity that the enemy were thrown into confusion and dislodged from their coverts. The English had seven men killed and fourteen wounded; among the latter was their brave commander, who received an arrow through his left arm. The loss of the enemy was thirty-two killed, and between sixty and seventy wounded.

On the 20th, information was forwarded to the governor and council, that the famous Philip, who had been for a long time skulking about in the woods near Mount Hope, much disheartened by the ill success of his countrymen, was the morning preceding discovered in a swamp near that place, attended by about ninety Seaconet Indians; on hearing which, the brave Capt. Church, with his little band of invincibles, were immediately despatched in pursuit of him. Capt. Church was accompanied as usual by a number of Mohegans, and a few friendly Seaconet Indians. On the 27th, they arrived in the neighborhood of the swamp, near the border of which he stationed several of the Mohegans and a few friendly Seaconet Indians to intercept Philip in case he should attempt an escape. Capt. Church, at the head of his little band, now, with unconquerable resolution, plunged into the swamp, and wading nearly to his waist in water, discovered the enemy. The Indians were nearly one hundred strong, but, being unexpectedly attacked, they made no resistance, but fled in every direction. The inaccessible state of the swamp, however, prevented the English from pursuing them with success. Their dependence was now upon their friends stationed without. Nor did it appear that those faithful fellows suffered so good an opportunity to pass unimproved. The reports of their muskets convinced Capt. Church that they were doing their duty, in confirmation of which he was very soon after presented with the head of King Philip.

Philip, it appeared, in attempting to fly from his pursuers, was recognised by one of the English, who had been stationed with the Mohegans to intercept him, and at whom he levelled his piece, but the priming being unfortunately wet, and preventing the discharge, the cunning sachem would have escaped had not one of the brave sons of Uncas, at this instant, given him the contents of his musket. The ball went directly through his heart. Thus fell, by the hands of a faithful Mohegan, the famous Philip; who was the projector and instigator of a war, which not only proved the cause of his own destruction, but that of nearly all his tribe—one of the most numerous of any inhabiting New England.

It was at this important instant that the English were made witnesses of a remarkable instance of savage customs. Oneco, on learning that Philip had fallen by the hand of one of his tribe, urged that, agreeably to their custom, he had an undoubted right to the body, and a right to feast himself with a piece of it! The English not objecting, he deliberately drew his long knife from the girdle, and cut a piece of flesh from the bleeding body of Philip, of about one pound weight, which he broiled and eat; in the mean time declaring that he had not for many moons eaten anything with so good an appetite! The head of Philip was severed from his body, and sent by Capt. Church to Boston, to be presented to the governor and council, as a valuable trophy.

The few hostile Indians that now remained within the united colonies, conscious that, if so fortunate as to evade the vigilance of the English, they must soon fall victims to the prevailing famine, fled with their families far to the westward. The English were disposed rather to facilitate than prevent their flight. Having been for a number of years engaged in a destructive and bloody war with them, they were willing that the few who remained alive should escape to a country so far distant that there was no probability of their returning to reassume the bloody tomahawk. Impressed with these ideas, and that the enemy was completely exterminated, they were about to bury the hatchet and turn their attention to agricultural pursuits; when by an express they were informed that the natives in the eastern part of the country, (province of Maine,) had unprovokedly attacked and killed a considerable number of the English in that quarter.

To quench the flames which appeared to be enkindling in the east, the governor despatched four companies of cavalry to the relief of the unfortunate inhabitants. The enemy, who were of the Kennebeck and Amoscoggin tribes, first áttacked with unprecedented fury the defenceless inhabitants settled on Kennebeck river, the most of whom were destroyed or dispersed by them.

On the 2d of November, about seven hundred of the enemy attacked, with their accustomed fury, the inhabitants of Newchewannick, an English settlement, situated a few miles from the mouth of the river Kennebeck. Before they had fully accomplished their hellish purpose, they were surprised by the troops sent from Boston, with whom a most bloody engagement ensued. The Indians, encouraged by their numbers, repelled the attack of the English in so heroic a manner, that the latter were very soon thrown into disorder, and driven out of town, where they again formed, faced about, and in turn charged the enemy with unconquerable resolution. The contest now became close and severe. The savages, with their terrific yells, dexterously hurled their tomahawks among the English, while the latter, with as much dexterity, attacked and mowed them down with their cutlasses. Each were apparently determined on victory or death. The English, at one moment, unable to withstand the impetuosity of the savages, would give ground; at the next, the latter, hard pushed by the cavalry, would fall back. Thus, for the space of two hours, did victory appear balancing between the two contending parties. The field of action was covered with the slain, while the adjacent woods resounded with shrieks and groans of the wounded. At this critical juncture, the English, when on the very point of surrendering, were providentially preserved by a stratagem. In the heat of the action, Maj. Bradford despatched a company of cavalry by a circuitous route to attack the enemy; suspecting this to be a reinforcement of the English, they fled in every direction, leaving the English masters of the field. Thus, after two hours' hard fighting, did the English obtain a victory at the expense of the lives of more than half their number. Their killed and wounded amounted to ninety-nine. The loss of the enemy was not ascertained; it was, however, probably three times greater than that of the English.

The day succeeding this bloody engagement, a lieutenant, with twelve men, was sent by the commander to the place of action to bury the dead. When within a few rods, they were suddenly attacked by about one hundred of the enemy, who had laid in ambush. The lieutenant ordered his men to reserve their fire until they could discharge with the best effect upon the enemy, by whom they were soon surrounded and furiously attacked on all sides; the savages yelling horribly, and brandishing their long knives in the air, yet crimsoned with the blood of their countrymen. The brave little band, however, remained firm and undaunted, and, as the savages approached them, each taking proper aim, discharged with so good effect upon them, that the Indians, amazed at the instantaneous destruction of so many of their comrades, fled in every direction. The English sustained no loss.

On the 5th, the enemy successfully attacked the inhabitants of the village of Casco, thirty of whom they killed, and made prisoners the family of a Mr. Bracket, who, on the 7th, made their escape, in the following manner: The Indians, on returning to their wigwams, learning that a detached party of their brethren had attacked with success and plundered the village of Arowsick, to enjoy a share of the spoil, hastened to join them, leaving the prisoners in the care of two old men and three squaws. Mr. Bracket, whose family consisted of himself, wife, three small children, and a negro lad, viewed this a favorable opportunity to escape; to effect which, he requested the lad to attempt an escape by flight, which he, being uncommonly active, easily effected. The plan of Mr. Bracket had now its desired effect; as the old men, pursuing the negro, left him and his family guarded only by three squaws, whom, (being intoxicated,) he soon despatched, and returned the day following, with his family, to Casco, where the negro lad had arrived some hours before.

On the 15th, the Indians attacked the dwelling-houses of a Capt. Bonithon and Maj. Philips, situated on the east side of Casco river. Having seasonable notice of the hostile views of the enemy, the family of the former, as a place of greater safety, had resorted to the house of the latter a few moments previous to the attack. The savages first communicated fire to the house of Capt. Bonithon, and next proceeded furiously to attack the dwelling of Maj. Philips, in which there were about twenty persons, by whom it was most gallantly defended. The enemy had their leader and a number of their party killed by the fire of the English. Despairing of taking the house by assault, they adopted a new plan of communicating fire thereto. They procured a carriage, on which they erected a stage, in front of which was a barricade, rendered bullet proof, to which poles were attached nearly twenty feet in length, and to the ends were affixed every kind of combustible, such as birch rinds, straw, pitch pine, &c. The Indians were sheltered by the barricade from the fire of the English, while they approached the walls of the house with their carriage. The English were now on the eve of despairing, when fortunately one of the wheels being brought in contact with a rock, the carriage was turned completely round, which exposed the whole body of Indians to their fire. This unexpected opportunity was improved with the greatest advantage by the English, who, with a few rounds, soon dispersed the enemy with no inconsiderable loss.

The day following, the Indians set fire to the house of a Mr. Wakely, whom, with his whole family, they murdered. A company of the English, apprized of their dangerous situation, marched to their relief, but arrived too late to afford assistance. They found the house reduced to ashes, and the mangled bodies of the unfortunate family half consumed by fire.

The savages, emboldened by their late success, on the 20th attacked a small settlement on the Piscataqua river, and succeeded in murdering a part, and carrying away the remainder of the inhabitants into captivity. As an instance of their wonted barbarity, it should be here mentioned, that after tomahawking and scalping one of the unfortunate women of the above place, they bound to her dead body her little infant; in which situation it was the succeeding day discovered by the English, attempting to draw nourishment from its mother's breast.

The governor and council of the united colonies, conceiving it their duty, if possible, to put a final stop to the ravages of the enemy in the east, and to prevent the further effusion of innocent blood, despatched Maj. Wallis and Maj. Bradford, with six companies under their command, to destroy, root and branch, the common enemy. On the 1st December, they arrived in the neighborhood of Kennebeck, near where they were informed the main body of the enemy were encamped. On the morning of the 3d, about the break of day, they fell in with and attacked them. The enemy, who were about eight hundred strong, appeared disposed to maintain their ground. They fought with all the fury of savages, and even assailed the English from the tops of lofty trees, which they ascended for the purpose. They were in possession of but few fire-arms, but hurled their tomahawks with inconceivable exactness, and checked the progress of the cavalry with long spears. Victory for a long time remained doubtful. The ground being covered with snow, greatly retarded the progress of the troops, who probably would have met with a defeat had not a fresh company of infantry arrived in time to change the fortune of the day. These, having remained inactive, as a body of reserve, the commander found himself under the necessity of calling to his aid. The enemy, disheartened at the unexpected arrival of the English, fled with precipitancy to the woods. But very few of them, however, escaped; more than two hundred of whom remained dead on the field of action, and double that number were mortally wounded. The loss of the English was fifty-five killed and ninety-five wounded. This engagement, which proved a decisive one, was of the greatest importance to the English. The great and arduous work was now completed. The few remaining Indians that inhabited the eastern country now expressed a desire to bury the bloody hatchet, and make peace with the English. Their request was cheerfully complied with, and they continued ever after the faithful friends of the English.

CHAP. V.

INVASION OF NEW YORK AND NEW ENGLAND, AND THE DESTRUCTION OF SCHENECTADY BY THE FRENCH AND INDIANS.

In the year 1690, the Mohawks having made several successful expeditions against the Canadians, the Count Frontenac, to raise the depressed spirits of the latter, despatched several parties of French and Indians to attack the frontier settlements of New York and New England. A detachment of nearly five hundred French and Indians, under the command of Messieurs P. Aillebout, De Waulet, and Le Wayne, were despatched from Montreal for this purpose. They were furnished with everything necessary for a winter campaign. After a march of twenty-two days, they, on the 8th February, reached Schenectady. They had on their march been so reduced as to harbor thoughts of surrendering themselves prisoners of war to the English; but their spies, having been several days in the village, entirely unsuspected, represented in such strong terms the defenceless state of the inhabitants, as determined them to make an immediate attack. They found the gates open and unguarded, which they entered about eleven o'clock at night; and the better to effect their hellish purpose, divided their main body into several parties of six or seven men each. The inhabitants were in a profound sleep, and unalarmed until the enemy had broken open their doors, and with uplifted tomahawks were surrounding their beds. Before they had time to rise, the savages began the perpetration of the most inhuman barbarities. No language can express the cruelties which were committed. In less than one hour, two hundred of the unfortunate inhabitants were slain, and the whole village wrapt in flames. A detail of the cruelties committed by the barbarians cannot be read without horror. They ravished, rifled, murdered and mutilated the inhabitants without distinction of age or sex; without any other provocation or excitement than brutal lust and wantonness of barbarity. Pregnant women were ripped open, and their infants cast into the fire or dashed against the posts of the doors. Such monsters of barbarity ought certainly to be excluded from all the privileges of human nature, and hunted down as wild beasts, without pity or cessation. A very few of the inhabitants escaped, who in their shirts fled to Albany in a severe and stormy night. Twenty-five of the fugitives in their flight perished with the cold. After destroying the inhabitants, the enemy killed all the horses and cattle they could find, with the exception of about thirty of the former, which they loaded with their plunder and drove off.

When the news of this horrid massacre reached Albany, a universal fear and consternation seized the inhabitants. The country became panic-struck, and many entertained thoughts of destroying the town and abandoning that part of the country to the enemy.

A second party of the enemy, which Count Frontenac had detached from the main body at the Three

Rivers, under the command of Sieur Hartel, an officer of distinguished character in Canada, on the 18th February fell upon Salmon Falls, a plantation on the river which divides New Hampshire from the province of Maine. This party consisted of about seventy men, more than half of whom were Indians. They commenced the attack at break of day, in three different places, and although the inhabitants were surprised, yet they flew to arms and defended themselves with a bravery that even their enemies applauded; but they were finally overpowered by numbers, when forty-three of them, consisting of men, women, and children, fell victims to savage barbarity.

The depredations of the French and Indians filled the people of the western country with fear and alarm. The assembly of New York conceived it necessary to make every exertion to prevent the settlement of the French at Albany. It was resolved that two companies, of one hundred men each, should be raised and sent forward for that purpose. For the defence of the frontier towns in New England, it was ordered that a constant watch should be kept in several towns; that all males above the age of eighteen and under sixty years should be kept in readiness to march at the shortest notice. On the 20th March, at a meeting of commissioners from New York and New England, a plan was proposed and adopted for invading Canada. Eight hundred men were ordered to be raised for the purpose, and the quotas of several colonies were fixed, and general rules adopted for the management of the army.

A small vessel was sent express to England, the beginning of April, carrying a representation of the exposed state of the colonies and the necessity of the reduction of Canada. A petition was also forwarded to the king for a supply of arms and ammunition, and a number of frigates to attack the enemy by water, while the colonial troops made an invasion by land. John Winthrop, Esq., was appointed major general and commander in chief of the land army, and arrived, with the troops under his command, near the falls at the head of Wood Creek*, early in August.

When the army arrived at the place appointed for the rendezvous of the Indians from the Five Nations, who had engaged to assist the English, instead of meeting with that powerful body which they expected, and which the Indians had promised, there were no more than seventy warriors from the Mohawks and Oneidas. When the general had advanced about one hundred miles, he found that there were not canoes sufficient to transport one half of the English across the lake. Upon representing to the Indians that it was impossible for the army to cross into Canada without a greater number, they replied that it was then too late in the season to make canoes, as the bark would not peel. In short, they artfully evaded every proposal, and finally told the general and his officers that they looked too high, advising them only to attack Chambly, and the out settlements on this side of the St. Lawrence. Thus did these Indians, who a few years before had so harassed all the French and Indians in Canada, exhibit the greatest proof of cowardice. The English, finding it impossible to cross the lake with advantage, returned to Albany. Thus the expedition unfortunately failed.

In the year 1693, Count Frontenac, finding that he could not accomplish a peace with the Mohawks, who, of all the Indians, had been by far the most destructive to the settlements in Canada, determined on their destruction. He collected an army of about seven hundred French and Indians, and, having supplied them with everything necessary for a winter campaign, sent them against the Mohawk castles. They commenced their march from Montreal on the 15th January, 1693. After enduring incredible hardships, they fell in with the first castle about the 10th February. The Mohawks, unprepared for an attack, had not any idea of the approach of the Canadians.

The enemy killed and captured about fifty of the Mohawks at this castle, and then proceeded for the second, at which they were equally successful. A great part of the Mohawks were at Schenectady, and the remainder thought themselves perfectly secure. When the enemy arrived at the third castle, they found about eighty warriors collected at a war-dance, as they designed the next day to go upon an expedition against their enemies. A conflict ensued, in which the Canadians, after losing about thirty men, were victorious, and the third castle was taken. The Canadians in their descent took near three hundred prisoners, principally women and children. The brave Col. Schuyler of Albany, receiving information of the approach of the enemy, at the head of a party of the volunteers, consisting of about four hundred English and Dutch, pursued them. On the 25th February, he was joined by about three hundred Indians, whom he found lodged in a fortified camp. The Canadians made three successive sallies upon the colonel, and were as often repulsed. He kept his ground, waiting for provisions and a reinforcement from Albany. The enemy at length, taking advantage of a violent snow-storm, escaped and marched to Canada. The day following, Capt. Sims, with a reinforcement and supply of provisions, arrived from Albany, and the next day the colonel reassumed the pursuit; but the Canadians, luckily finding a cake of ice across the north branch of Hudson river, made their escape; they were, however, so closely pursued by the English and Dutch that they could not prevent the escape of most of their prisoners, all of whom, with the exception of nine or ten, returned in safety to their country. Col. Schuyler lost twelve of his party, and had nineteen wounded. According to the report of the captives, the enemy lost fifty men, five of whom were French officers, and two Indian guides, and about seventy wounded. On their return, the Mohawks found more than forty dead bodies of the enemy, which, after they had scalped, so great was their hunger, they devoured.

CHAP. VI.

MASSACRE OF THE INHABITANTS OF DEERFIELD, AND CAPTIVITY OF THE REV. JOHN WILLIAMS AND FAMILY, BY THE SAVAGES.—CONTINUATION OF INDIAN HOSTILITIES.

On the 19th February, 1703, a large body of Indians from the frontiers made an attack on Deerfield. They entered the town about midnight, and commenced an indiscriminate butchery of the defenceless inhabitants. Among others, they attacked the house of the Rev. Mr. Williams, pastor of the parish. The following are the particulars of this melancholy transaction, as related by Mr. Williams.

"They came to my house in the beginning of the onset, and, by their violent endeavors to break open doors and windows with axes and hatchets, awaked me out of sleep; on which I leaped out of bed, and running towards the door, perceived the enemy making their entrance into the house. I called to awaken two soldiers in the chamber, and returned towards my bedside for my arms. The enemy immediately broke into the room, I judge to the number of twenty, with painted faces and hideous acclamations. I reached up my hands to the bed-tester for my pistol, uttering a short petition to God for everlasting mercy for me and mine, on account of the merits of our blessed Redeemer. Taking down my pistol, I cocked it, and put it to the breast of the first Indian who came up; but my pistol missing fire, I was seized by three Indians, who disarmed me, and bound me naked, as I was in my shirt, and so I stood for the space of an hour. While binding me, they told me that I was to be carried to Quebec. My pistol missing fire was the occasion of my life's being preserved, since which I have also found it profitable to be crossed in my own will. The judgment of God did not long slumber against one of the three which took me, who was a captain, for by sunrise he received a mortal shot from my next neighbor's house; who opposed so great a number of French and Indians as three hundred, and yet were no more than seven men in an ungarrisoned house.

"I cannot relate the distressing care I had for my dear wife, who had lain in but a few weeks before, and for my poor children, family, and christian neighbors. The enemy fell to rifling the house, and entered in great numbers into every room of the house. I begged of God to remember mercy in the midst of judgment; that he would so far restrain their wrath as to prevent their murdering us; that we might have grace to glorify his name, whether in life or death; and, as I was able, committed our state to God. The enemies who entered the house were all of them Indians and Macquas, exulting over me a while, holding up hatchets over my head, threatening to burn all I had; but yet God, beyond all expectation, made us in great measure to be pitied; for though some were so cruel and barbarous as to take and carry to the door two of my children, and murder them, as also a negro woman, yet they let me put on my clothes, keeping me bound with a cord on one arm till I put on my clothes to the other, and then changing my cord, they let me dress myself, and then pinioned me again; and gave liberty to my dear wife to dress herself and our children About an hour after sunrise, we were all carried out of the house for a march, and saw many of my neighbors' houses in flames, perceiving the whole fort, one house excepted, to be taken. Who can tell what sorrow pierced our souls when we saw ourselves carried from God's sanctuary, to go into a strange land, exposed to so many trials? the journey being at least three hundred miles we were to travel; the snow up to the knees, and we never inured to such hardships and fatigues; the place we were to be carried to, a popish country. Upon my parting from the town, they fired my house and barn. We were carried over the river to the foot of the mountain, about a mile from my house, where we found a great number of our christian neighbors, men, women, and children, to the number of one hundred, nineteen of whom were afterwards murdered by the way, and starved to death near Coos, in a time of great scarcity or famine which the savages underwent there. When we came to the foot of the mountain, they took away our shoes, and gave us in the room of them Indian shoes, to prepare us for our travel. Whilst we were there, the English beat out a company that remained in the town, and pursued them to the river, killing and wounding many of them; but the body of the army being alarmed, they repulsed those few English that pursued them. After this, we went up to the mountain, and saw the smoke of the fires in the town, and beheld the awful desolation of Deerfield; and before we marched any farther, they killed a sucking child of the English. There were slain by the enemy, of the inhabitants of the town, to the number of thirty-eight, besides nine of the neighboring towns.

"When we came to our lodging-place the first night, they dug away the snow and made some wigwams; cut down some of the small branches of spruce trees to lie down on, and gave the prisoners somewhat to eat; but we had but little appetite. I was pinioned and bound down that night, and so I was every night whilst I was with the army. Some of the enemy, who brought drink from the town, fell to drinking, and in their drunken fit they killed my negro man—the only dead person I either saw at the town or on the way. In the night an Englishman made his escape. In the morning I was called for, and ordered by the general to tell the English, that if any more made their escape, they would burn the rest of the prisoners. He that took me was unwilling to let me speak with any of the prisoners as we marched; but early on the second day, he being appointed to the rear guard, I was put into the hands of my other master, who permitted me to speak to my wife, when I overtook her, and to walk with her, to help her on her journey."

After a fatiguing journey of ten or twelve days, the

Indians reached their village with their prisoners, whom they held in captivity, enduring almost incredible hardships, until the 25th of October following; when an ambassador from Boston, Samuel Appleton, Esq., arrived, who had been despatched to redeem such as had survived. They took passage at Quebec, and, to the number of fifty-seven, arrived in safety at Boston on the 21st of November.

The Indians continued their depredations upon the defenceless inhabitants on the frontiers until the year 1725, when a treaty of peace was signed between commissioners appointed by the general court at Boston, and the chiefs of the hostile Indian tribes. A long peace followed, and the Indians generally manifested a disposition to remain on friendly terms with the English, and it was supposed that they never would again be disposed to hostilities, had they not been under the immediate influence of French interest.

War was declared between France and England in March, 1744. The first year of the war, no Indians made their appearance in this part of the country. They had found by experience, that to maintain an open trade with the English was greatly to their interest, and consequently at first entered into the war with reluctance.

The first mischief done by them in this part of the country, in the course of the war, was in July, 1745; when a few Indians came to a place called the Great Meadow, about sixteen miles above Fort Dummer, on Connecticut river. Two of them captured William Phipps as he was hoeing his corn.

October 11th, the fort at the Great Meadow was attacked by a large party of French and Indians. The attack was bold and furious, but without success. No lives were lost. Nehemiah Howe was taken captive and carried to Quebec, where he soon died. The enemy, on their return, met one David Rugg, with another person, passing down Connecticut river in a canoe. Rugg was killed and scalped, but the other with some difficulty made his escape.

14

On the 22d of the same month, a large party of the enemy came to the Upper Ashwolot, with a design to have taken the fort by surprise, but being discovered by a person who was providentially at that time at a little distance from the garrison, they were disconcerted. An action, however, ensued, which continued for some time. The enemy finally withdrew. In this action, John Bullard was killed, Nathan Blake captured, and the wife of Daniel M'Kinne, being out of the fort, was overtaken and stabbed. Before the enemy retired, they burnt several buildings, which was supposed to have been done not so much for the sake of mischief as to conceal their dead, there being many human bones afterwards found among the ashes.

August 3d, a body of the enemy appeared at Number Four. Suspicions of their approach were excited by the howling of dogs. A scout, being sent out from the fort, had proceeded but a few rods before they were fired upon. Ebenezer Phillips was killed, and the remainder made their escape to the fort. The enemy surrounded the garrison, and endeavored for three days to take it, but, finding their efforts ineffectual, withdrew, after having burnt several buildings, and killed all the cattle, horses, &c., they could find.

August 11th, Benjamin Wright, of Northfield, riding in the woods, was fired on, mortally wounded, and died in a few hours after.

In the month of August, M. Rigaud De Vaudreuil marched from Crown Point, with about eight hundred French and Indians, and invested fort Massachusetts on the 20th. The garrison, at this time, consisted of only twenty-two effective men, under the command of sergeant, afterwards Lieut. Col. John Hawks.

Notwithstanding the inferiority of his force, the brave sergeant rejected the proposals of the French commander, and resolved to defend the place to the last extremity. For twenty-eight hours, with small arms only, and a scanty supply of ammunition, he resisted the efforts of the enemy, and kept them at a respectful distance. Habituated to sharp shooting, the garrison singled out the assailants whenever they exposed themselves, and brought them down at long shot. Instances occurred in which the enemy were thus killed at the extraordinary distance of sixty rods; and they often fell when they supposed themselves in perfect security. Having at length expended most of his ammunition, the brave commander reluctantly consented to submit, and a capitulation was agreed upon, by which the garrison was to remain prisoners of war until exchanged or redeemed, to be humanely treated, and none to be delivered to the Indians. Vaudreuil, however, the next day, in violation of the articles of capitulation, delivered one half of the captives into the hands of the irritated Indians, by whom a sick man was immediately murdered; but the others were treated with humanity, carried to Crown Point, thence to Canada, and afterwards redeemed. Hawks lost but one man during the siege, but the enemy, according to information afterwards obtained, had forty-seven killed or badly wounded.

Immediately after the capture of the fort, a party of about fifty Indians went for the purpose of committing depredations upon Deerfield. They came first upon a hill at the southwest corner of the south meadow, where they discovered ten or twelve men and children at work, in a situation in which they might all with ease be made prisoners. Had they succeeded in their design, which was to obtain prisoners rather than scalps, it is probable that events would not have been so disastrous as they proved. They were disconcerted by the following circumstance: Mr. Eleazer Hawks was out that morning a fowling, and was providentially at the foot of the hill when the enemy came down; who, seeing him, supposed they were discovered, and immediately fired upon him, killed, and scalped him. This gave an alarm to the people in the meadow, some of whom were but a few rods distant. The enemy were now sensible that what they did must be done with despatch. Accordingly, they rushed into the meadow, fired on Simeon Amsden, a lad, beheaded, and scalped him. Messrs. Samuel Allen, John Sadler, and Adonijah Gillet, ran a few rods and made a stand under the bank of the river, where they were attacked with fury, and fought a little time with great bravery; they were, however, soon overpowered with numbers. Allen and Gillet fell. Sadler, finding himself alone, ran across the river and made his escape, amidst a shower of balls. While this was passing, Oliver Amsden was pursued a few rods, overtaken, and stabbed, after having his hands and fingers cut in pieces by endeavoring to defend himself against the knives of the enemy. At the same time, three children, by the name of Allen, were pursued. Eunice, one of the three, was struck down with a tomahawk, which was sunk into her head; but by reason of the haste in which the enemy retreated, she was left unscalped, and afterwards recovered. Caleb Allen, of Deerfield, made his escape; and Samuel was taken captive, who was the only prisoner taken at this time.

This lad, after a year and nine months, was redeemed. Col. Hawks, who was sent to Canada for the purpose of redeeming captives, inquiring for the lad, was informed, that he was unwilling to be seen, and that he expressed great dissatisfaction on hearing of his arrival. When he was brought into the presence of Col. Hawks, he was unwilling to know him, although he was his uncle, and had always been acquainted with him in Deerfield. Neither would he speak in the English tongue; not that he had forgotten it, but to express his unwillingness to return. He made use of various arts that he might not be exchanged; and finally could not be obtained but by threats, and was brought off by force. In this we see the surprising power of habit. This youth had lost his affection for his country and friends in the course of one year and nine months, and had become so attached to the Indians, and their mode of living, as to consider it the happiest life. This appears the more surprising, when we consider that he fared extremely hard, and was reduced almost to a skeleton.

In the various attacks upon small parties by surprise, the enemy had generally been successful; but scouting parties, under brave and cautious officers, sometimes turned the scales against them. A gallant case of this kind occurred about this time. Capt. Humphrey Hobbs, with forty men, was ordered from Charlestown, through the woods, to fort Shirley, in Heath, one of the posts on the Massachusetts line. The march was made without interruption until Hobbs arrived at what is now Marlborough, in Vermont, about twelve miles northwest of fort Dummer, where he halted, on the 26th of June, to give his men an opportunity to refresh themselves. A large body of Indians, under a resolute chief by the name of Sackett, a half-breed, discovered Hobbs' trail, and made a rapid march to cut him off. Without being apprized of the pursuit of the enemy, Hobbs had circumspectly posted a guard on his trail, and his men were regaling themselves at their packs, on a low piece of ground, covered with alders, intermixed with large trees, and watered by a rivulet. The enemy soon came up, and drove in the guard, which first apprized Hobbs of their proximity. Without the least knowledge of their strength, he instantly formed for action, each man selecting his tree for a cover. Confident of victory, from their superiority of numbers, the enemy rushed up, and received Hobbs' well-directed fire, which cut down a number, and checked their impetuosity. Covering themselves, also, with trees and brush, the action became warm, and a severe conflict ensued between sharp shooters. The two commanders had been known to each other in time of peace, and both bore the character of intrepidity. Sackett, who could speak English, in a stentorian voice frequently called upon Hobbs to surrender, and threatened, in case of refusal, to rush in and sacrifice his men with the tomahawk. Hobbs, in a voice which shook the forest, as often returned a defiance, and urged his enemy to put his threats in execution. The action continued with undaunted resolution, and not unfrequently the enemy approached Hobbs' line, but were driven back to their first position by the fatal fire of his sharp-sighted marksmen; and thus about four hours elapsed without either side giving up an inch of their original ground. At length, finding Hobbs determined on death or victory, and that his own men had suffered severely, Sackett ordered a retreat, carrying off his dead and wounded, and leaving his antagonist to continue his march without further molestation.

This battle was often mentioned by the old people of the vicinity with great exultation, as exhibiting a masterpiece of persevering bravery. Sackett's number has not been accurately given, but it is pretty certainly ascertained that they were at least four to one of the English.

August 29th, about two hundred of the enemy made their appearance at fort Massachusetts, which was then under the command of Capt. Ephraim Williams. A scout was first fired upon, which drew out Capt. Williams, with about thirty men. An attack began, which continued for some time, but finding the enemy numerous, Capt. Williams fought upon the retreat till he had again recovered the fort. The enemy soon withdrew, and with what loss was unknown. In this action one Abbot was killed, and Lieut. Howley and Ezekiel Wells were wounded, but recovered.

This is the last instance of mischief done by the enemy in the western frontiers in what is called the first French war. Peace, however, was not finally settled with the Indians until October, 1749, when a treaty was held at Falmouth, by commissioners from the general court and the chiefs of the Indian tribes, by whom a former treaty, with some additions, was renewed.

From this important period, which being the 15th day of October, 1749, ought the peace and prosperity of the now flourishing states of New England to receive their date. It was at this period that her hardy sons quit the sanguinary field, and exchanged their implements of death for such as were better calculated for the cultivation and tillage of their farms. The forests, with which they were encompassed, no longer abounded with fierce and untutored savages; the Indian death-song and war-whoop were no longer heard; the greater part of the Indians that survived the many bloody engagements had sought peace and retirement far westward; and the prisoners which the English had captured were liberated, on condition of resorting to and remaining with them. They proved faithful to their promise. They took possession of the country bounding on the great lakes, and in possession of which their descendants remain to the present day; a description of whose manners and customs will be found in a succeeding chapter.

CHAP. VII.

REMARKS RELATIVE TO THE STATE, CUSTOMS, AND LUDICROUS OPINIONS OF THE NATIVES IN NEW ENGLAND WHEN FIRST VISITED BY OUR FOREFATHERS, AND THEIR RAPID DEPOPULATION SINCE THAT PERIOD.

We cannot even hazard a conjecture respecting the Indian population of New England at the time of its first settlement by the English. Capt. Smith, in a voyage to this coast in 1614, supposed that on the Massachusetts islands there were about three thousand Indians. All accounts agree that the sea-coast and neighboring islands were thickly inhabited.

Three years before the arrival of the Plymouth colony, a very mortal sickness, supposed to have been the plague or yellow fever, raged with great violence among those in the eastern parts of New England. Whole towns were depopulated. The living were not able to bury the dead; and their bones were found lying above ground many years after. The Massachusetts Indians are said to have been reduced from thirty thousand to three hundred fighting men. In 1633, the small pox swept off great numbers in Massachusetts.

In 1763, on the island of Nantucket, in the space of four months, the Indians were reduced by a mortal sickness from three hundred and twenty to eighty-five souls. The hand of Providence is notable in these surprising instances of mortality among the Indians to make room for the whites. Comparatively few have perished by wars, and the descendants of the few that were not driven to the westward by the English, waste and moulder away, and in a manner unaccountably disappear.

The number in the state of Connecticut in 1774 was one thousand three hundred and sixty-three. The principal part of their population in this state is at Mohegan, in the county of New London. These are the descendants of the Mohegans, of whom frequent mention is made in the foregoing pages as being very serviceable, under the command of Uncas, to the English in their many engagements with the natives. The Mohegans have ever exhibited great reverence for the descendants of their royal sachem. After the death of Uncas, his body, by his request, was conveyed to Norwich, and there interred in the neighborhood of one of his forts. This spot was selected by him previous to his death, and it was his dying request that the whole family of Uncas should there be buried; a request which has been strictly complied with by the Mohegans, who, although the distance is seven miles from their own burying-ground, have and continue to deposite there the descendants of their revered sachem.

The number of Indians in Rhode Island in 1783 was only five hundred and twenty-five. More than half these lived in Charlestown, in the county of Washington. In 1774 their number was one thousand four hundred and eighty-two; so that in nine years the decrease was nine hundred and fifty-seven. We have not been able to ascertain the exact state of the Indian population of Massachusetts and New Hampshire. In 1784, there was a tribe of about forty Indians at Norridgewalk, in the province of Maine, with some few other scattering remains of tribes in other parts, and a number of towns thinly inhabited near Cape Cod.

When the English first arrived in America, the Indians had no times or places set apart for religious worship. The first settlers in New England were at great pains to introduce among them the habits of civilized life, and to instruct them in the christian religion. A few years' intercourse with them induced them to establish several good and natural regulations.

The Rev. Mr. Elliot, of Roxbury, near Boston, who has been styled the great Indian apostle, with much labor learned the Natic dialect. He published an Indian grammar, and preached in Indian to several tribes, and in 1664 translated the Bible and several religious books into the Indian language. He relates several pertinent queries of the Indians respecting the christian religion; among others, Whether Jesus Christ, the mediator or interpreter, could understand prayer in the Indian language? If the father be bad and the child good, why should God in the second commandment be offended with the child? How the Indians came to differ so much from the English in the knowledge of God and Jesus Christ, since they all sprung from one Father? Mr. Elliot was indefatigable in his labors, and travelled through all parts of Massachusetts and Plymouth colonies, as far as Cape Cod. The colony had such a veneration for him, that in an act of the general assembly, relating to the Indians, they expressed themselves thus:—"By the advice of the said magistrates and of Mr. Elliot."

Concerning the religion of the untaught natives of New England, who once held to a plurality of deities, after the arrival of the English they supposed there were only three, because they saw people of three

15

kinds of complexion, viz. English, negroes, and themselves.

It was a notion pretty generally prevailing among them, that it was not the same God that made them who made us, but that they were created after the white people; and it is probable they supposed their god gained some special skill by seeing the white people made, and so made them better; for it is certain they looked upon themselves, and their methods of living, which they say their god expressly prescribed for them, as vastly preferable to the white people and their methods.

With regard to a future state of existence, many of them imagined that the chichung, that is, the shadow or what survived the body, would at death go southward, and, in an unknown but curious place, would enjoy some kind of happiness, such as hunting, feasting, dancing, and the like. And what they supposed would contribute much to their happiness was, that they should there never be weary of those entertainments.

The natives of New England believed not only in a plurality of gods, who made and governed the several nations of the world, but they made deities of everything they imagined to be great and powerful, beneficial or hurtful to mankind; yet they conceived an almighty being, whom they called Kichtau, who at first, according to their tradition, made a man and woman out of stone, but, upon some dislike, destroyed them again, and then made another couple out of a tree, from whom descended all the nations of the earth; but how they came to be scattered and dispersed into countries so remote from one another, they could not tell. They believed their supreme god to be a good being, and paid a sort of acknowledgment to him for plenty, victory, and other benefits.

The immortality of the soul was universally believed among them. When good men died, they said their souls went to Kichtau, where they met with their friends, and enjoyed all manner of pleasures; when the wicked died, they went to Kichtau also, but were commanded to walk away, and so wander about in restless discontent and darkness forever.

The natives of New England in general were quick of apprehension, ingenious, and when pleased nothing could exceed their courtesy and friendship. Gravity and eloquence distinguished them in council, address and bravery in war. They were not more easily provoked than the English, but when once they received an injury, it was never forgotten. In anger, they were not like the English, talkative and boisterous, but sullen and revengeful. The men declined all labor, and spent their time in hunting, fishing, shooting, and warlike exercise. They imposed all the drudgery upon their women, who gathered and brought home their wood, and planted, dressed, and gathered their corn. When they travelled, the women carried their children, packs, and provisions, and submitted patiently to such treatment. This ungenerous usage of their husbands they repaid with smiles and good humor.

The clothing of the natives was the skins of wild beasts. The men threw a mantle of skins over them, and wore a small flap, which was termed Indian breeches. The women were much more modest. They wore a coat of skins, girt about their loins, which reached down to their hams, which they never put off in company. If the husband chose to dispose of his wife's beaver petticoat, she could not be persuaded to part with it until he had provided her another of some sort. In the winter, their blankets of skins, which hung loose in summer, were tied or wrapped more closely about them. The old men in the severe seasons also wore a sort of trowsers made of skins and fastened to their girdles, and on their feet they wore moccasons made of moose leather, and their chiefs or sachems wore on their heads a cap decorated with feathers.

Their houses or wigwams were at best but miserable cells. They were constructed generally like arbors, or small young trees bent and twisted together, and so curiously covered with mats or bark that they were tolerably dry and warm. They made their fires in the centre of the house, and there was an opening at the top which emitted the smoke. For the convenience of wood and water, these huts were commonly erected in groves, near some river, brook, or living spring. When either failed, the family removed to another place.

They lived in a poor, low manner. Their food was coarse and simple, without any kind of seasoning, having neither spice, salt, or bread. Their food was principally the entrails of moose, deer, bears, and all kinds of wild beasts and fowls. Of fish and snakes they were extremely fond. They had strong stomachs, and no kind of food came amiss. They had no set meals, but, like all other wild creatures, ate when they were hungry and could find anything to satisfy the cravings of nature. They had but little food from the earth except what it spontaneously produced. Indian corn, beans, and squashes were the only eatables for which the natives of New England labored.

Their household furniture was of but small value. Their beds were composed of mats or skins. They had neither chairs or stools, but commonly sat upon the ground, with their elbows upon their knees. A few wooden and stone vessels and instruments served all the purposes of domestic life. Their knife was a sharp stone, shell, or kind of reed, which they sharpened in such a manner as to cut their hair, make their bows and arrows, &c. They made their axes of stone, which they shaped somewhat similar to our axes, but with the difference of their being made with a neck instead of an eye, and fastened with a withe, like a blacksmith's chisel.

The manner of the courtship and marriage of the natives manifested the impurity of their morals. When a young Indian wished for marriage, he presented the girl with whom he was enamored with bracelets, belts, and chains of wampum. If she received his presents, they cohabited together for a time upon trial.

If they pleased each other, they joined in marriage; but if, after a few weeks, they were not suited, the man, leaving his presents, quitted the girl, and sought another mistress, and she another lover. In this manner they courted until two met who were agreeable to each other.

The natives of New England, although they consisted of a great number of different nations and clans, appear to have spoken the same language. From Piscataqua to Connecticut, it was so nearly the same that the different tribes could converse tolerably together. The Mohegan or Pequot language was essentially that of all the Indians in New England. The word Mohegan is a corruption of Muhhekaneew in the singular, or of Muhhekaheek in the plural number. The Penobscots bordering on Nova Scotia, the Indians of St. Francis in Canada, the Delawares in Pennsylvania, the Shawnese on the Ohio, and the Chippewas at the westward of lake Huron, all now speak the same radical language.

CHAP. VIII.

REMARKS ON THE INDIAN CUSTOMS AND MODE OF WARFARE, AND THE CHANGE THAT TOOK PLACE IN CONSEQUENCE OF THEIR INTERCOURSE WITH THE FRENCH, WITH A HISTORY OF THEIR ATTACKS ON THE FRONTIER SETTLEMENTS DURING THE FRENCH WAR.—EXPEDITION TO NORRIDGEWOG, AND DEATH OF THE JESUIT RALLE, AND A DESCRIPTION OF LOVEWELL'S FIGHT.—BRAVE DEFENCE OF THE FORT AT CHARLESTOWN, BY CAPT. STEVENS.

After the destruction of Philip and those tribes of Indians who joined him in his wars against the English, the inhabitants of the New England colonies were in a great measure relieved from the terrors and vexations which they had for so long a time suffered from the hostilities which had existed with the Indians from the time they first landed at Plymouth. The remnants of those tribes which had been subdued, fled to the far west and to Canada. Those who had been friendly to the English remained, and had a portion of their lands assigned them, that they might exist upon, with certain privileges of hunting, fishing, peeling bark, &c.; but the change that took place in their habits and mode of life in consequence of their intercourse with the English, has proved about as destructive to them as their wars. At the present time, there are a few miserable remnants of them remaining in different parts of the country.

The French having possession of the Canadas and Nova Scotia, gave them great advantages in getting a complete control over the Indian tribes on all the frontiers of the north and east. They pursued a very different course toward them from that of the English. Instead of destroying them, they adopted the plan of conciliating and improving their condition. Missionaries were sent out from France by the Jesuits, who adopted their manner of living, and established themselves at the various posts throughout the country; introducing among them the Roman Catholic religion, which they readily embraced, it being more congenial to their ideas of worship than any other that they had a knowledge of. All the Indian tribes in Canada and Nova Scotia, at the present time, strictly conform to the Catholic faith, and have their churches and priests. One of their sachems, being asked why they were so strongly attached to the French, from whom they could not expect to receive so much benefit as from the English, gravely answered, "Because the French have taught us to pray to God, which the English never did."

It was the policy of the French government, in the settlement of the Canadas, to gain an ascendency and control over all the Indian tribes, in order to make them subservient to their plans, in aiding them in their conquests, and in enabling them to keep possession of the country. For this purpose, they not only converted them to their religion, but those who came out to settle in the country were not permitted to bring women with them; in order that they might be induced to form a closer alliance, by taking to themselves Indian wives. From this cause many of the French Canadians are of a mixed blood.

The great plan of the French was to establish a line of posts from the mouth of the St. Lawrence to the mouth of the Mississippi; by which means, with the aid of the savage tribes, they would have been able to control the destinies of North America, and have placed the English colonies in a very uncertain position; and would also have given them the whole of the fur trade, which was a very important object. This would probably have been effected, had the government of France given that aid to the plan that was expected. The colonies were sensible of their danger, and the English government was finally induced to take measures for the conquest of Canada.

When the French first settled in this country, they commenced an extensive traffic with the Indians, and supplied them with fire-arms, ammunition, and other weapons of war; and also introduced among them a better system than they had before known, by organizing them into companies and smaller parties, under proper officers; which caused an entire change in their mode of warfare. This made them a much more formidable enemy than they had before been, with their bows and tomahawks, and their irregular manner of attack. In their later wars, they were generally led by French officers, who had a complete control over them; and a liberal price being paid them for prisoners and scalps, this, with their natural savage ferocity, made them so sanguinary and desperate in their attacks on the inhabitants of the frontier towns, that it struck a general terror throughout the country. Besides, they were taught by their priests that the English were heretics, and to destroy them was a religious duty.

The head-quarters of the savage tribes who continued the war against the English was at Montreal and its vicinity. A large establishment of them had been collected on the St. Francis, a river that empties into the St. Lawrence a few miles below Montreal, who were called the St. Francis Indians. They were composed of the fragments of the different tribes, who had fled to the French for protection, from New England, and still retained their hatred to the English, and thirst for revenge. The Cahnawaghas, a numerous and warlike tribe, which had always been at war with the English, were also established near Montreal. There were other tribes to the north and west of Montreal, and between there and Quebec; which enabled the French to assemble, at short notice, any number of Indian warriors they might wish, to carry on the war against the English.

The great extent of frontier, from the Penobscot river to the Hudson, made it impossible to establish any formidable means of defence against the inroads and frequent attacks made by the French and Indians upon the inhabitants of our scattered settlements. There were, it is true, several forts, at what were considered the most exposed situations; but these were so far apart that they formed no barrier to the incursions of the enemy, who would conceal themselves in the woods till a favorable opportunity offered, when they would fall upon the defenceless settlements, destroy them, murder or make prisoners the inhabitants, committing the most savage barbarities, and retreat, before a force could be collected sufficient to oppose them. In many places there were block-houses, and also dwelling-houses, which were generally built of logs and surrounded with palisadoes, and being a safe defence against musket balls, afforded a protection to the inhabitants who fled to them in case of alarm.

The expeditions against our frontiers were planned and fitted out at Montreal, and were composed of a portion of French Canadians, with as many of the Indian warriors as were deemed necessary to effect their savage atrocities. They were well armed, and under the command of distinguished French officers, who were acquainted with the country, and the mode of warfare best calculated to insure success to their sanguinary and horrid incursions. They had also the advantage of the knowledge of those Indians who had fled from New England, acting as their guides, and who were well acquainted with all the best routes through what was then a vast wilderness, between Canada and the frontier settlements of Massachusetts and New Hampshire, and with all the rivers and lakes that were more or less navigable for their light, birch-bark canoes. These canoes were easily carried round the rapids, and from one stream to another, which afforded great facilities in their expeditions. By sending out small parties of these Indians, they could at all times get information of the situation of the whole extent of the frontier, and form their plans accordingly.

There were two main routes which were in most cases taken in these expeditions. One was by passing up the river St. Francis to lake Memphremagog, where they could strike upon and go down the Connecticut or the Merrimack rivers, or pass on farther east to other streams emptying into the Atlantic. They would often, when the main body arrived at lake Memphremagog, divide themselves into smaller parties, and take different routes, falling upon several places near the same time, and uniting again on their retreat. The other was by going up lake Champlain, which was then in possession of the French, and either passing up Onion river and down White river to the Connecticut, or else Otter Creek, and then down other streams to the same river, more to the south. Either would bring them near the English settlements on the northwest frontier of Massachusetts and New Hampshire. By one or the other of these routes, the enemy were in the habit of making frequent attacks on these settlements, the inhabitants of which were made to suffer very severely from their barbarities.

16

Several fortifications and other means of defence were erected, to guard against these incursions of the enemy, and to protect the inhabitants, as far as the nature of their defenceless situation would admit; but with all that could be done, it gave them very little security against their foes, so long as they possessed the advantages above described; for the enemy could fall upon them at such place and at any time they chose, commit their savage barbarities with impunity, and make good their retreat, with little molestation. To pursue them was useless, for it is believed there never has been an instance, where the Indians have had a few hours the start, that they have ever been overtaken. In some few cases they have, by being vigorously pursued, been compelled to leave their plunder and prisoners behind; though the latter were generally killed and their scalps taken, for which they were paid a liberal reward.

Deerfield and Northfield were for many years the frontier towns on the valley of the Connecticut; a few houses had been built, however, at Greenfield. A strong fort was erected on the west bank of Connecticut river, about six miles above Northfield, furnished with a garrison, and named Fort Dummer; and soon after some families settled in the vicinity—the first settlement made in Vermont. This afforded some protection to the towns on the river below, but those to the east and west were in a defenceless state, and suffered great hardships.

To defend the inhabitants on the western frontiers from the frequent incursions made by the enemy from Crown Point, a fort was erected in the town of Adams, which was named Fort Massachusetts. Several other small fortifications were established between Fort Dummer and Hoosac. These works were erected and garrisoned by Massachusetts colony, and afforded some protection to the suffering settlers; notwithstanding which, however, frequent attacks were made upon them by the savages, and many prisoners and scalps were taken, and much property destroyed.

One of the most important forts erected on the frontier was that at Number Four, so called from its being the fourth town on the river in New Hampshire, above Massachusetts line, and since named Charlestown. This is the first town on the river above Bellows' Falls, and formed a sort of connecting link between the settlements below and the extensive valley of the Connecticut above, which was called the Coos country. At this place the enemy, in their expeditions against that part of the frontier, had heretofore made a rendezvous, from which to make their attacks on the settlements, and from which they could retreat in canoes up the river, or take such other route as they chose on their return to Canada.

For many years previous to the conquest of Canada by the united forces of England and the New England colonies, the inroads of the French and Indians upon our frontier settlements were frequent and sanguinary. Very few seasons passed without the commission of some acts of the most savage barbarity. The defenceless state of the settlements on the frontiers made the inhabitants liable, at all times, not only to suffer by the tomahawk and scalping-knife, the destruction of their property, the carrying off their dearest friends as captives to Canada; but were kept in continual fear and alarm, never laying their heads on their pillows at night to sleep without the apprehension of being waked by the yells of the savage foe.

Some account of these sufferings have been given in a former chapter, and a detail of all the particulars of every case would, we believe, be unimportant at the present day; but to keep up a connection in the historical events of the times, we shall give some of the most important and interesting descriptions of such as are thought worthy of being preserved.

One of the expeditions sent out from Canada descended the Merrimack river, and made an attack on Andover, Haverhill, and other places in that vicinity; burnt and destroyed much property, and took a number of prisoners; but apprehending they were pursued by a large force, in their hurry suffered the prisoners to escape; but a party of them soon after made another attack on Haverhill, burnt nine houses, and killed and captured about forty of the inhabitants. Among the prisoners was Mrs. Hannah Dustan, who had recently lain in, and her infant and nurse. Her children had escaped from the house on the first approach of the Indians, and their father, who was at labor in his field, came to their assistance, and by placing himself in their rear, receiving and returning the fire of the enemy, conducted them to a place of safety. A small party carried off Mrs. Dustan, the nurse, and the infant; the latter they soon despatched; and after several days of tedious travelling, they arrived at an island situated at the junction of the Contoocook and Merrimack rivers, where the prisoners were compelled to run the gauntlet, according to the Indian custom. The party now consisted of an Indian family of two men, three women, and seven children, besides an English lad who had been with them some time.

At night, the whole retired to rest, without a watch, and a little before day, Mrs. Dustan arose from her couch, and, finding the Indians in a sound sleep, waked the nurse and boy, whom she engaged to aid her, and seizing the hatchets, fell resolutely upon the Indians, and despatched all excepting a boy and an old woman, who escaped, after being severely wounded. Taking off the scalps, and embarking in a canoe, they paddled down the river, and at length arrived safely at Haverhill. A reward of fifty pounds was granted to the heroine by the general court of Massachusetts, and many valuable presents were made to her by individuals. The brave act was the topic of conversation throughout the country.

The usual route of the Indians, on their way to the frontiers of New Hampshire, was by the way of Winnipiseogee lake. The distance from Cochecho falls, in the town of Dover, to the southeast bay of that lake, is about thirty miles. In one of their incursions, they made their first appearance at Dover, where they surprised and killed Joseph Ham, and took three of his children; the rest of the family escaped to the garrison. Their next onset was at Lamprey river, where they killed Aaron Rawlins and one of his children, taking his wife and three children captive.

His brother Samuel also lived about half a mile distant on the same river. It seems the Indian scout consisted of eighteen, who probably had been reconnoitring some time, and intended to have destroyed both the families, and for that purpose divided, and nine went to each house; but the party that went to Samuel Rawlins', beating in the windows, and finding the family gone, immediately joined their companions, who were engaged at Aaron's. His wife went out at the door, which perhaps in some degree hastened their assault upon the house, and was immediately seized, and one or two of her children who followed her. Her husband, being alarmed, secured the door before they could enter, and with his eldest daughter, about twelve years old, stood upon his defence, repeatedly firing wherever they attempted to enter, and at the same time calling earnestly to his neighbors for help; but the people in the several garrisoned houses near, apprehending, from the noise and incessant firing, the number of the enemy to be greater than it was, and expecting every moment to be attacked themselves, did not venture to come to his assistance. Having for some time bravely withstood such unequal force, he was at last killed by their random shots through the house, which they then broke open, and killed his daughter. They scalped him, and cut off his daughter's head, either through haste, or probably being enraged against her on account of the assistance she had afforded her father in their defence, which evidently appeared by her hands being soiled with powder. His wife and two children, a son and daughter, they carried to Canada. The woman was redeemed in a few years. The son was adopted by the Indians, and lived with them all his days. He came to Penacook, with the Indians, after the peace, and expressed to some people, with whom he conversed, much resentment against his uncle Samuel Rawlins, on supposing he had detained from his mother some property left by his father, but manifested no desire of returning to Newmarket again. The daughter married with a Frenchman, and, when she was near sixty years old, returned with her husband to her native place, in expectation of recovering the patrimony she conceived was left at the death of her father; but the estate having been sold, they were disappointed, and after a year or two went back to Canada.

Within the town of Dover were many families of Quakers; who, scrupling the lawfulness of war, could not be persuaded to use any means for their defence; though equally exposed with their neighbors to an enemy who made no distinction between them. One of these people, Ebenezer Downs, was taken by the Indians, and grossly insulted and abused by them, because he refused to dance, as the other prisoners did, for the diversion of their savage captors. Another of them, John Hanson, who lived on the outside of the town, in a remote situation, could not be persuaded to remove to a garrison, though he had a large family of children. A party of thirteen Indians, called French Mohawks, had marked his house for their prey, and lay several days in ambush, waiting for an opportunity to assault it. While Hanson with his eldest daughter were gone to attend the weekly meeting of Friends, and his two eldest sons were at work in a meadow at some distance, the Indians entered the house, killed and scalped two small children, and took his wife, with her infant of fourteen days old, her nurse, two daughters and a son, and, after rifling the house, carried them off. This was done so suddenly and secretly that the first person who discovered it was the eldest daughter, at her return from the meeting before her father. Seeing the two children dead at the door, she gave a shriek of distress, which was distinctly heard by her mother, then in the hands of the enemy among the bushes, and by her brothers in the meadow. The people being alarmed, went in pursuit; but the Indians, cautiously avoiding all paths, went off with their captives undiscovered. The woman, though of a tender constitution, had a firm and vigorous mind, and passed through the various hardships of an Indian captivity with much resolution and patience. When her milk failed, she supported her infant with water, which she warmed in her mouth and dropped on her breast, until the squaws taught her to beat the kernel of walnuts and boil it with bruised corn, which proved a nourishing food for her babe. They were all sold to the French, in Canada. Hanson went the next spring and redeemed his wife, the three younger children, and the nurse, but he could not obtain the elder daughter, of seventeen years old, though he saw and conversed with her. After this disaster had befallen his family, Hanson removed the remainder of them to the house of his brother, who, though of the same religious persuasion, yet had a number of lusty sons, and always kept his fire-arms in good order, for the purpose of shooting game.

These and other insolences of the enemy being daily perpetrated on the frontiers, caused the governments to resolve on an expedition to Norridgewog. The captains Moulton and Harman, both of York, each at the head of a company of one hundred men, executed their orders with great address. They completely invested and surprised that village; killed the obnoxious Jesuit, with about eighty of his Indians; recovered three captives; destroyed the chapel, and brought away the plate and furniture of the altar, and the devotional flag, as trophies of their victory. When the attack commenced, the noise and tumult gave Father Rasles notice of the danger his converts were in. Not intimidated, he went out to meet the assailants, in hopes to draw all their attention to himself and secure his flock, at the peril of his own life. He was not disappointed. As soon as he appeared, the English set up a shout, which was followed by a shower of shot, and he fell near a cross which he had erected in the middle of the village, and with him seven Indians, who had accompanied him to shelter him with their own bodies. The Indians, in the greatest consternation at his death, immediately took to flight, and crossed the river, some by fording, and others swimming. The enemy pursued them until they entered far into the woods; and then returned, and pillaged and burnt the church and the wigwams. Ralle was then in the sixty-eighth year of his age, and had resided in his mission at Norridgewog twenty-six years; having before spent six years in travelling among the Indian nations, in the interior parts of America.

Sebastian Rasles, or Ralle, was of a respectable family in Franche-Compte, and was born about the year 1657. Being appointed a missionary from the society of Jesuits to the Indians of North America, he embarked at Rochelle, in France, on the 23d of July, 1689, and arrived at Quebec in October following. He immediately applied himself to learning the language of the *Abnakis*; and went to reside in their village, containing two hundred inhabitants, and situated about three leagues from Quebec, in the midst of a forest. Among the various tribes of Indians he passed the rest of his life, conforming to their customs, living upon their unpalatable food, in irregular and uncertain supplies, taking long journeys through a rugged wilderness, without shelter or comfortable repose by night, and with incessant fatigue by day. He is said to have been a man of superior sense and profound learning, and particularly skilled in Latin, which he wrote with classic purity.

The success of the forces at Norridgewog, and the large premium offered for scalps, having induced several volunteer companies to go out, they visited, one after another, several of the Indian villages, but found them deserted. The fate of Norridgewog had struck such a terror into the enemy, that they did not think themselves safe at any of their former places of abode, and occupied them as resting places only, when they were scouting or hunting.

One of these volunteer companies, under the command of Captain John Lovewell, of Dunstable, was greatly distinguished, first by their success, and afterwards by their misfortunes. This company consisted of thirty. At their first excursion to the northward of Winnipiseogee lake, they discovered an Indian wigwam, in which were a man and a boy. They killed and scalped the man, and brought the boy alive to Boston, where they received the reward promised by law, and a handsome gratuity besides.

By this success, his company was augmented to seventy. They marched again, and visiting the place where they had killed the Indian, found his body as they had left it two months before. Their provision falling short, thirty of them were dismissed by lot and returned. The remaining forty continued their march till they discovered a track, which they followed till they saw a smoke, just before sunset, by which they judged that the enemy were encamped for the night They kept themselves concealed till after midnight, when they silently advanced, and discovered ten Indians asleep, round a fire, by the side of a frozen pond. Lovewell now determined to make sure work; and placing his men conveniently, ordered a part of them to fire, five at once, as quick after each other as possible, and another part to reserve their fire: he gave the signal by firing his own gun, which killed two of them; the men firing according to order, killed five more on the spot; the other three starting up from their sleep, two of them were immediately shot dead by the reserve. The other, though wounded, attempted to escape by crossing the pond, but was seized by a dog and held fast till they killed him. Thus in a few minutes the whole company was destroyed, and that attempt against the frontiers of New Hampshire prevented; for these Indians were marching from Canada, well furnished with new guns and plenty of ammunition; they had also a number of spare blankets, moccasons and snow-shoes, for the accommodation of the prisoners whom they expected to take, and were within two days' march of the frontiers. The pond where this exploit was performed is at the head of a branch of Salmonfall river, in the township of Wakefield, and has ever since borne the name of Lovewell's Pond. The action is spoken of by elderly people, at this distance of time, with an air of exultation; and considering the extreme difficulty of finding and attacking Indians in the woods, and the judicious manner in which they were so completely surprised, it was a capital exploit.

The brave company, with the ten scalps stretched on hoops, and elevated on poles, entered Dover in triumph, and proceeded thence to Boston; where they received the bounty of one hundred pounds for each, out of the public treasury.

Encouraged by this success, Lovewell marched a third time; intending to attack the villages of Pequawket, on the upper part of the river Saco, which had been the residence of a formidable tribe, and which they still occasionally inhabited. His company at this time consisted of forty-six, including a chaplain and surgeon. Two of them proving lame, returned; another falling sick, they halted and built a stockade fort on the west side of great Ossipee pond; partly for the accommodation of the sick man, and partly for a place of retreat in case of any misfortune. Here the surgeon was left with the sick man, and eight of the company for a guard. The number was now reduced to thirty-four. Pursuing their march to the northward, they came to a pond, about twenty-two miles distant from the fort, and encamped by the side of it. Early the next morning, while at their devotions, they heard the report of a gun, and discovered a single Indian, standing on a point of land, which runs into the pond, more than a mile distant. They had been alarmed the preceding night by noises round their camp, which they imagined were made by Indians, and this opinion was now strengthened. They suspected that the Indian was placed there to decoy them, and that a body of the enemy was in their front. A consultation being held, they determined to march forward, and, by encompassing the pond, to gain the place where the Indian stood; and that they might be ready for action, they disencumbered themselves of their packs, and left them without a guard at the northeast end of the pond, in a pitch-pine plain, where the trees were thin, and the brakes, at that time of the year, small. It happened that Lovewell's march had crossed a carrying-place, by which two parties of Indians, consisting of forty-one men, commanded by Paugus and Wahwa, who had been scouting down Saco river, were returning to the lower village of Pequawket, distant about a mile and a half from this pond. Having fallen on his track, they followed it till they came to the packs, which they removed; and counting them, found the number of his men to be less than their own. They therefore placed themselves in ambush, to attack them on their return. The Indian who stood on the point, and was returning to the village by another path, met them, and received their fire, which he returned, and wounded Lovewell and another with small shot. Lieutenant Wyman firing again, killed him, and they took his scalp. Seeing no other enemy, they returned to the place where they had left their packs, and while they were looking for them, the Indians rose and ran toward them with a horrid yelling. A smart firing commenced on both sides, it being now about ten o'clock. Captain Lovewell and eight more were killed on the spot. Lieut. Farwell and two others were wounded. Several of the Indians fell; but, being superior in number, they endeavored to surround the party, who, perceiving their intention, retreated; hoping to be sheltered by a point of rocks which ran into the pond, and a few large pine trees standing on a sandy beach. In this forlorn place, they took their station. On their right was the mouth of a brook, at that time unfordable; on their left was the rocky point; their front was partly covered by a deep bog and partly uncovered, and the pond was in their rear. The enemy galled them in front and flank, and had them so completely in their power, that had they made a prudent use of their advantage, the whole company must either have been killed, or obliged to surrender at discretion; being destitute of a mouthful of sustenance, and an escape being impracticable. Under the conduct of Lieut. Wyman, they kept up their fire, and showed a resolute countenance, all the remainder of the day; during which, their chaplain, Jonathan Frye, Ensign Robbins, and one more, were mortally wounded. The Indians invited them to surrender, by holding up ropes to them, and endeavored to intimidate them with their hideous yells; but they determined to die rather than yield; and by their well-directed fire the number of the savages was thinned, and their cries became fainter, till, just before night, they quitted their advantageous ground, carrying off their killed and wounded, and leaving the dead bodies of Lovewell and his men unscalped.

The shattered remnant of this brave company collected themselves together, found three of their number unable to move from the spot, eleven wounded but able to march, and nine who had received no hurt. It was melancholy to leave their dying companions behind, but there was no possibility of removing them. One of them, Ensign Robbins, desired them to lay his gun by him charged, that, if the Indians should return before his death, he might be able to kill one more. After the rising of the moon, they quitted the fatal spot, and directed their march toward the fort, where the surgeon and guard had been left. To their great surprise, they found it deserted. In the beginning of the action, one man (whose name has not been thought worthy to be transmitted to posterity) quitted the field, and fled to the fort; where, in the style of Job's messenger, he informed them of Lovewell's death, and the defeat of the whole company; upon which they made the best of their way home, leaving a quantity of bread and pork, which was a seasonable relief to the retreating survivors. From this place, they endeavored to get home. Lieutenant Farwell and the chaplain who had the journal of the march in his pocket, and one more, perished in the woods, for want of dressing for their wounds

The others, after enduring the most severe hardships, came in one after another, and were not only received with joy, but were recompensed for their valor and sufferings; and a generous provision was made for the widows and children of the slain.

The fort at Charlestown, which had been abandoned during the winter previous to March, 1747, was then re-occupied by thirty men, and placed under the command of Captain Stevens, who had been its former commander; and scarcely had he commenced his usual duties, when it was invested by a large body of French and Indians, under the command of Mons. Debeline.

On first arriving before the place, the enemy, secreting themselves, lay some time before they were discovered by the garrison; nor was their proximity conjectured until the dogs in the fort indicated something singular in their conduct. Suspicions being thus raised, the gate of the fort was cautiously opened, the garrison put on the alert, and no one allowed to go at a distance. At length one of the men, desirous of ascertaining the ground of the suspicions, ventured out about twenty rods, discharged his musket, and sent forward his dogs. Believing they were discovered, a party of the enemy, concealed behind a log, rose, fired, and slightly wounded the man, who, by a rapid retreat to the fort, saved his life. The whole body of the enemy now rose from their covert, and with horrid yells poured a general fire on the fort; but their resolution was not equal to an attempt to carry it by storm.

The fort being constructed of combustible materials, the enemy believed it possible to set it on fire, and thereby compel the garrison to surrender without further opposition. To effect this, the neighboring fences and a log hut, about forty rods to windward, were soon set on fire, and as the wind was brisk, the flames approached and covered the fort with a dense body of smoke, through which was heard the terrifying yell of the savages, and a constant roar of musketry, and the balls like hail showered upon the fort.

Undaunted, the brave little garrison resolved to defend their post to the last extremity, and a novel scheme was adopted to extinguish the approaching flames, which now began to threaten destruction. By great exertions, no less than eleven passages, or subterranean galleries, were carried under the parapet, of such a depth, that men standing in them on the exterior of the fort were completely protected from the shot of the enemy. Buckets of water from a well within were handed to the men, who kept the parapet constantly moistened. Several hundred barrels were thus expended, and the fort rendered perfectly secure from the approaching flames. In the mean time, a brisk fire was continued upon the enemy, when they could be distinguished through the smoke. Thus baffled in his plan, Debeline resolved to carry the place by other means; a sort of mantelet was prepared, and loaded with dry fagots, set on fire, and forced towards the fort; flaming arrows were also tried; but his efforts to fire the place proved abortive.

On the second day, Debeline proposed a cessation of hostilities, until sunrise the next morning, with which Stevens complied, and in the morning, before the time had expired, Debeline approached with fifty men, under a flag, which he planted within twenty rods of the fort. A parley was then agreed on, and Stevens admitted a lieutenant and two men into the fort as hostages, and the same number were sent out to Debeline, who demanded that the garrison should lay down their arms, pack up their provisions in blankets, surrender the fort, and be conducted prisoners to Montreal; and Stevens was requested to meet him without the fort, and give an answer. Stevens accordingly met the French commander, but before he had time to return his answer, Monsieur threatened that if the terms were rejected, the fort should be stormed, and in case any of his men should be killed, the garrison should be put to the sword. Stevens coolly replied, that as he had been intrusted by his government with the command of the fort, he should hearken to no terms until he was satisfied that he could no longer defend it; and added, that it was but a poor inducement to surrender, if all were to be put to the sword for killing one of his men, when it was probable he had already despatched several. Debeline replied, "Do as you please—I am resolved to have the fort, or die; go and see if your men dare fight any longer, and give me a quick answer." Stevens returned to the fort, and found his men unanimously determined to defend the place or die in the attempt. This resolution was communicated to the French commander about noon; the hostages were exchanged, and the firing was renewed, with a shout from the Indians, and it continued until day-light the next morning, when Stevens was familiarly saluted with "good morning," from the enemy, when a proposition was made for a cessation of arms for two hours. Soon after two Indians approached with a flag, and promised, if Stevens would sell them provisions, they would leave the place without further efforts. In reply, they were told that five bushels of corn would be given for each captive in Canada, for whom they should give hostages, to remain until the captives should be delivered. Debeline, convinced that he could not operate upon the fears of his enemy, or gain possession of the place without an assault, continued a distant fire a short time; then reluctantly withdrew from the fort.

In the attack, which continued three days, Stevens states that thousands of balls were poured upon the fort, yet not a man of the garrison was killed, and only two wounded. When the intelligence of this brave defence was received at Boston, Commodore Sir Charles Knowles, who happened to be at that station, was so highly gratified at the conduct of Stevens, that he sent him an elegant sword; and Number Four, when incorporated into a town in 1753, was called after the commodore's name, Charlestown.

CHAP. IX.

PLAN FOR ESTABLISHING A MILITARY SETTLEMENT ON THE RICH INTERVALS OF COOS.—JOHN KILBURN'S BRAVE DEFENCE OF HIS GARRISON.—MASSACRE OF PRISONERS BY THE INDIANS AT FORT WILLIAM HENRY.—THE VILLAGE OF ST. FRANCIS DESTROYED BY ROGERS' RANGERS.—QUEBEC TAKEN BY GEN. WOLF.

During the cessation of hostilities which took place after the treaty of peace with the Indians, in 1749, measures were taken for extending settlements up Connecticut river, and towns were granted on both banks not long after. A plan was also proposed for establishing a military settlement on the rich intervals at Coos. A road was to be cut out to that place, two towns laid out, one on each side of the river, opposite to each other, (now Newbury and Haverhill,) and stockades, with lodgments for two hundred men, in each township to be erected, enclosing a space of fifteen acres; in the centre of which was to be a citadel, containing the public buildings, and granaries sufficient to receive the inhabitants and movable effects, in case of necessity. Courts of justice were to be established, and other civil privileges granted to the people; and they were to be under strict military discipline.

A large number of people engaged in the enterprise; and in the spring of 1752 a party was sent up to view Coos meadows, and lay out the proposed townships. The movements were noticed by the Indians, and a party of the St. Francis tribe was deputed to remonstrate against the project. They came to Charlestown, and informed Capt. Stevens, that if the English encroached on the lands, which they pretended to claim, they should resist by force. This determination was communicated to the governor of New Hampshire, and the scheme was laid aside.

The savage nations in the French interest were always ready, on the first appearance of a rupture, to take up the hatchet. It was the policy of the French government to encourage their depredations on the frontiers of the English colonies, to which they had a native antipathy. By this means, the French could make their enemies pay the whole expense of a war; for all the supplies which they afforded to the Indians were amply compensated by the ransom of captives. In these later wars, therefore, we find the savages more dexterous in taking captives, and more tender of them when taken, than in former wars; which were carried on with circumstances of greater cruelty.

No sooner had the alarm of hostilities, which commenced between the English and French in the western part of Virginia, spread through the continent, than the Indians renewed their attacks on the frontiers of New Hampshire. A party of them made an assault on a family at Bakerstown, on Pemigewasset river, where they killed a woman, and took several captives. Within three days, they killed a man and a woman at Stevenstown, in the same neighborhood; upon which the settlements were broken up, and the people retired to the lower towns for safety, and the government was obliged to post soldiers in the deserted places. After a few days more, they broke into the house of James Johnson, at Number Four, early in the morning, before any of the family were awake, and took him, with his wife and three children, her sister Miriam Willard, and two men, Peter Laboree and Ebenezer Farnsworth. The surprise was complete and bloodless, and they carried them off undisturbed. The next day, Johnson's wife was delivered of a daughter, who from the circumstance of its birth was named Captive. The Indians halted one day, on the woman's account, and the next day resumed their march, carrying her on a litter, which they made for the purpose, and afterwards put her on horseback. On their march, they were distressed for provision, and killed the horse for food. The infant was nourished by sucking pieces of its flesh. When they arrived at Montreal, Johnson obtained a parole, of two months, to return and solicit the means of redemption. He applied to the assembly of New Hampshire, and after some delay obtained one hundred and fifty pounds sterling. But the season was so far advanced, and the winter proved so severe, that he did not reach Canada till the spring. He was then charged with breaking his parole; a great part of his money was taken from him by violence, and he was shut up with his family in prison, where they took the small-pox, which they happily survived. After eighteen months, the woman, with her sister and two daughters, were sent in a cartel ship to England, and thence returned to Boston. Johnson was kept in prison three years, and then, with his son, returned and met his wife in Boston, where he had the singular ill fortune to be suspected of designs unfriendly to his country, and was again imprisoned; but no evidence being produced against him, he was liberated. His eldest daughter was retained in a Canadian nunnery.

Soon after this, a party from St. Francis made several attacks upon the western frontier of New Hampshire, and committed many savage acts at Keene, Walpole, and other places in that vicinity. They afterwards, being joined by other Indians, made an assault on the garrison of John Kilburn, in which were himself, John Peak, two boys, and some women; who bravely defended the house, and obliged the enemy to retire, with considerable loss.

The defence of Kilburn's garrison was one of the most heroic and successful efforts of personal courage and valor recorded in the annals of Indian warfare. The number of Indians was about two hundred, against whom, John Kilburn, his son John, in his eighteenth year, John Peak and his son, and the wife and daughter of Kilburn, were obliged to contend for their lives. The leader of the Indians, named Philip, was well acquainted with Kilburn, and having approached near the garrison, and secured himself behind a tree, called out to those in the house to surrender. "Old John, young John," said he, "I know you; come out here; we give you good quarter." "Quarter!" vociferated Kilburn, with a voice of thunder; "you black rascals, be gone, or we'll quarter you." The Indians soon rushed forward to the attack, but were repulsed by Kilburn and his men, who were aided by the females in running bullets and in loading their guns, of which they had several in the house. All the afternoon, one incessant firing was kept up till near sundown, when the Indians began to disappear; and as the sun sunk behind the western hills, the sound of the guns and the cry of the war-whoop died away in silence. Peak, by an imprudent exposure before the port-hole, received a ball in his hip, which, for want of surgical aid, proved fatal on the fifth day.

The New Hampshire soldiers had become so noted for hardy courage and agility, so habituated to fatigue and danger, and so well acquainted with the Indian mode of warfare, that, by the express desire of Lord Loudon, three ranging companies were formed of them. They were eminently useful in scouring the woods, procuring intelligence, and skirmishing with detached parties of the enemy. These companies were afterwards formed into one body, and were called Rogers' Rangers, Maj. Robert Rogers being appointed to the command, and in which John Stark, afterwards the hero of Bennington, was captain. He had been taken by the Indians, and was for some time a prisoner among them, but had fortunately made his escape.

Maj. Rogers was an officer of daring courage, and indefatigable in the execution of all enterprises entrusted to him. He adopted the plan of advancing against the enemy in two columns of single files, parallel to each other, within hailing distance; by which means they were in little danger from ambuscades, or from attacks in front, or on either flank. This plan has since been generally practised by our commanders, in their wars with the Indians; and had Gen. Braddock adopted it, agreeably to Washington's advice, he would most probably have saved his army.

This corps of rangers were of great service in the defence of our frontiers against the French and Indians, and their daring exploits were the common theme of conversation at that time throughout the country. Many who served in it were afterwards commissioned, and became distinguished officers in the continental army of the revolution.

During the absence of Lord Loudon, who had been sent with a large force against Louisburg, the main body of Canadians and Indians, under the command of Montcalm, made an attack on fort William Henry, commanded by Col. Monroe, a British officer. Gen. Webb at this time lay at fort Edward, with the main army, consisting principally of provincial troops. The force under Col. Monroe consisted of two thousand and two hundred regulars and provincials; four hundred and forty-nine of whom were posted in the fort, and the remainder in a fortified camp, on the eminence where fort George was subsequently built. The siege, which was continued for six days, was vigorously pressed, and Monroe defended his fort and fortified camp with spirit; but having burst many of his guns and mortars, and expended most of his ammunition, he was compelled to surrender. A capitulation was signed on the ninth, by which the troops were allowed to retain their arms, and were to be escorted to fort Edward.

Soon after the capitulation was signed, a detachment of the French army took possession of Monroe's works. About the same time the Indians rushed over the parapets, and began to plunder such small articles as they could seize with impunity, and at length commenced their depredations on the officers' baggage. To prevent the Indians from becoming intoxicated, the whole of the remaining liquor, both in the fort and camp, was stove. Col. Monroe, perceiving their conduct, gave orders for marching about midnight, and at the time assigned the troops were drawn up and put in motion; but being informed that a large body of savages were on the road for the purpose of intercepting the march, gave orders for the troops to return to camp, where they continued without shelter till morning; the Indians in the mean time hovering about the lines, indicating their savage designs.

Early the next morning, the troops were ordered to prepare for the march; but it was observed that the Indians indicated more ferocity than in the preceding night, each carrying a tomahawk, or other weapon of death, in his hand; and they continued to plunder the baggage of the officers. Col. Monroe complained of a breach of the articles of capitulation, but to no effect. He was told by the French officers, that the savages might be appeased by giving up the private property of the troops; to which he consented, and the plan was generally adopted. But the blood-thirsty tigers were not so easily glutted. They soon seized the officers' hats, guns, and swords, and violently forced off their clothing, in some instances not sparing even their shirts, and this was soon followed by a scene which beggars description. They rushed upon the sick and wounded, whom they butchered and scalped, in the presence of the troops; the negroes, mulattoes and friendly Indians were next dragged from the ranks, and shared the same fate; one of the latter they burnt to death. At length, with great difficulty, the troops left the entrenched camp, but without the promised escort, and had barely cleared it, when the rear of the column was attacked, and many killed and scalped, without discrimination. Monroe then brought the troops to a halt, but in great confusion. As soon as the men in front perceived the danger in the rear, they pressed forward until they reached a French guard at La Corne's camp, followed by the savages, who continued their murders by stabbing, tomahawking, and scalping all within their power. The women accompanying the troops, unable to resist, were seized, their throats cut, their bodies ripped open, and their bowels torn out and thrown in their faces; the children were taken by the heels, and their brains dashed out against rocks and trees; and it is stated that many of the savages drank the hearts' blood of their victims, as it flowed reeking from the horrid wounds.

Protection was now demanded from the French guard, but it was refused, and the unfortunate troops were told that they must scatter in the woods, and seek their own safety. Finding no alternative, they rushed desperately through the savages, attempting to escape by flight, but being pursued, many were tomahawked, while others were so fortunate as to outstrip their pursuers, and to reach fort Edward, but in a horrible plight, after secreting themselves through the following night in the thick woods and swamps, stripped even to nudity. Col. Monroe, and several of his officers and men, were carried back to the French camp, where they remained until an escort was furnished them to fort Edward.

During these horrid transactions, the French troops remained idle spectators of the scene. La Corne, who had great influence among the savages, probably foreseeing the massacre, immediately after the capitulation was signed, sent for Col. Frye, commanding the Massachusetts regiment, and informed him that he well remembered the humanity he had shown to his countrymen in Nova Scotia; that he should embrace the present opportunity to express his gratitude, and reward his humanity; and that neither he nor any of the Massachusetts troops should receive insult or injury from the Indians. But during the whole transaction, he kept at a distance, nor did he send a party to afford the promised protection, or use his influence to moderate the vengeance of the Indians.

On receiving intelligence of the capitulation, Gen. Webb ordered five hundred men to meet the French escort, and conduct the captured troops into his camp; but to his surprise, instead of meeting the escort, the captives were discovered flying through the woods singly or in small parties, in the greatest distress and consternation; many exhibiting the horrid cuts of the knife and tomahawk, and some in a state of delirium, and nearly exhausted.

The individual exploits of several of the captives may not be uninteresting. In the confusion consequent upon the attack upon the defenceless troops, an Indian chief seized Col. Frye, plundered and stripped him of his clothes, even to his shirt, and then led him into the woods, in a direction and manner which left no doubt as to the design of the ferocious chief. Arriving at a secluded spot, where the colonel expected to meet his fate, he determined to make one effort for his life, and roused by desperation, with no other arms than those nature gave him, he sprang upon the savage, overpowered and killed him on the spot, and fleeing rapidly into a thick wood, he eluded the search of the other Indians. After wandering in various directions for several days, subsisting wholly on whortleberries, he reached fort Edward, and joined his suffering companions.

Capt. John Burk, of Frye's regiment, was seized, and, after a violent struggle, stripped of the whole of his clothes, and afterwards escaped into the woods. Straying in various directions, he was overtaken by darkness in the margin of a morass, and unable to direct his course, lay down in the thick grass and passed the night, covered only by the damp vapor of the swamp. The next day he renewed his march, and fortunately arrived safely at fort Edward.

At the time Col. Monroe consented to the delivery of the private baggage to the Indians, as has been related, Lieut. Selah Barnard, another of Frye's officers, having with him a small trunk containing his effects, resolutely determined not to part with it, unless by force. The trunk soon attracted the attention of the savages, and two stout fellows approaching to seize it, the lieutenant, springing upon it, threatened them with instant death if they persisted in their design, and for some time held the trunk from their grasp. At length, others coming up, he was seized by each arm by two savages, plundered, and led off, as he supposed, to be butchered. Being athletic, and remarkably nervous in his arms, rousing his whole strength, he sent them in different directions, and by a rapid flight rejoined his fellow-sufferers. The savages returned and took possession of the trunk, and submitted to his escape; and he reached fort Edward without further misfortune.

Capt. Jonathan Carver, of the same regiment, after being stripped of his clothes, broke from the savages and regained a body of his companions. In attempting afterwards to escape through the woods, he was again seized, and led off towards a swamp by two Indians; an English gentleman happening to pass by, one of the Indians relinquished his hold, and seized the gentleman, who, proving too strong, threw him upon the ground, on which the other Indian flew to the assistance of his comrade, and the captain, seizing the opportunity, escaped, and after two or three days arrived at fort Edward.

The number that fell in the massacre has not been accurately ascertained. Dr. Belknap says the New Hampshire regiment lost eighty out of two hundred; but these, being in the rear, suffered more severely than other regiments. Captain Carver estimates the whole loss at fifteen hundred; but this is evidently an exaggeration. In a letter from a gentleman in Albany, inserted in the London Magazine for 1757, the number is much diminished. From a comparison of all the accounts that have reached us, it is probable that the whole number massacred and carried off by the savages was less than three hundred.

After Gen. Amherst had taken command of the English and provincial forces, they were eminently successful, and had taken from the French all their strong works on lake Champlain. The capture of these important posts immediately relieved the frontiers of New England from incursions from the western quarter; and a general joy spread through the long distressed colonies. Crown Point had been in the possession of the French for nearly thirty years, and from that place predatory parties had issued, and involved the frontiers of Massachusetts and New Hampshire in blood and slaughter; and numerous were the prisoners who had there suffered the disgraceful and cruel treatment of the savages. One other post from which the colonies of New Hampshire and Massachusetts had suffered similar cruelties, still remained in the hands of the enemy. This was the village of St. Francis, situated at the mouth of the river of that name, between Montreal and Quebec. From its easy communication with the upper part of Connecticut river, this place had long been a focus of murder and devastation, and many a captive had there suffered barbarities intolerable, and the place was loaded with the plunder of the English colonies. Gen. Amherst now resolved to put an end to these barbarities, by destroying the place. Maj. Rogers, who had so ably and frequently distinguished himself as a partisan during the war, was selected for the arduous service, with his hardy rangers and a detachment of regular troops.

To prevent a discovery of the expedition, it was kept profoundly secret from the army; and in the preceding day's orders, Rogers had been destined to the command of a party to march in a different direction, while he had private orders to proceed directly to St. Francis.

In pursuance of his orders, Maj. Rogers left Crown Point in the evening, on board of whale-boats, and proceeded down the lake, on his adventurous expedition. The distance to Missisque bay was not far short of one hundred miles, and as parties of the enemy were often on the lake, the greatest circumspection was required to avoid a discovery. The fifth day after his departure, being encamped on the east shore, a keg of gunpowder accidentally took fire, and wounded Capt. Williams and several men, whom Rogers sent back, with part of the detachment, to Crown Point, which reduced his number to one hundred and forty-two, including officers. Pursuing his voyage, Rogers arrived at Missisque bay on the twentieth, without discovery, where he secreted his boats, and provisions sufficient for his men on their return, under the bank of a creek, overhung with brush, and left two trusty Indians to watch them, with orders, should the boats be discovered by the enemy, to follow his trail, and give him the information.

The country between the bay and St. Francis village was covered with woods, and intersected by swamps and rivulets; but, notwithstanding these impediments, Rogers pressed his march with considerable expedition. The second day after quitting the boats, the two Indians, who had been left to watch them, came up with Rogers, and informed him that four hundred French and Indians had discovered and taken possession of the boats, and that two hundred were in rapid pursuit on his trail. The intelligence was embarrassing, and the circumstances of the detachment critical. But, fertile in resources, Rogers devised means to overcome his difficulties, and to prosecute his expedition. Lieut. M'Mullen and ten men were detached, with orders to proceed through the woods to Crown Point, to inform Gen. Amherst of the misfortune, and to request him to forward provisions from Charlestown, up the Connecticut, to the mouth of Great Ammonoosuc river, near Coos intervals, by which route Rogers proposed to return, after the destruction of the Indian village, as ordered. He then renewed his march, resolving to outstrip his pursuers; but was much retarded by the sunken nature of the country, which in many places was covered with water mid-leg deep, and often a spruce bog, in which it became necessary to prepare a sort of hammock, from the boughs of trees, to enable the men to repose at night; and this, after a hard day's march, continued from early dawn until darkness commenced.

The tenth day after leaving the bay, Rogers struck St. Francis river, about fifteen miles above the village, and with some difficulty forded it, where the water was five feet, and running in a rapid current. The ground now being firm, the march was pressed with celerity, and on the fourth of October, at eight in the evening, Rogers came within sight of the village, halted, and directed his men to refresh themselves, while he, with

Lieut. Turner and Ensign Avery, reconnoitred the place. The Indians were found in a high frolic or dance, and appeared to entertain no apprehensions of an enemy in the vicinity. Returning to his men about two o'clock in the morning, Rogers marched them within five hundred yards of the village, lightened them of their packs, and prepared for the attack. It was now about three o'clock, and an hour after, the Indians broke up their dance, and retired to their cabins for repose, and all was calm in the village. About half an hour before sunrising, the troops advanced in three divisions, and made simultaneous attacks in as many directions. The Indians were completely surprised, and incapable of much resistance. Well acquainted with the Indian mode of attack on similar occasions, the rangers dealt death and destruction in all directions, and with unsparing hands. Nor was it possible to distinguish age or sex, and an indiscriminate butchery followed in the true savage style. Many were killed in their cabins; others, attempting to fly, were shot or knocked on the head, and few escaped. At sunrise the scene was truly horrible, and but for the sight of six or seven hundred of the scalps of their countrymen, suspended upon poles, and waving in the air, the trophies of the former cruelty of the Indians, the assailants would have been excited to pity. This horrid spectacle added new vigor, and sympathy for the sufferers found no place in the breasts of the rangers, and in too many instances they continued to despatch women and children indiscriminately; and a general conflagration of the cabins ended the scene, about seven o'clock in the morning. Out of about three hundred inhabitants of the place, two hundred were killed; twenty women and children captured, and five English prisoners, residing in the village, set free; but most of the women and children were soon liberated.

The village appeared to have been in a very flourishing condition. Many of the cabins were well furnished, and the church was handsomely adorned with plate, and the whole place had been enriched by the scalps and plunder taken from the English in the various wars. Two hundred guineas were found in money, and a silver image, weighing ten pounds, besides a large quantity of wampum, clothing, and some provisions.

On assembling his troops, Rogers found Capt. Ogden and six privates wounded, and one Stockbridge Indian killed; and after an hour's rest, to refresh his men and collect the provisions remaining in the village, he commenced his march up the St. Francis, and by Memphremagog lake, for Coos, on Connecticut river. The detachment continued in a body eight days, at the expiration of which the provisions were entirely expended, and Rogers found it necessary to divide into several parties, that the men might more easily procure subsistence by hunting, giving them orders to assemble at the junction of the great Ammonoosuc and Connecticut rivers, where he expected to find provisions forwarded by order of Gen. Amherst.

Two days after separating, a party under Ensign Avery was overtaken by the pursuing Indians, and seven captured, but two fortunately escaped. Another party of about twenty, under Lieutenants Dunbar and Turner, was attacked, and the principal part killed or taken, including the two officers. The party under Rogers, after several days of fatiguing march, and in a state of starvation, reached Coos meadows, where he entertained little doubts of meeting with ample supplies of provisions. But here he was disappointed. Provisions had been sent to that place by Amherst's orders, under an officer and party of men from Charlestown, but after remaining several days without meeting Rogers, or gaining intelligence of his party, they had returned down the river, only a few hours before Rogers arrived at the place, and their fires were found still burning where they had encamped.

Reduced to this deplorable situation, and little or no game to be found in the woods, Rogers had recourse to ground-nuts and lily roots, which were collected, boiled to a mucilaginous consistence resembling soup, and dealt out to the men, and this was found to preserve life; but a future supply was precarious, and little prospect remained of reaching Charlestown before they should famish. Rogers at length contrived to construct a raft of dry pines, on which he, with Capt. Ogden, one ranger and a captive boy, embarked and floated down the Connecticut, leaving Lieut. Grant in command of the remaining party. At White river falls, the raft was unfortunately lost, and a new one constructed by the slow process of burning down trees, and separating them into logs of a proper length. With much difficulty the raft was conducted over Waterqueechy falls; and after meeting many other embarrassments, and passing other rapids, they arrived near Charlestown, where they were relieved by some people who were out from that place cutting timber, and conducted to the town. Canoes loaded with provisions were immediately sent up the river for the relief of the other sufferers, who arrived at various points on the river in a starving condition, after having lost many in the woods. A few reached Crown Point, subsisting wholly on roots and game procured on the route.

After collecting his scattered survivors at Charlestown, Rogers marched for Crown Point, where he arrived the first of December, and joined Gen. Amherst's army. The whole loss of the detachment, after leaving the ruins of St. Francis, was three officers and forty-six non-commissioned officers and privates. In relating their individual sufferings, one of the rangers stated that the party to which he was attached, having expended the last morsel of food, was on the point of starvation, when fortunately an owl was discovered perched upon a tree. Instantly the bird was brought down by the eager shot of several of the men, dissected, and distributed by the well-known method of "Who shall have this?" He shared a leg, which he devoured without cooking; and by this refreshment the party were enabled to continue the march, and at length arrived without the loss of a man.

During the operations of Amherst at lake Champlain, Gen. Wolf, with about eight thousand men, sailed from

Louisourg, under Admirals Saunders and Holmes, and landed near Quebec; and after many difficulties thrown in his way, and a severe repulse at Montmorency, he by a daring movement gained the plains of Abraham, in the vicinity of Quebec, and brought Montcalm to a general action, in which the French were decisively defeated, and both commanders killed; and a few days subsequently Quebec surrendered to the British arms.

The joy spread over the colonies, at the conquest of Canada, is hardly to be described. From the commencement of King William's war, in 1689, with the exception of a few short intervals, to this event, the frontier people of the English northern provinces were doomed to destruction, captivity, and slaughter. Relieved from their embarrassments, they re-occupied their plantations, and new ones were commenced, and population began to spread.

CHAP. X.

REMARKS ON INDIAN HOSTILITIES AT THE COMMENCEMENT OF THE WAR OF THE REVOLUTION, AND SETTLEMENT OF THE NEW HAMPSHIRE GRANTS IN THE COOS COUNTRY.—BATTLE OF BENNINGTON, WITH ITS RESULTS.—BURNING OF ROYALTON.

After the conquest of Canada by the English, in which the New England colonies were actively engaged, and in which they bore a large proportion of the burthen, Indian depredations and attacks on our frontiers ceased. The inhabitants were relieved from the distresses and horrors of a savage warfare, in which they had suffered almost incredible hardships, from the first settlement of the country. The enterprising settlers could now push their fortunes into the wilderness, fell the trees, and establish themselves wherever they thought it would most conduce to their comfort and prosperity, and where they could pursue their labors in peace. The anxious mother could now lay her head upon her pillow and take her rest, without the fear of being disturbed by the war-whoop of the savage, and was relieved from that dreadful apprehension of danger, which caused her, when awakened by the whistling of the winds through the forest, to hug her infant closer to her breast.

Emigrations now took place rapidly into the wilderness, in every direction. The hardy sons of New England penetrated the forests, and formed settlements on all the best lands on the streams to the north and west of the old settlements, which had before been prevented by the hostilities of the savage tribes. Many new towns had been granted, and the most liberal terms offered for their settlement. The wilderness now literally blossomed as the rose; and where, a short time before, they were only inhabited by the savage beast of prey, or the more savage Indian, were now becoming the abode of industry, civilization, and prosperity. At no period of our existence as a nation has the increase of population and accumulation of wealth been more rapid, than what took place between the peace of 1763 and the commencement of the war of the revolution.

The most extensive and important settlements that were made at this time were in the great valley of Connecticut river, above Charlestown, then called the Upper Coos, which had been till now unoccupied, in consequence of its having been the principal thoroughfare of the French and Indians, in their attacks upon the frontiers of Massachusetts and New Hampshire; but in the various military expeditions through the country our people had discovered the richness of the soil, and a strong desire was felt to get possession of the land. The governor of New Hampshire had previously caused a survey of Connecticut river to be made, for sixty miles, and three lines of townships on each side to be laid out. By procuring the signatures of a certain number of petitioners for these townships, grants were readily obtained, on very easy conditions, which were nothing more than to have a certain number of settlers in each town in a given time; and the expense to each was only the charter fee, which was but half a dollar; and this entitled the original proprietors to three hundred and forty acres of land.

These easy terms induced a great number from Massachusetts and Connecticut to become settlers, and the river towns were soon taken up by their most industrious and enterprising sons. New Hampshire claimed the jurisdiction as far as to within twenty miles of the Hudson river, from thence westerly to lake Champlain, and then northerly to the forty-fifth degree of latitude. This was disputed by New York, who pretended to claim as far east as Connecticut river. This dispute, however, rather facilitated than otherwise the settlement of the country. Both parties continued to give grants of the lands, and to encourage their settlement; and the dispute was never finally put at rest till the territory was by act of Congress admitted into the Union as an independent state, under the name of Vermont. All those towns that lie between Connecticut river and the Green mountains were for many years known only by the name of the New Hampshire Grants, and acknowledged no other jurisdiction but of that colony.

These settlements continued to prosper and increase in population for several years, and nothing took place which in the least tended to retard this prosperity, until the commencement of the revolutionary struggle between the colonies and the mother country. This event produced a new order of things throughout the country. The inhabitants of these parts generally took sides with the colonies, and were very active and zealous in the cause of independence. Many of them, however, and among these some of the most respectable and wealthy, were opposed to the separation from England. They were willing to agree not to take part on either side, and to remain neutral; but this, under the popular feelings of the times, could not be permitted; for the principle adopted by the patriotic party was, "Whoever is not for us is against us." Those who adhered to the royal cause were stigmatized by the name of tories, and those on the other side styled themselves whigs; and bitter were the feelings of animosity between the two parties.

The tories were deprived of their arms, and many of them were thrown into prison; tarring and feathering were in some cases introduced, and their suffering, with that of their families, was very great. They were finally driven from the country, and took refuge in Canada, where they were protected by the British, and furnished with the means of subsistence. Their feelings were, of course, very bitter against the whigs, whom they considered the cause of all their sufferings; and threats were made that, with the assistance of the Canada Indians, they should overrun the Coos settlements, and take ample revenge for their injuries, by despoiling the country. These threats were often received and circulated through the settlements, which kept the inhabitants in a constant state of alarm; but the country was now too thickly inhabited, and too formidable, to make such an attempt, with any chance of success, without a large force, which could not at that time be spared.

The refugees, who were now in Canada, were, however, formed into a regiment, and the command given to Col. John Peters, a gentleman who had been conspicuous among the settlers of the Coos country, and from which he had been driven on account of his political principles. This regiment was well officered and armed, to act as a partisan corps, and it was intended that it should co-operate with the Indians, in excursions into the Coos settlements, whenever a suitable opportunity should occur. After events, however, frustrated all these plans, and their services proved to be of very little use to the cause of the English, more than to keep the scattered settlements in a constant state of alarm, by their threats of revenge.

The situation of the whole country was at this time very peculiar. The declaration of independence had dissolved all allegiance to England, and there had not been time in some sections of the country to establish any permanent form of government. This was particularly the case with the New Hampshire Grants; for their territorial jurisdiction was in dispute, and they were under the necessity of forming a temporary system of government for the time being. For this purpose a general committee was appointed, and other committees were chosen by the people in different sections, who were styled committees of safety, to whom was intrusted the whole management of public affairs. Their authority was absolute, and their decrees and acts were the only law of the land. Though some of their acts were rather arbitrary and severe, particularly towards the tories, and from which there was no appeal, yet their orders were readily obeyed by the people. They not only took effectual measures to protect their own frontier, but provided large supplies for the government, and furnished more recruits for the army than any other section of the country of the same number of inhabitants. As an evidence of this, one fact will be given: that when the late pension law was passed by Congress, there were very few men among them, who where old enough to bear arms in the continental army, but what were entitled to a pension.

Nothing of much importance took place in these parts, until Gen. Burgoyne took command of the English army in Canada, and commenced his march to overrun and conquer the colonies. He was accompanied by the refugees and a large body of Indians, who were to act, as circumstances required, in scouring the country and plundering the inhabitants. After he had taken Ticonderoga, a plan was formed, at the request of the tories, to detach a large force from his regulars, who, with the refugees and Indians, were to proceed to the Coos country, to plunder and destroy it; and so sanguine were they of success, that a list of the heads of families in the principal towns was made out, and furnished for each officer who was to have any command, with each one's doom marked against his name, of those that were to be saved, and those that were to be attacked and plundered.

Information of this plan being communicated to the inhabitants of these settlements, caused great alarm among them; and the committee of the New Hampshire Grants immediately wrote, in the most pressing terms, to the committee of safety at Exeter, for assistance, and said that if none should be afforded to them, they should be obliged to retreat to the New England states for safety. When the news of this affair reached New Hampshire, the assembly had finished their spring session, and returned home. A summons from the committee brought them together again; and in a short session, of three days only, they took the most effectual and decisive steps for the defence of the country. They formed the whole militia of the state into two brigades; of the first, they gave the command to William Whipple, and of the second, to John Stark. They ordered one fourth part of Stark's brigade, and one fourth of three regiments of the other brigade, to march immediately, under his command, to stop the progress of the enemy on our western frontiers. They ordered the militia officers to take away arms from all persons who scrupled or refused to assist in defending the country.

The appointment of Stark to this command, with the same pay as a brigadier in the continental service, was peculiarly grateful to the people, as well as to himself. In an arrangement of general officers, in the preceding year, Poor, a junior officer, had been promoted, whilst he was neglected. He had written on this subject to Congress, and his letters were laid on the table. He therefore quitted the army, and retired to his own state. He was now, by the unanimous voice of his fellow-citizens, invested with a separate command, and received orders to repair to Charlestown, on Connecticut river, there to consult with a committee of New Hampshire Grants respecting his future operations and the supply of his men with provisions; to take the command of the militia, and march into the Grants; to act in conjunction with the troops of that new state, or any other of the states, or of the United States, or separately, as it should appear expedient to him, for the protection of the people and the annoyance of the enemy.

In a few days he proceeded to Charlestown, and as fast as his men arrived he sent them forward to join the forces of the new state, under Col. Warner, who had taken post at Manchester, twenty miles northward of Bennington. Here Stark joined him, and met with Gen. Lincoln, who had been sent from Stillwater by Gen. Schuyler, commander of the northern department, to conduct the militia to the west side of Hudson's river. Stark informed him of his orders, and of the danger which the inhabitants of the Grants apprehended from the enemy and from their disaffected neighbors; that he had consulted with the committee, and it was the determination of the people, in case he should join the continental army and leave them exposed, that they would retire to the east of Connecticut river; in which case New Hampshire would be a frontier. He therefore determined to remain on the flank of the enemy, and to watch their motions. For this purpose he collected his force at Bennington, and left Warner with his regiment at Manchester. A report of this determination was transmitted to Congress, and the orders on which it was founded were by them disapproved; but the propriety of it was evinced by the subsequent facts.

Gen. Burgoyne, with the main body of the British army, lay at fort Edward. Thence he detached Lieut. Col. Baum and about fifteen hundred of his German troops, with the refugees and a large body of Indians, to pervade the Grants as far as Connecticut river, with a view to plunder the country. He was to persuade the people among whom he should pass, that his detachment was the advanced guard of the British army, which was marching to Boston. He was accompanied by Col. Skeene, who was well acquainted with the country.

The Indians who preceded this detachment, being discovered about twelve miles from Bennington, Stark detached Col. Gregg, with two hundred men, to stop their march. In the evening of the same day he was informed that a body of regular troops, with a train of artillery, was in full march for Bennington. The next morning he marched with his whole brigade and some of the militia of the Grants, to support Gregg, who found himself unable to withstand the superior number of the enemy. Having proceeded about four miles, he met Gregg retreating, and the main body of the enemy pursuing, within half a mile of his rear. When they discovered Stark's column, they halted in an advantageous position; and he drew up his men on an eminence in open view, but could not bring them to an engagement. He then marched back about a mile and encamped, leaving a few men to skirmish with them, who killed thirty of the enemy and two of the Indian chiefs. The next day was rainy. Stark kept his position, and sent out parties to harass the enemy. Many of the Indians took this opportunity to desert, because, as they said, "the woods were full of Yankees."

On the following morning, Stark was joined by a company of militia from the Grants, and another from the county of Berkshire, in Massachusetts. His whole force amounted to about sixteen hundred. He sent Col. Nichols, with two hundred and fifty men, to the rear of the enemy's left wing, and Col. Hendrick, with three hundred, to the rear of their right. He placed three hundred to oppose their front and draw their attention. Then, sending Cols. Hubbard and Stickney, with two hundred to attack the right wing, and one hundred more to reinforce Nichols in the rear of their left, the attack began in that quarter precisely at three of the clock in the afternoon. It was immediately seconded by the other detachments; and at the same time Stark himself advanced with the main body. The engagement lasted two hours, at the end of which he forced their breastworks, took two pieces of brass cannon and a number of prisoners; the rest retreated.

Just at this instant he received intelligence that another body of the enemy was within two miles of him. This was a reinforcement for which Baum had sent, when he first knew the force which he was to oppose. It was commanded by Col. Breyman. Happily, Warner's regiment from Manchester came up with them and stopped them. Stark rallied his men and renewed the action; it was warm and desperate; he used with success the cannon which he had taken, and at sunset obliged the enemy to retreat. He pursued them till night, and then halted, to prevent his own men from killing each other in the dark. He took from the enemy two other pieces of cannon, with all their baggage, wagons, and horses. Two hundred and twenty-six men were found dead on the field. Their commander, Baum, was taken, and died of his wounds; besides whom, thirty-three officers and above seven hundred privates were made prisoners. Of Stark's brigade, four officers and ten privates were killed, and forty-two were wounded.

In the account of this battle which Stark sent to the committee of New Hampshire, he said, "Our people behaved with the greatest spirit and bravery imaginable. Had every man been an Alexander, or a Charles of Sweden, they could not have behaved better." He was sensible of the advantage of keeping on the flank of the enemy's main body, and therefore sent for one thousand men, to replace those whose time had expired, but intimated to the committee that he himself should return with the brigade. They cordially thanked him "for the very essential service which he had done to the country," but earnestly pressed him to continue in the command, and sent him a reinforcement, "assuring the men that they were to serve under Gen. Stark." This argument prevailed with the men to march, and with Stark to remain.

The prisoners taken in this battle were sent to Boston. The trophies were divided between New Hampshire and Massachusetts. But Congress heard of this victory by accident. Having waited some time in expectation of letters, and none arriving, inquiry was made why Stark had not written to Congress. He answered that his correspondence with them was closed, as they had not attended to his last letters. They took the hint; and though they had but a few days before resolved that the instructions which he had received were destructive of military subordination, and prejudicial to the common cause, yet they presented their thanks to him, and to the officers and troops under his command, and promoted him to the rank of brigadier general in the army of the United States.

This victory gave a severe check to the hopes of the enemy, and raised the spirits of the people after long depression. It wholly changed the face of affairs in the northern department. Instead of disappointment and retreat, and the loss of men by hard labor and sickness, we were now convinced, not only that our militia could fight without being covered by intrenchments, but that they were able, even without artillery, to cope with regular troops in their intrenchments. The success thus gained was regarded as a good omen of further advantages. "Let us get them into the woods," was the language of the whole country.

The inhabitants of the New Hampshire Grants were relieved by this decisive battle from all fears of an invasion from any considerable force of the enemy. The hopes of the tories were now completely blasted, and their hopes of revenge by overrunning the country were at an end. But still they were enabled to keep the people in a constant state of alarm, by their threats to bring the savage foe in detached parties among them, to plunder the settlements, and carry into captivity such of the leading men among the patriots of the day as they considered to be the cause of their sufferings, in being forced to leave the country.

This state of things continued for a considerable length of time. Small bodies of Indians were frequently known to be prowling about the settlements, concealing themselves in the woods during the day-time, and at night committing depredations by plundering and destroying property; but no attack was made upon the inhabitants. It was well known at the time that their principal object was to take captive and carry to Canada certain leading men, who were the most influential and active in maintaining the cause of independence, for each of whom they were to receive a large reward. Every man was obliged to keep himself well armed, and never suffer himself to sleep without a loaded gun standing by his bed; and many of those who had reason to believe themselves to be marked as victims for captivity, dared not sleep in their own houses, but for safety were compelled to change their place of rest every night, sleeping in barns and other places of concealment.

No adequate means could be adopted to guard the inhabitants against these dangers, for they were so scattered that it would be impossible to collect a number sufficient to afford protection to such an extensive frontier, every point of which was equally liable to be attacked by the enemy. Each one was, therefore, obliged to depend on himself, with the assistance of his neighbors, to repel any assault that might be made upon him by the Indians. The committee of safety took every means in their power to afford assistance and protection to the inhabitants. A brigade of militia was organized of all who were able to bear arms, and the officers appointed, residing in the different towns, who had orders, whenever there should be an alarm, to muster all the force in their neighborhoods, and march immediately to the place of danger, and, as the parties arrived, the senior officer present to take command, and proceed against the enemy.

Gen. Jacob Bailey, of Newbury, was appointed to the command—a man of tried courage and long experience, in whom the people had great confidence. Frequent attempts were made by the Indian scouts to take him prisoner, but he eluded all their stratagems and kept clear of them. On one occasion, his house was surrounded by a party of Indians in the night, and a demand made for him, with a threat, that, if he was not surrendered, they would burn the house and destroy all within. His heroic wife answered that he was not at home; on which she was told to tell where he was, or they would commence an immediate attack on the house. Her answer was, that she knew not where he was, but she hoped he was where they would not find him; that she was prepared for their attack, and should defend the house to the last extremity; on which they retired.

No military event of any importance took place in the towns on the river, within the Grants, during the remainder of the war, though some towns in the neighborhood did not wholly escape the common calamities. In the month of October, 1780, a party, consisting of about three hundred refugees and Indians, commanded by Lieut. Horton, an officer in the British army, made an incursion into the settlements, and destroyed Royalton, a flourishing town on White river, about twenty miles from its junction with the Connecticut. They plundered the inhabitants of everything valuable that they could carry off, burnt twenty-one houses, with all their barns and stacks of hay and grain, and took fourteen men prisoners, most of them heads of families; these they carried to Canada, except two, who were found murdered and scalped in their camp, after their retreat.

This event caused great alarm throughout the country, and many speculative opinions were formed as to the reasons why this town should be singled out for destruction, while others were passed by the enemy and left unmolested. Subsequently a circumstance became known, which was supposed to be the cause. A gentleman had taken up his residence in that town, who was a land-owner to a considerable extent in that part of the country, and took great interest in promoting its prosperity. He often gave assistance to the inhabitants, who were at that time very poor. He made it his home in the family of a man whom he had often assisted, and shown many acts of kindness. When the revolutionary troubles commenced, this gentleman, not wishing to take a part, was proscribed as a tory; and for safety was obliged to conceal himself in the woods, where he remained till compelled by hunger to seek some relief, for which he secretly applied to the man with whom he had resided, begged for food, and that he would afford him such assistance as would enable him to make his escape. This was promised, and he was told to hide himself in the barn, while this man said he would keep him there concealed till some plan could be devised for his escape. Instead of this, however, this treacherous friend immediately informed against him to the committee, who sent a guard and took him prisoner. This gentleman was treated with great indignity, and suffered many hardships, but finally made his escape and got safe to Canada.

There was no doubt at the time of this man being one of the party that attacked Royalton. One thing is a fact, that the house of his betrayer was the first that was destroyed, and the owner owed his life to a remarkable circumstance. Awaking, on the morning of the attack, a little before daylight, he thought he heard strange noises, which induced him to believe that some wild animal had got among his flock. He arose and went out to see to them, and on returning found his house on fire and surrounded by the enemy. He fled to the woods, and was closely pursued by some Indians, but was enabled to make his escape by secreting himself under a log, and so closely concealed himself that some of the enemy even passed over him.

No correct account has ever before been published of the measures adopted, and the conduct of those who turned out and marched against the enemy on this occasion, though a very false one was printed and circulated by a religious fanatic, who had no means of knowing anything more than from hearsay reports, which reflected with some severity upon those who were engaged in the expedition, because they did not pursue and kill every one of the enemy. The following particulars are made from the statements of those who were present and took an active part in the whole affair; one of whom was the late Dr. Thomas Baldwin, who then resided in Canaan, about thirty miles from the scene of action, and who shouldered his gun, and marched with his neighbors in defence of his country.

The enemy encamped in a thick wood the night before the attack, about two miles from the village, and commenced their depredations at daylight in the morning. They were divided into parties, and began their assault upon the inhabitants in different parts of the village at the same time. Most of the women, with the children, fled to the woods, and some of the young men made their escape down the river and gave the alarm. The senior officer of that section was Col. John House, who resided at Hanover, twenty-four miles distant from the scene of action. He received the news by express in the afternoon, and immediately sent runners to all the towns in the neighborhood with the information, and orders for every man able to bear arms to repair to the place of rendezvous with all possible haste. He was enabled to march with a considerable force the next morning at daylight, occasionally being joined by others on the route, and arrived at Royalton in the afternoon; but the enemy had left the place a few hours before, and there was nothing to be discovered but the burning ruins of the settlement.

The men were mustered and formed into companies, and everything arranged for a pursuit of the enemy. Scouts were sent out to gain information of them, but they missed their track, and did not return till the next day. No certain information could be obtained of the route they had taken, but it was determined to commence the pursuit in such a direction as it was thought they would be most likely to fall in with the enemy. They were fortunate enough to hit upon their trail, and followed on with all possible haste; but they were in a thick wood, and the night was very dark, so that their progress was slow. The first discovery that they made of the enemy was by being fired on by their rear guard, by which a lieutenant was severely wounded. The party was immediately formed in order of battle, and moved on till they received the fire of the main body of the Indians, who were formed in a half circle. The fire was returned with spirit, and a sharp engagement commenced; but it was soon found that the enemy had retreated. It was so dark that nothing could be seen but the flashes from the muskets, from which the commander discovered that there was danger of the parties getting into a position which might cause them to mistake each other for the enemy; and it was with great difficulty that he was enabled to put a stop to the firing, and to get the men into order, for the purpose of advancing against the enemy. This being effected, they pursued them, and on arriving at their encampment, found that they had left it, and made a hasty retreat, leaving a great part of their plunder behind them. Even their camp-kettles were left over the fire, in which they were cooking their breakfasts. A council of the officers was held, whose opinion was, that to pursue the enemy further would be useless, and, an arrangement being made that the property found in the camp should be restored to the owners, the men were dismissed and returned to their homes.

Two circumstances occurred during the time the enemy were plundering and burning the village which are thought worthy of being stated. A Mrs. Handy had a son, ten years old, taken by the Indians, and she had the courage to attempt his liberation. To effect this, she repaired to the head-quarters of the enemy, in doing which she had to wade across the river. She sought out the English commander, and, with the feelings of a mother, plead her cause so well that she effected his release; but finding there nine other boys about the same age, and knowing all their mothers, her feelings of sympathy were too strong to permit her to leave them. She plead for them, one by one, till she obtained the release of the whole. The commander ordered a fire to be made, by which they could warm themselves, and gave them some food, telling her to remain there till the scouts all came in, or they might be taken again. After they came in, he made the Indians carry them on their backs across the river, and they were all landed safely on the other side.

The other case was as follows: A party of Indians entered a house where there was a woman somewhat advanced in pregnancy. One of them seized hold of her with one hand, and in the other held a large knife in such a manner that she supposed his aim was to cut her throat, at which she fainted and fell to the floor.

On recovering, however, she found that all the damage she had received was the loss of a string of gold beads, which was round her neck; but the most remarkable part of the case was, that when her child was born, which was a boy, he had perfectly the fierce look and complexion of the savage. He lived to manhood, and was a respectable head of a family, but always retained this singular mark.

CHAP. XI.

SOME ACCOUNT OF THE DIFFERENT TRIBES OF INDIANS INHABITING THE WESTERN COUNTRY.

BEING about to speak of the wars with the savages in the western country, we shall commence with a description of their prevailing customs and habits.

They are the descendants of those who once inhabited the sea-coasts, and who were driven by the English far to the westward; so that but few of their descendants are now to be found within less than two or three hundred miles of the sea; for though many of them have been instructed in the knowledge of Christianity, and districts of land have been allotted them in several of the British colonies, where they have been formed into societies, it has been found that, in proportion as they lay by their ancient customs and conform to the manners of civilized life, they dwindle away, either because the change is prejudicial to their constitutions, or because when settled among the English they have great opportunities of procuring spirituous liquors, of which both sexes are in general inordinately fond; very little care being ever taken to prevent those who are inclined to take advantage of this in trade from basely intoxicating them. This has a powerful effect on their constitutions, and soon proves fatal, producing diseases to which they were formerly strangers. Thus, where a few years ago there were considerable settlements, their name is almost forgotten; and those who still remain have, for the most part, joined themselves to other nations, in the interior part of the country, on the banks of the lakes and rivers.

The Indians in Canada, and to the south of it, are tall and straight beyond the proportion of most other nations. Their bodies are strong, but, as has been before observed, this is a strength rather suited to endure the exercise of the chase than much hard labor. They have generally supple limbs, and the smallest degree of deformity is rarely seen among them. Their features are regular, their complexion somewhat of a copper color, or reddish brown. Their hair, which is long, black, and lank, is as strong as that of a horse. They carefully eradicate the hair from every part of the body except the head, and they confine that to a tuft at the top; whence an erroneous idea has much prevailed, that the men of this country are naturally destitute of beards, but it is unquestionable that it is only an artificial deprivation.

They generally wear only a blanket wrapped about them, or a shirt, both of which they purchase of the English traders. When the Europeans first came among them, they found some nations entirely naked, and others with a coarse cotton cloth, woven by themselves, put round the waist; but in the northern parts, their whole bodies were in winter covered with skins.

The Huron Indians possess a very pleasant and fertile country, on the eastern side of the lake which bears the same name. Half a century ago, they were very numerous, and could raise six or seven hundred warriors; but they have suffered greatly from the attacks of neighboring tribes. They differ in their manners from any of the Indian tribes with which they are surrounded. They build regular houses, which they cover with bark; and are considered as the most wealthy Indians on the continent, having not only horses, but some black cattle and swine. They likewise raise corn, so that, after providing for their own wants, they are enabled to barter the remainder with other tribes. Their country extends one hundred and fifty miles eastward of the lake, but is narrower in the contrary direction. The soil is not exceeded by any in this part of the world. The timber is tall and beautiful; the woods abound with game, and abundance of fish may be obtained from the rivers and lakes; so that, if it were to be well cultivated, the land would equal that of any part of the sea-coast of North America. A missionary, of the order of Carthusian Friars, by permission of the bishop of Canada, resides among them, and is by them amply rewarded for his services.

Those tribes of Indians who inhabit the banks of lakes Champlain, George, and Ontario, were formerly called Iroquots, but have since been known by the name of the Five Mohawk Nations, and the Mohawks of Canada. The former are called Onondagoes, Oneidas, Senecas, Tuscarories, and Troondocks. These fought on the side of the English in the contest for territory with France. The Cohnawaghas and St. Francis Indians joined the French.

The knowledge which we have of the Indians further to the southwest, beyond forty-five degrees north latitude, is chiefly obtained from that worthy provincial officer, Maj. Carver, who travelled into those parts in the year 1776; whose placid manners and artless sincerity could not fail of recommending him to men whom nature alone had instructed. He visited twelve nations of Indians, among which the following appear to be the most considerable: the Chippeways, who dwell to the southward of lake Superior, and the Ottawas; the Winnebagoes, to the west of lake Michigan, who, with the Saukies and Otignanmies, occupy the whole extent of country from the lake to the Mississippi, below forty-two degrees north latitude, where the Wisconsin river discharges itself. The Nandowesse, the most numerous and extended Indian nation, inhabit the country to the west of the river Mississippi, on the borders of Louisiana.

The Indians in general are strangers to the passion of jealousy, and the most profligate of their young men very rarely attempt the virtue of married women; nor do such often put themselves in the way of solicitation, although the Indian women in general are amorous, and before marriage not less esteemed for gratifying their passions. It appears to have been a very prevalent custom with the Indians of this country, before they became acquainted with the Europeans, to compliment strangers with their wives; and the custom still prevails, not only among the lower rank, but even among the chiefs themselves, who consider such an offer as the greatest proof of courtesy they can give a stranger.

The men are remarkable for their indolence, on which they even seem to value themselves, saying that labor would degrade them, and belongs solely to the women, while they are formed only for war, hunting, and fishing, to form their canoes and build their houses. But they frequently make the women assist them in these, besides attending to all domestic affairs and cultivating the land. They have a method of lighting up their huts with torches, made of the splinters cut from the pine or birch tree.

The Indians have generally astonishing patience and equanimity of mind, with the command of every passion except revenge. They bear the most sudden and unexpected misfortune with calmness and composure, without uttering a word, or the least change of countenance. Even a prisoner, who knows not whether he may not in a few hours be put to the most cruel death, seems entirely unconcerned, and eats and drinks with as much cheerfulness as those into whose hands he has fallen. Their resolution and courage under sickness and pain are really astonishing. Even when under the shocking torture to which prisoners are frequently exposed, they will not only make themselves cheerful, but provoke and irritate their tormentors by the most severe reproaches.

They are graceful in their deportment upon serious

occasions, observant of those in company, respectful to the old, of a temper cool and deliberate, by which they are never in haste to speak before they have well thought of the matter, and sure that the person who spoke before them has finished all that he had to say. In their public councils, every man is heard in his turn, according to his years, his wisdom, or as his services to his country have ranked him. Not a whisper nor a murmur is heard from the rest while he speaks; no indecent commendations, no ill-timed applause. The young attend for their instruction; for here they learn the history of their nation, are animated by those who celebrate the warlike actions of their ancestors, and taught what is the interest of their country, and how to cultivate and pursue it.

Hospitality is exercised among them with the utmost generosity and good will. Their houses, their provisions, and even their young women, are presented to a guest. To those of their own nation they are likewise very humane and beneficent. If any of them succeed ill in hunting, if the harvest fails, or his house is burnt, he feels no other effect of his misfortune than its giving him an opportunity of experiencing the benevolence and regard of his countrymen; who, for that purpose, have almost everything in common. But to the enemies of his country, or to those who have privately offended him, the native American is implacable. He never, indeed, makes use of oaths, or indecent expressions, but cruelly conceals his sentiments till, by treachery or surprise, he can gratify his revenge. No length of time is sufficient to allay his resentment; no distance of place is great enough to protect the object. He crosses the steepest mountains, pierces forests, and traverses the most hideous deserts; bearing the inclemency of the season, the fatigues of the expedition, the extremes of hunger and thirst, with patience and cheerfulness, in hopes of surprising his enemy, and exercising upon him the most shocking barbarities. When these cannot be effected, the revenge is left as a legacy transferred from generation to generation, from

22

father to son, till an opportunity offers of taking what they think ample satisfaction. To such extremes do the Indians push their friendship or their enmity; and such indeed is in general the character of all uncivilized nations. They, however, esteem nothing so unworthy a man of sense as a peevish temper, and a proneness to sudden and rash anger.

On the other hand, they are highly sensible of the utility and pleasures of friendship; for each of them, at a certain age, make choice of some one nearly of the same standing in life to be their most intimate and bosom friend. These two enter into mutual engagements, by which they oblige themselves to brave any danger, and run any risk, to assist and support each other. This attachment is even carried so far as to overcome the fear of death, which they consider as only a temporary separation; being persuaded that they shall meet and be united in friendship in the other world, never to be separated more, and that there they shall need one another's assistance as well as here.

It does not appear that there is any Indian nation that has not some sense of a Deity, and a kind of superstitious religion. Their ideas of the nature and attributes of God are very obscure, and some of them absurd; but they conceive of him as the Great Spirit, and imagine that his more immediate residence is on the island of the great lakes. They seem to have some idea that there are spirits of a higher order than man; and, supposing them to be everywhere present, frequently invoke them, and endeavor to act agreeably to their desires. They likewise imagine that there is an evil spirit, who they say is always inclined to mischief, and bears great sway in the creation. This, indeed, is the principal object of their devotion. They generally address him most heartily, beseeching him to do them no harm. But supposing the others to be propitious, and ever inclined to do good, they intreat those spirits to bestow blessings upon them, and prevent the evil spirit from hurting them. Maj. Carver relates, that one of the most considerable chiefs among the Ottawas, with whom he remained a night, on attending him to his canoe the next morning, with great solemnity, and in an audible voice, offered up a fervent prayer, as he entered his canoe, "that the Great Spirit would favor him with a prosperous voyage; that he would give him an unclouded sky and smooth waters by day, and that he might lie down by night on a beaver blanket, enjoying uninterrupted sleep and pleasant dreams; and also that he might find continual security under the great pipe of peace." To procure the protection of the Good Spirit, they imagine it necessary to distinguish themselves, and that they must, above all other attainments, become good warriors, expert hunters, and steady marksmen.

Their priests often persuade the people that they have revelations of future events, and are authorized to command them to pursue such and such measures. They also undertake to unfold the mysteries of religion, and to solve and interpret all their dreams. They represent the other world as a place abounding with an inexhaustible plenty of everything desirable, where they shall enjoy the most full and exquisite gratification of their senses. This is doubtless the motive that induces the Indian to meet death with such indifference and composure; none of them being in the least dismayed at the news that he has but a few hours or minutes to live; but with the greatest intrepidity sees himself upon the brink of being separated from all terrestrial things, and with great serenity talks to all around him. Thus a father leaves his dying advice to his children, and takes a formal leave of all his friends.

They testify great indifference for the productions of art: "It is pretty, I like to look at it;" but express no curiosity about its construction. Such, however, is not their behavior when they are told of a person who distinguishes himself by agility in running; is well skilled in hunting; can take a most exact aim; work a canoe along a rapid with great dexterity; is skilled in all the arts which their stealthy mode of carrying on a war is capable of; or is acute in discovering the situation of a country, and can without a guide pursue his proper course through a vast forest, and support hunger, thirst, and fatigue with invincible firmness;—at such a relation their attention is aroused. They listen to the interesting tale with delight, and express in the strongest terms their esteem for so great and so wonderful a man.

They generally bury their dead with great decency, and deposite in the grave such articles as the deceased had made the greatest use of and been most attached to—as his bows and arrows, pipes, tobacco, &c.—that he may not be in want of anything when he comes to the other country. The mothers mourn for their children a long time, and the neighbors make presents to the father, and he in return gives them a feast.

Every band has a leader, who bears the name of sachem or chief warrior, and is chosen for his tried valor or skill in conducting the war. To him is entrusted all military operations; but his authority does not extend to civil affairs, that pre-eminence being given to another, who possesses it by a kind of hereditary claim, and whose assent is necessary to render valid all conveyances of land, or treaties of whatever kind, to which he affixes the mark of the tribe or nation. Though these military and civil chiefs are considered the heads of the band, and the latter is usually styled king, yet the American Indians consider themselves as controlled by neither civil or military authority. Every individual regards himself as free and independent, and would never renounce the idea of liberty; therefore injunctions, conveyed in the style of a positive command, would be disregarded and treated with contempt. Nor do their leaders assume an ascendency repugnant to these sentiments, but merely advise what is necessary to be done, which is sufficient to produce the most prompt and effectual execution, never producing a murmur.

Their great council is composed of the heads of

tribes and families, and of those whose capacity has raised them to the same degree of consideration They meet in a house built in each of their towns for that purpose, and also to receive ambassadors, to deliver them an answer, to sing their traditionary songs, or to commemorate the dead. In these councils they propose all such matters as concern the state, and which have already been digested in the secret councils, at which none but the head men assist. The chiefs seldom speak much themselves at these general meetings, but entrust their sentiments with a person who is called their speaker or orator, there being one of this profession in every tribe or town; and their manner of speaking is natural and easy, their words strong and expressive, their style bold, figurative, and laconic; whatever is told tending either to the judgment or to rouse the passions.

When any business of consequence is transacted, they appoint a feast upon the occasion, of which almost the whole nation partakes. Before the entertainment is ready, the principal person begins with a song on the remarkable events of their history, and whatever may tend to their honor or instruction. The others sing in their turn. They also have dances, chiefly of a martial kind; and no solemnity or public business is carried on without songs and dances.

As the Indians are high-spirited and soon irritated, the most trifling provocations frequently rouse them to arms, and prove the occasion of bloodshed and murder. Their petty private quarrels are often decided this way, and expeditions undertaken without the knowledge or consent of the general council. These private expeditions are winked at and excused, as a means of keeping their young men in action, and inuring them to the exertions of war.

But when war becomes a national affair, it is entered upon with great deliberation. They first call an assembly of sachems or chief warriors, to deliberate upon the affair, and everything relating to it. In this general congress, among the northern Indians and Five

Nations, the women have a voice as well as the men. When they are assembled, the chief sachem or president proposes the affair they have met to consult upon, and, taking up the tomahawk which lies by him, says, "Who among you will go and fight against such a nation? Who among you will bring captives from thence to replace our deceased friends, that our wrongs may be revenged, and our name and honor maintained as long as the rivers flow, the grass grows, or the sun and moon shall endure?" Then one of the principal warriors, rising, harangues the whole assembly, and afterwards, addressing himself to the young men, inquires who will go with him and fight their enemies; when they generally rise, one after another, and fall in behind him, while he walks round the circle, till he is joined by a sufficient number.

On such occasions they usually have a deer, or some other beast, roasted whole; and each of them, as they consent to go to war, cuts off a piece and eats, saying, "Thus will I devour our enemies;" mentioning the nation they are going to attack. The ceremony being performed, the dance commences, and they sing their war-song, which has relation to their intended expedition and conquest, or to their own skill, courage, and dexterity in fighting, and the manner in which they will vanquish their enemies. Their expressions are strong and pathetic, and are accompanied with a tone that inspires terror.

Such is the influence of their women in these consultations, that the issue depends much upon them. If any one of them, in conjunction with the chiefs, has a mind to excite one who does not immediately depend upon them to take an active part in the war, she presents, by the hands of some trusty young warrior, a string of wampum to the person whose help she solicits, which seldom fails of producing the desired effect. But when they solicit an offensive or defensive alliance with a whole nation, they send an embassy with a large belt of wampum and a bloody hatchet, inviting them to come and drink the blood of their enemies.

The wampum used on these and other occasions, before their acquaintance with Europeans, was only small shells, which they picked up by the sea-coasts and on the banks of the lakes. It now consists principally of a kind of cylindrical beads, made of white and black shells, which are esteemed among them as silver and gold are among us. The black they think the most valuable. Both of them are their greatest riches and ornaments, answering all the ends of money among us. They have the art of stringing, twisting, and interweaving them into their belts, collars, blankets, &c., in ten thousand different sizes, forms, and figures, so as not only to be ornaments for every part of dress, but expressive of all their important transactions. They die the wampum of various colors and shades; and so they are made significant of almost anything they please. By these their records are kept, and their thoughts communicated to one another, as ours are by writing. Thus the belts that pass from one nation to another, in all important transactions, are carefully preserved in the cabin of their chiefs, and serve both as a kind of record or history and as a public treasure. Hence they are never used on trifling occasions.

The calumet, or pipe of peace, is of no less importance, nor is it less revered among them. The bowl is made of a kind of soft red stone, easily wrought and hollowed out; the stem is of cane or light wood, painted with different colors, and adorned with the heads, tails, and feathers of the most beautiful birds, &c. The use of the calumet is to smoke either tobacco, or some other herb used instead of it, when they enter into an alliance or any solemn engagement; this being esteemed the most sacred oath that can be taken, the violation of which is thought to be most infamous, and deserving severe punishment in the other life. When they treat of war, the whole pipe and all its ornaments are red; sometimes it is red only on one side, and by the disposition of the feathers, &c., a person acquainted with their customs knows at first sight the intentions or desires of the nation which presents it. Smoking the calumet is also upon some occasions, and in all treaties, considered as a sacred oath, as a seal of their decrees, and a pledge of their performance of them. The size and decorations of their calumets are commonly proportioned to the importance of the occasion, to the quality of the persons to whom they are presented, and to the esteem and regard they have for them.

Another instrument of great importance among them is the tomahawk. This is an ancient weapon, used by them in war before they were taught the use of iron or steel; since which, hatchets have been substituted in the room of them; but it retains its use and importance in public transactions, and, like the pipe, is very significant. This instrument is formed in some respects like a hatchet, having a long handle; the head, which is a round knob of solid wood, calculated to knock a man down, has on the other side a point bending a little toward the handle; and near the centre, where the handle pierces the head, another point projects forward, of considerable length, which serves to thrust with, like a spear. The tomahawk is also ornamented with painting and feathers, disposed and variegated in many significant forms, according to the occasion and end for which they are used; and on it are kept a kind of journal of their marches and most important occurrences in a kind of hieroglyphics. When the council is called to deliberate on war, the tomahawk is colored red; and when the council sits it is laid down by the chief, and if war be concluded upon, the captain of the young warriors takes it up, and, holding it in his hand, dances and sings the war-song. When the council is over, this, or some other one of the same kind, is sent by the hands of the same warrior to every tribe concerned; who with it presents a belt of wampum, and delivers his message, throwing a tomahawk on the ground, which is taken up by one of the most expert warriors, if they choose to join; if not, it is returned with a belt of their wampum, suited to the occasion.

Each nation or tribe has its distinct ensign, generally consisting of some beast, bird, or fish. Thus the Five Nations have the bear, otter, wolf, tortoise, and eagle. By these names the tribes are generally distinguished, and the shapes of these animals are pricked and painted on several parts of their bodies. Generally, when they march through the woods, at every encampment they cut the figure of their arms on the trees, especially when they have had a successful campaign, that travellers may know they have been there; recording also in their way the number of prisoners and scalps they have taken.

Their military appearance is very odd and terrible. They cut off all their hair, except a spot on the crown of their head, and pluck out their eyebrows. The lock left upon the head is divided into several parcels, each of which is stiffened and intermixed with beads and feathers of various shapes and colors, the whole twisted and connected together. They paint themselves with a red pigment down to the eyebrows, which they sprinkle over with white down. The gristle of their ears are slit almost quite round, and hung with ornaments that have generally the figure of some bird or beast drawn upon them. Their noses are likewise bored and hung with beads, and their faces painted with various colors. On their breasts is a gorget or medal of brass, copper, or some other metal; and by a string which goes round their necks is suspended that horrid weapon called the scalping-knife.

Thus equipped, they march forth, singing their war-song till they lose sight of their village; and are generally followed by their women, who assist them in carrying their baggage, whether by land or water, but commonly return before they proceed to action.

They have in most cases one commander for ten men; and if the number amount to one hundred, a general is appointed over the others, not for the purpose of command, but to give his opinion. They have no stated rules of discipline, or fixed methods of carrying on a war, but make their attacks in as many different ways as there are occasions, but generally in flying parties equipped for that purpose.

The weapons used by those who trade with the English and French are commonly a firelock, a hatchet, and a scalping-knife; but the others use bows, tomahawks, and pikes. As the commander in chief governs only by advice, and can neither reward nor punish, every private may return home when he pleases, without assigning any reason for it; or any number may leave the main body and carry on a private expedition, in whatever manner they please, without being called to account for their conduct.

When they return from a successful campaign, they contrive their march so as not to approach their village till towards the evening. They then send two or three forward to acquaint their chief and the whole village with the most material circumstances of their campaign. At daylight the next morning, they give the prisoners new clothes, paint their faces with various colors, and put into their hands a white staff, tasselled round with the tails of deer. This being done, the war-captain sets up a cry, and gives as many yells as he has taken prisoners and scalps, and the whole village assemble at the water-side. As soon as the warriors appear, four or five of their young men, well clothed, get into a canoe, if they come by water, or, otherwise, march by land; the two first, carrying a calumet, go out singing to search the prisoners, whom they lead in triumph to the cabin where they are to receive their doom. The owner of this cabin has the power of determining their fate, though it is often left to some woman who has lost a husband, brother, or son, in the war; and when this is the case, she generally adopts him in the place of the deceased. The prisoner has victuals immediately given him, and while he is at his repast a consultation is held; and if it be resolved to save his life, two young men untie him, and take him by the hands, leading him to the cabin of the person into whose family he is to be adopted, and there he is received with all imaginable marks of kindness. He is treated as a friend, as a brother, or as a husband, and they soon love him with the same tenderness as if he stood in the place of one of their friends. In short, he has no other marks of captivity except his not being suffered to return to his own nation; for his attempting this would be punished with certain death.

But if the sentence be death, how different their conduct. These people, who behave with such disinterested affection to each other, with such tenderness to those whom they adopt, here show that they are truly savages. The dreadful sentence is no sooner passed, than the whole village set up the death-cry, and, as if there were no medium between the most generous friendship and the most inhuman cruelty, the execution of him whom they had just before deliberated upon admitting into their tribe, is no longer deferred than whilst they can make the necessary preparations for rioting in the most diabolical cruelty. They first strip him, and fixing two posts in the ground, fasten to them two pieces from one to the other—one about two feet from the ground, the other about five or six feet higher—then, obliging the unhappy victim to mount upon the lower cross-piece, they tie his legs to it a little asunder. His hands are extended and tied to the angles formed by the upper piece. In this posture, they burn him all over the body, sometimes first daubing him with pitch. The whole village, men, women, and children, assemble round him, every one torturing him in what manner they please; each striving to exceed the other in cruelty, as long as he has life. But if none of the bystanders are inclined to lengthen out his torments, he is either shot to death, or enclosed with dry bark, to which they set fire; they then leave him on the frame, and in the evening run from cabin to cabin, superstitiously striking, with small twigs, the furniture, walls, and roofs, to prevent his spirit from remaining there to take vengeance for the evils committed on his body. The remainder of the day and the night following are spent in rejoicing.

This is the most usual method of murdering their

prisoners; but sometimes they fasten them to a single stake, and build a fire around them. At other times, they cruelly mangle their limbs, cut off their fingers and toes joint by joint, and sometimes scald them to death.

What is most extraordinary, if the sufferer be an Indian, there seems, during the whole time of his execution, a contest between him and his tormentors, which shall outdo the other, they inflicting the most horrid pains, or he in enduring them. Not a groan, nor a sigh, nor a distortion of countenance, escapes him in the midst of his torments. It is even said that he recounts his own exploits, informs them what cruelties he has inflicted upon their countrymen, and threatens with the revenge that will attend his death; that he even reproaches them for their ignorance of the art of tormenting; points out methods of more exquisite torture, and more sensible parts of the body to be afflicted.

The scalps, those dreadful proofs of the barbarity of these Indians, are valued and hung up in their houses as the trophies of their bravery; and they have certain days when the young men gain a new name or title of honor, according to the qualities of the persons to whom these scalps belonged. This name they think a sufficient reward for the dangers and fatigues of many campaigns, as it renders them respected by their countrymen, and terrible to their enemies.

In the American Revolution, Britain had the inhumanity to reward these sons of barbarity for depredations committed upon those who were struggling in the cause of liberty. The widow's wail, the virgin's shriek, and the infant's trembling cry, were music in their ears. In cold blood they sunk their cruel tomahawks into the defenceless head of a Miss M'Kray, a beautiful girl, who was that very day to have been married. The particulars of the inhuman transaction follow: Previous to the war between America and Great Britain, a British officer, by the name of Jones, an accomplished young man, resided near fort Edward. His visits thither became more frequent, when he found himself irresistibly drawn by charms of native worth and beauty. Miss M'Kray, whose memory is dear to humanity and true affection, was the object of his peregrinations. Mr. Jones had not taken the precaution necessary in hazardous love, but had manifested to the lady, by his constant attention, undissembled and ingenuous demeanor, that ardent affection which a susceptible heart compelled her implicitly to return. In this mutual interchange of passions, they suffered themselves to be transported on the ocean of imagination, till the unwelcome necessity of a separation cut off every springing hope. The war between Great Britain and America commenced. A removal from this happy spot was in consequence suggested to Mr. Jones as indispensable. Nothing could alleviate their mutual horror but duty; nothing could allay their reciprocal grief, so as to render a separate corporeal existence tolerable, but solemn vows, with ideas of a future meeting. Mr. Jones repaired to Canada, where all intercourse with the Provincials was prohibited. Despair, which presented itself in aggravated colors when Gen. Burgoyne's expedition through the States was fixed, succeeded to his former hopes. The British army being encamped about three miles from the fort, a descent was daily projected. Here Mr. Jones could not but recognise the spot on which rested all his joys. He figured to his mind the dread which his hostile approach must raise in the breast of her whom, of all others, he thought it his highest interest to protect. In spite of arrest and commands to the contrary, he found means secretly to convey a letter, entreating her not to leave the town with the family, assuring her that, as soon as the fort should surrender, he would convey her to an asylum where they might peaceably consummate the nuptial ceremony. Far from discrediting him who could not deceive her, she heroically refused to follow the flying villagers. The remonstrances of a father, or the tearful entreaties of a mother and numerous friends, could not avail! It was enough that her lover was her friend. She considered herself protected by the love and voluntary assurances of her youthful hero. With the society of a servant-maid, she impatiently waited the desired conveyance. Mr. Jones, finding the difficulty into which he was brought, at length, for want of better convoy, hired a party of twelve Indians to carry a letter to Miss M'Kray, with his own horse, for the purpose of carrying her to the place appointed. They set off, fired with the anticipation of their promised premium, which was to consist of a quantity of spirits, on condition that they brought her off in safety, which to an Indian was the most cogent stimulus the young lover could have named. Having arrived in view of her window, they sagaciously held up the letter, to prevent the fears and apprehensions which a savage knows he must excite in the sight of tenderness and sensibility. Her faith and expectations enabled her to divine the business of these ferocious missionaries, while her frightened maid uttered nought but shrieks and cries. They arrived, and, by their signs, convinced her from whom they had their instructions. If a doubt could remain, it was removed by the letter; —it was from her lover. A lock of his hair, which it contained, presented his manly figure to her gloomy fancy.

Here, reader, guess what must have been her ecstasy. She, indeed, resolved to brave even the most horrid aspect which might appear between her and him, whom she considered already hers, without a sigh. She did not for a moment hesitate to follow the wishes of her lover, and took her journey with these bloody messengers, expecting very soon to be shielded in the arms of legitimate affection. A short distance only then seemed to separate two of the happiest of mortals. Alas! how soon are the most brilliant pictures of felicity defaced by the burning hand of affliction and wo!

Having risen the hill, at about equal distance from the camp and her former home, a second party of Indians, having heard of the captivating offer made by Mr.

Jones, determined to avail themselves of the opportunity. The reward was the great object. A clashing of real and assumed rights was soon followed by a furious and bloody engagement, in which several were killed on each side. The commander of the first party, perceiving that nought but the lady's death could appease the fury of either, with a tomahawk deliberately knocked her from her horse, and mangled her scalp from her beautiful temples, which he exultingly bore as a trophy of zeal to the expectant and anxious lover! It was with the utmost difficulty that Mr. Jones could be kept from total delirium. His horror and indignation could not be appeased. His remorse for having risked his most valuable treasure in the hands of savages drove him almost to madness. When the particulars of this melancholy event reached Gen. Burgoyne, he ordered the survivors of both these parties to immediate execution.

Many persons suppose that the idea that the American Indians are descended from the ancient Jews is a novel one. This is not the fact. Many writers have suggested this opinion. Among others, James Adair, Esq., who had resided among the North American Indians forty years, and paid particular attention to their language, laws, customs, manners, dress, ceremonies, &c., and whose account of them was published in London, in 1775, seems to have been fully convinced of the fact himself; and if his arguments do not convince others, they will at least stagger their incredulity. The following extract from the contents of his work will show the course he takes to establish his opinion.

"Observations and arguments in proof of the American Indians being descended from the Jews.

1. Their division into tribes.
2. Their worship of Jehovah.
3. Their notion of a theocracy.
4. Their belief in the ministration of angels.
5. Their language and dialects.

6. Their manner of counting time.
7. Their prophets and high priests.
8. Their festivals, fasts, and religious rites.
9. Their daily sacrifice.
10. Their ablutions and anointings.
11. Their laws of uncleanness.
12. Their abstinence from unclean things.
13. Their marriages, divorces, and punishment of adultery.
14. Their several punishments.
15. Their cities of refuge.
16. Their purifications and ceremonies preparatory to war.
17. Their ornaments.
18. Their manner of curing the sick.
19. Their burial of the dead.
20. Their mourning for their dead.
21. Their raising seed to a departed brother.
22. Their choice of name adapted to their circumstances and the times.
23. Their own traditions, the accounts of our English writers, and the testimonies which the Spanish and other authors have given concerning the primitive inhabitants of Peru and Mexico."

Under each of these heads the author gives us such facts as a forty years' residence among them, at a time when their manners, customs, &c., had not been greatly corrupted or changed by intercourse with Europeans, had enabled him to collect; and he assures us they are "neither disfigured by fable nor prejudice." The rest of his work is taken up with accounts of the different nations among whom he had been, with occasional reflections on their laws, &c.

The following list of names of the various Indian nations in North America, in 1794, with the number of their fighting men, was obtained by a gentleman, Mr. Benjamin Hawkins, employed in a treaty then made with them.

The Choctaws or Flat Heads, 4500; Natches, 150; Chickasaws, 750; Cherokees, 2500; Catabas, 150; Piantas, a wandering tribe, 800; Kisquororas, 600; Hankashaws, 250; Oughtenons, 400; Kikapous, 505; Delawares, 300; Shawnese, 300; Miamies, 800; Upper Creeks, Middle Creeks, and Lower Creeks, 4000; Cowitas, 7000; Alabamas, 600; Akinsaws, 200; Ansaus, 1000; Padomas, 600; white and freckled Pianis, 4000; Cauzes, 1600; Osages, 600; Grand Saux, 1000; Missouri, 3000; Saux of the wood, 1800; Biances, or white Indians with beard, 1500; Asinbols, 1500; Christian Cauzes, 3000; Ouiscousas, 500; Mascotins, 500; Lakes, 400; Muherouakes, 230; Folle Avoines or Wildoats, 350; Puans, 700; Powatamig, 550; Missagues, a wandering tribe, 2000; Otabas, 900; Chiewas, 5000; Wiandots, 300; Six Nations, 1500; Round Heads, 3500; Algoquins, 2000; Nepisians, 400; Chalsas, 130; Amitestes, 550; Muckniacks, 700; Abinaguis, 350; Consway Hurins, 200. Total, 58,780.

CHAP. XII.

WASHINGTON'S EXPEDITION, AND DEFEAT OF GEN. BRADDOCK BY THE INDIANS.

In 1753, the French and Indians began to make inroads on our western frontiers along the Ohio. Gov. Dinwiddie, of Virginia, was very desirous to get a letter of remonstrance to their commander in chief. He had applied to several young gentlemen of his acquaintance, but they were all so deficient in courage that they could not be prevailed on, for love or money, to venture out among the savages. Our beloved Washington, happening to hear of it, instantly waited on his

24

excellency, and offered his services, but not without being terribly afraid lest his want of a beard should go against him. However, the governor was so charmed with his modesty and manly air, that he never asked him a syllable about his age, but, after thanking him for his offer, calling him "a noble youth," and insisting on his taking a glass of wine with him, slipped a commission into his hand. The next day, he set out on his expedition, which was, from start to pole, disagreeable and dangerous. Soaking rains, chilling blasts, roaring floods, pathless woods, and mountains clad in snows, opposed his course,—but opposed in vain. The glorious ambition to serve his country rendered him superior to all difficulties.

Returning homeward, he was waylaid and shot at by a French Indian, and though the copper-colored ruffian was not fifteen steps distant when he fired at him, yet not even so much as the smell of lead passed on the clothes of our young hero. On his return to Virginia, it was found that he had executed his negotiations, both with the French and Indians, with such fidelity and judgment, that he received the heartiest thanks of the governor and council for the very important services he had done his country.

He was now (in the twentieth year of his age) appointed major and adjutant general of the Virginia forces. Soon after this, the Indians continuing their encroachments, orders were given by the English government for the colonies to arm and unite in one confederacy. Virginia took the lead, and raised a regiment of four hundred men, at the head of which was placed Washington.

With this handful of brave fellows, Col. Washington, not yet twenty-three years of age, boldly pushed out into the Indian country, and there, for a considerable time, maintained the war against three times their number of French and Indians. At the Red Stones he came up with a strong party of the enemy, whom he engaged and effectually defeated, after having killed and taken thirty-one men. From his prisoners he obtained undoubted intelligence that the French forces on the Ohio consisted of upwards of a thousand regulars and many hundreds of Indians. But, notwithstanding this disheartening advice, he still pressed on undauntedly against the enemy, and at a place called the Little Meadows built a fort, which he called Fort Necessity. Here he waited, hourly and anxiously looking for succors from New York and Pennsylvania; but in vain. No one came to his assistance. Not long after this, his small force, now reduced to three hundred men, were attacked by an army of eleven hundred French and Indians. Never did the true Virginian valor shine more gloriously than on this trying occasion.

To see three hundred young fellows, commanded by a smooth-faced boy, all unaccustomed to the terrors of war, far from home, and from all hopes of help, shut up in a dreary wilderness, and surrounded by four times their number of savage foes, and yet, without sign of fear, without thought of surrender, preparing for mortal combat! Scarcely since the days of Leonidas and his three hundred deathless Spartans had the sun beheld its equal. With hideous whoops and yells, the enemy came on like a host of tigers. The woods and rocks, and tall tree-tops, (as the Indians, climbing to the tops of the trees, poured down their bullets into the fort,) were in one continued blaze and crash of fire-arms. Nor were our young warriors idle, but, animated by their gallant chief, plied their rifles with such spirit that their little fort resembled a volcano in full blast, roaring and discharging thick sheets of liquid fire among their foes. For three hours, enveloped in smoke and flame, they sustained the attack of the enemy's whole force, and laid two hundred of them dead on the spot. Discouraged by such desperate resistance, the French general, the Count de Villiers, sent in a flag to Washington, extolling his gallantry to the skies, and offering him the most honorable terms. It was stipulated that Col. Washington and his little band of heroes should march away, with all the honors of war, and carry with them their military stores and baggage.

In the spring of 1755, Washington, while busied in the highest military operations, was summoned to attend Gen. Braddock, who, in the month of February, had arrived at Alexandria with two thousand British troops. The assembly of Virginia had appointed eight hundred provincials to join him. The object of this army was to march through the country, by the way of Will's Creek, to fort Duquesne, (now Pittsburgh or fort Pitt.) As no person was so well acquainted with the frontier country as Washington. and none stood so high in military fame, it was thought he would be infinitely serviceable to Gen. Braddock. At the request of the governor and council, he cheerfully quitted his own command to act as volunteer aid-de-camp to that very imprudent and unfortunate general. The army, near three thousand strong, marched from Alexandria, and proceeded unmolested within a few miles of fort Pitt.

On the morning of the 9th of July, when they had arrived within seven miles of fort Duquesne, the provincial scouts discovered a large party of French and Indians lying in ambush. Washington, with his usual modesty, observed to Gen. Braddock what sort of enemy he had now to deal with—an enemy who would not, like the Europeans, come forward to a fair contest in the field, but, concealed behind rocks and trees, carry on a deadly warfare with their rifles. He concluded with begging that Gen. Braddock would grant him the honor to let him place himself at the head of the Virginia riflemen, and fight them in their own way. And it was generally thought that our young hero and his eight hundred hearts of hickory would very easily have beaten them; for they were not superior to the force which, with only three hundred, he had handled so roughly twelve months before. But Gen. Braddock, who had all along treated the American officers and soldiers with infinite contempt, instead of following this truly salutary advice, swelled and reddened with most unmanly rage. "High times, by G—d!" he exclaimed, strutting to and fro, with arms akimbo, "high times! when a young buckskin can teach a British general how to fight!" Washington withdrew, biting his lips with grief and indignation, to think what numbers of brave fellows would draw short breath that day, through the pride and obstinacy of their commander. The troops were ordered to form and advance in columns through the woods. In a little time the ruin which Washington had predicted ensued. This poor devoted army, pushed on by their haughty general, fell into the fatal snare which was laid for them. All at once a thousand rifles began the work of death. The ground was instantly covered with the dying and dead. The British troops, thus slaughtered by hundreds, and by an enemy whom they could not see, were thrown irrecoverably into panic and confusion; and in a few minutes their general, with twelve hundred of his brave but unfortunate countrymen, were killed.

Poor Gen. Braddock closed the tragedy with great decency. He was mortally wounded in the beginning of the action, and Washington had him placed in a cart, ready for retreat. Close on the left, where the weight of the French and Indian fire principally fell, Washington, at the head of his Virginia riflemen, who were dressed in blue, sustained the shock. At every discharge of their rifles the wounded general cried out, "O, my brave Virginia blues! would to God I could live to reward you for such gallantry." But he died. Washington caused him to be buried in the road, and to save him from discovery and the scalping-knife ordered the wagons on their retreat to drive over his grave.

Amidst all this fearful consternation and carnage, with all the uproar and horrors of a rout, rendered still more dreadful by the groans of the dying, the screams of the wounded, the piercing shrieks of the women, and the yells of the furious assaulting savages, Washington, calm and self-collected, rallied his faithful riflemen, led them on to the charge, killed numbers of the enemy who were rushing with tomahawks, checked their pursuit, and brought off the shattered remains of the British army.

With regard to our beloved Washington, we cannot but here mention two extraordinary speeches that were uttered about him at this time, and which, as things have turned out, look a great deal like prophecies. A famous Indian warrior, who assisted in the defeat of Braddock, was often heard to say, that Washington was not born to be killed by a bullet; "for," he continued, "I had seventeen fair fires at him with my rifle, and after all I could not bring him to the ground." And, indeed, whoever considers that a good rifle, levelled by a sure marksman, hardly ever misses its aim, will readily enough conclude, with this unlettered savage, that some invisible hand must have turned aside the bullets.

The Rev. Mr. Davis, in a sermon occasioned by Gen. Braddock's defeat, has these remarkable words: "I beg leave to point the attention of the public to that heroic youth, Col. George Washington, whom I cannot but hope Providence has preserved for some great service to his country."

CHAP. XIII.

ADVENTURES OF CAPT. DANIEL BOON, COMPRISING AN ACCOUNT OF THE WARS WITH THE INDIANS ON THE OHIO, FROM 1769 TO 1782; WRITTEN BY HIMSELF.

It was on the first of May, 1769, that I resigned my domestic happiness, and left my family and peaceable habitation on the Yadkin river, in North Carolina, to wander through the wilderness of America, in quest of the country of Kentucky, in company with John

Finley, John Stuart, Joseph Holden, James Monay, and William Cool.

On the 7th June, after travelling in a western direction, we found ourselves on Red river, where John Finley had formerly been trading with the Indians, and from the top of an eminence saw with pleasure the beautiful level of Kentucky. For some time we had experienced the most uncomfortable weather. We now encamped, made a shelter to defend us from the inclement season, and began to hunt and reconnoitre the country. We found abundance of wild beasts in this vast forest. The buffaloes were more numerous than cattle on our settlements, browsing on the leaves of the cane, or cropping the herbage on these extensive plains. We saw hundreds in a drove, and the numbers around the salt springs were amazing. In this forest, the habitation of beasts of every American kind, we hunted with great success until December.

On the 22d December, John Stuart and I had a pleasing ramble; but fortune changed the day at the close of it. We passed through a great forest, in which stood myriads of trees, some gay with blossoms, others rich with fruits. Nature was here a series of wonders, and a fund of delight. Here she displayed her ingenuity and industry in a variety of flowers and fruits, beautifully colored, elegantly shaped, and charmingly flavored; and we were favored with numberless animals presenting themselves perpetually to our view. In the decline of the day, near Kentucky river, as we ascended the brow of a small hill, a number of Indians rushed out of a cane-brake and made us prisoners. The Indians plundered us and kept us in confinement seven days. During this time we discovered no uneasiness or desire to escape, which made them less suspicious; but in the dead of night, as we lay by a large fire, in a thick cane-brake, when sleep had locked up their senses, my situation not disposing me to rest, I gently awoke my companion. We seized this favorable opportunity and departed, directing our course toward the old camp; but we found it plundered, and our company destroyed or dispersed.

About this time, as my brother with another adventurer, who came to explore the country shortly after us, were wandering through the forest, they accidentally found our camp. Notwithstanding our unfortunate circumstances, and our dangerous situation, surrounded by hostile savages, our meeting fortunately in the wilderness gave us the most sensible satisfaction.

Soon after this, my companion in captivity, John Stuart, was killed by the savages, and the man who came with my brother, while on a private excursion, was soon after attacked and killed by the wolves. We were now in a dangerous and helpless situation, exposed daily to perils and death, among savages and wild beasts, not a white man in the country but ourselves.

Although many hundred miles from our families, in the howling wilderness, we did not continue in a state of indolence, but hunted every day, and prepared a little cottage to defend us from the winter.

On the 1st of May, 1770, my brother returned home for a new recruit of horses and ammunition; leaving me alone, without bread, salt, or sugar, or even a horse or a dog. I passed a few days uncomfortably. The idea of a beloved wife and family, and their anxiety on my account, would have disposed me to melancholy if I had further indulged the thought.

One day, I undertook a tour through the country, when the diversity and beauties of nature I met with, in this charming season, expelled every gloomy thought. Just at the close of the day the gentle gales ceased; a profound calm ensued; not a breath shook the tremulous leaf. I had gained the summit of a commanding ridge, and looking around with astonishing delight, beheld the ample plains and beauteous tracts below. On one hand I surveyed the famous Ohio, rolling in silent dignity, and marking the western boundary of Kentucky with inconceivable grandeur. At a vast distance I beheld the mountains lift their venerable brows and penetrate the clouds. All things were still. I kindled a fire near a fountain of sweet water, and feasted on the loin of a buck which I had killed a few hours before. The shades of night soon overspread the hemisphere, and the earth seemed to gasp after the hovering moisture. At a distance I frequently heard the hideous yells of savages. My excursion had fatigued my body and amused my mind. I laid me down to sleep, and awoke not until the sun had chased away the night. I continued this tour, and in a few days explored a considerable part of the country, each day equally pleasing as the first; after which, I returned to my old camp, which had not been disturbed in my absence. I did not confine my lodging to it, but often reposed in thick cane-brakes, to avoid the savages, who, I believe, frequently visited my camp, but, fortunately for me, in my absence. No populous city, with all its varieties of commerce and stately structures, could afford such pleasure to my mind as the beauties of nature which I found in this country.

Until the 27th of July, I spent my time in an uninterrupted scene of sylvan pleasures, when my brother, to my great felicity, met me, according to appointment, at our old camp. Soon after, we left the place and proceeded to Cumberland river, reconnoitring that part of the country, and giving names to the different rivers.

In March, 1771, I returned home to my family, being determined to bring them as soon as possible, at the risk of my life and fortune, to reside in Kentucky, which I esteemed a second paradise.

On my return I found my family in happy circumstances. I sold my farm on the Yadkin, and what goods we could not carry with us, and on the 25th of September, 1773, we took leave of our friends, and proceeded on our journey to Kentucky, in company with five more families, and forty men that joined us in Powel's valley, which is one hundred and fifty miles from the new-settled parts of Kentucky. But this promising beginning was soon overcast with a cloud of adversity.

On the 10th of October, the rear of our company was attacked by a party of Indians, who killed six, and wounded one man. Of these, my oldest son was one that fell in the action. Though we repulsed the enemy, yet this unhappy affair scattered our cattle and brought us into extreme difficulty. We returned forty miles to the settlement on Clench river. We had passed over two mountains, Powel's and Walden's, and were approaching Cumberland mountain, when this adverse fortune overtook us. These mountains are in the wilderness, in passing from the old settlement in Virginia to Kentucky; are ranged in a southwest and northeast direction; are of great length and breadth, and not far distant from each other. Over them, nature hath formed passes less difficult than might be expected from the view of such huge piles. The aspect of these cliffs is so wild and horrid, that it is impossible to behold them without terror.

Until the 6th of June, 1774, I remained with my family on the Clench, when myself and another person were solicited by Gov. Dunmore, of Virginia, to conduct a number of surveyors to the falls of Ohio. This was a tour of eight hundred miles, and took sixty-two days.

On my return, Gov. Dunmore gave me the command of three garrisons, during the campaign against the Shawanese. In March, 1775, at the solicitation of a number of gentlemen of North Carolina, I attended their treaty, at Wataga, with the Cherokee Indians, to purchase the lands on the south side of Kentucky river. After this, I undertook to mark out a road in the best passage from the settlements through the wilderness to Kentucky.

Having collected a number of enterprising men, well armed, I soon began this work. We proceeded until we came within fifteen miles of where Boonsborough now stands, where the Indians attacked us, and killed two and wounded two more of our party.

This was on the 22d of March, 1775. Two days after, we were again attacked by them, when we had two more killed and three wounded. After this we proceeded on to Kentucky river without opposition.

On the 1st of April, we began to erect the fort of Boonsborough, at a salt lick, sixty yards from the river, on the south side. On the 4th, the Indians killed one of our men. On the 14th of June, having completed the fort, I returned to my family on the Clench, whom I soon after removed to the fort. My wife and daughter were supposed to be the first white women that ever stood on the banks of Kentucky river.

On the 24th of December, the Indians killed one of our men and wounded another; and on the 15th of July, 1776, they took my daughter prisoner. I immediately pursued them with eight men, and on the 16th overtook and engaged them. I killed two of them, and recovered my daughter.

The Indians, having divided themselves into several parties, attacked in one day all our infant settlements and forts, doing a great deal of damage. The husbandmen were ambushed, and unexpectely attacked, while toiling in the field. They continued this kind of warfare until the 15th of April, 1777, when nearly one hundred of them attacked the village of Boonsborough, and killed a number of its inhabitants. On the 16th, Col. Logan's fort was attacked by two hundred Indians. There were only thirteen men in the fort, of whom the enemy killed two and wounded one.

On the 20th of August, Col. Bowman arrived with one hundred men from Virginia, with which additional force we had almost daily skirmishes with the Indians, who began now to learn the superiority of the "long knife." They termed us the Virginians, being outgeneraled in almost every action. Our affairs began now to wear a better aspect, the Indians no longer daring to face us in open field, but sought private opportunities to destroy us.

On the 7th of February, 1778, while on a hunting

excursion alone, I met a party of one hundred and two Indians and two Frenchmen, marching to attack Boonsborough. They pursued and took me prisoner, and conveyed me to Old Chilicothe, the principal Indian town on the Sciota river, where we arrived on the 18th of February, after an uncomfortable journey. On the 10th of March, I was conducted to Detroit, and while there was treated with great humanity by Gov. Hamilton, the British commander at that port, and intendant for Indian affairs.

The Indians had such an affection for me that they refused one hundred pounds sterling, offered them by the governor, if they would consent to leave me with him, that he might be enabled to liberate me on my parole. Several English gentlemen then at Detroit, sensible of my adverse fortune, and touched with sympathy, generously offered to supply my wants, which I declined with many thanks, adding, that I never expected it would be in my power to recompense such unmerited generosity.

On the 10th of April, the Indians returned with me to Old Chilicothe, where we arrived on the 25th. This was a long and fatiguing march, although through an exceedingly fertile country, remarkable for springs and streams of water. At Chilicothe, I spent my time as comfortably as I could expect; was adopted, according to their custom, into a family, where I became a son, and had a great share in the affection of my new parents, brothers, sisters, and friends. I was exceedingly familiar and friendly with them, always appearing as cheerful and contented as possible, and they put great confidence in me. I often went a hunting with them, and frequently gained their applause for my activity at our shooting-matches. I was careful not to exceed many of them in shooting, for no people are more envious than they in this sport. I could observe in their countenances and gestures the greatest expressions of joy when they exceeded me, and when the reverse happened, of envy. The Shawanese king took great notice of me, and treated me with profound respect and entire friendship, often entrusting me to hunt at my liberty. I frequently returned with the spoils of the woods, and as often presented some of what I had taken to him, expressive of duty to my sovereign. My food and lodging was in common with them; not so good, indeed, as I could desire, but necessity made everything acceptable.

I now began to meditate an escape, and carefully avoided giving suspicion. I continued at Chilicothe until the first day of June, when I was taken to the salt springs east of the Sciota, and there employed ten days in the manufacturing of salt. During this time, I hunted with my Indian masters, and found the land, for a great extent about this river, to exceed the soil of Kentucky.

On my return to Chilicothe, one hundred and fifty of the choicest Indian warriors were ready to march against Boonsborough. They were painted and armed in a frightful manner. This alarmed me, and I determined to escape.

On the 18th of June, before sunrise, I went off secretly, and reached Boonsborough on the 20th, a journey of one hundred and sixty miles, during which I had only one meal. I found our fortress in a bad state; but we immediately repaired our flanks, gates, and posterns, and formed double bastions, which we completed in ten days. One of my fellow-prisoners escaped after me, and brought advice that, on account of my flight, the Indians had put off their expedition for three weeks.

About the first of August, I set out with nineteen men to surprise Point-Creek Town, on Sciota, within four miles of which we fell in with forty Indians, going against Boonsborough. We attacked them, and they soon gave way, without any loss on our part. The enemy had one killed and two wounded. We took three horses and all their baggage. The Indians having evacuated their town, and gone, altogether, against Boonsborough, we returned, passed them on the 6th, and on the 7th arrived safe at Boonsborough.

On the 9th, the Indian army, consisting of four hundred and forty-four men, under the command of Capt. Duquesne, and eleven other Frenchmen and their own chiefs, arrived, and summoned the fort to surrender. I requested two days' consideration, which was granted. During this we brought in through the posterns all the horses and other cattle we could collect.

On the 9th, in the evening, I informed their commander that we were determined to defend the fort while a man was living. They then proposed a treaty; they would withdraw. The treaty was held within sixty yards of the fort, as we suspected the savages. The articles were agreed to and signed; when the Indians told us it was their custom for two Indians to shake hands with every white man in the treaty, as an evidence of friendship. We agreed to this also. They immediately grappled us to take us prisoners, but we cleared ourselves of them, though surrounded by hundreds, and gained the fort safe, except one man, who was wounded by a heavy fire from the enemy.

The savages now began to undermine the fort, beginning at the water mark of Kentucky river, which is sixty yards from the fort; this we discovered by the water being muddy by the clay. We countermined them by cutting a trench across their subterraneous passage. The enemy discovering this by the clay we threw out of the fort, desisted. On the 20th of August, they raised the siege, during which we had two men killed and four wounded. We lost a number of cattle. The loss of the enemy was thirty-seven killed, and a much larger number wounded. We picked up one hundred and twenty-five pounds of their bullets, besides what stuck in the logs of the fort.

In July, 1779, during my absence, Col. Bowman, with one hundred and sixty men, went against the Shawanese of Old Chilicothe. He arrived undiscovered. A battle ensued, which lasted until ten in the morning, when Col. Bowman retreated thirty miles. The Indians collected all their strength and pursued him, when another engagement ensued for two hours, not to Col. Bowman's advantage. Col. Harrod proposed to mount a number of horses, and break the enemy's line, who at this time fought with remarkable fury. This desperate measure had a happy effect, and the savages fled on all sides. In these two engagements we had nine men killed and one wounded. Enemy's loss uncertain. Only two scalps were taken.

June 23d, 1780, five hundred Indians and Canadians, under Col. Bird, attacked Riddle and Martin's station, on the forks of Licking river, with six pieces of artillery. They took all the inhabitants captives, and killed one man and two women, loading the others with the heavy baggage, and such as failed in the journey were tomahawked.

The hostile disposition of the savages caused Gen. Clark, the commandant at the falls of Ohio, to march with his regiment and the armed force of the country against Peccaway, the principal town of the Shawanese, on a branch of the Great Miami, which he attacked with great success, took seventy scalps, and reduced the town to ashes, with the loss of seventeen men.

About this time, I returned to Kentucky with my family; for, during my captivity, my wife, thinking me killed by the Indians, had transported my family and goods on horses through the wilderness, amidst many dangers, to her father's house in North Carolina.

On the 6th of October, 1780, soon after my settling again at Boonsborough, I went with my brother to the Blue Licks, and on our return he was shot by a party of Indians, who followed me by the scent of a dog, which I shot and escaped. The severity of the winter caused great distress in Kentucky, the enemy during the summer having destroyed most of the corn. The inhabitants lived chiefly on buffalo's flesh.

In the spring of 1782, the Indians harassed us. In May they killed and scalped a woman and her two daughters near Ashton's station, and took a negro prisoner. Capt. Ashton pursued them with twenty-five men, and in an engagement, which lasted two hours, his party were obliged to retreat, having eight killed, and four mortally wounded. Their brave commander fell in the action.

August 18th, two boys were carried off from Major Hoy's station. Capt. Holden pursued the enemy with seventeen men, who were also defeated, with the loss of seven killed and two wounded. Our affairs became more and more alarming. The savages infested the country, and destroyed the whites as opportunity presented. In a field near Lexington an Indian shot a man, and, running to scalp him, was himself shot from the fort, and fell dead upon the ground. All the Indian nations were now united against us.

August 15th, five hundred Indians and Canadians came against Briat's station, five miles from Lexington. They assaulted the fort and all the cattle round it; but, being repulsed, they retired the third day, having about eighty killed; their wounded uncertain. The garrison had four killed and nine wounded.

August 18th, Colonels Todd and Trigg, Maj. Harland and myself, speedily collected one hundred and seventy-six men, well armed, and pursued the savages. They had marched beyond the Blue Licks, to a remarkable bend of the main fork of Licking river, about forty-three miles from Lexington, where we overtook them on the 19th. The savages, observing us, gave way, and we, being ignorant of their numbers, passed the river. When they saw our proceedings, having greatly the advantage in situation, they formed their line of battle from one end of the Licking to the other, about a mile from the Blue Licks. The engagement was close and warm for about fifteen minutes, when we, being overpowered by numbers, were obliged to retreat, with the loss of sixty-seven men, seven of whom were taken prisoners. The brave and much lamented Cols. Todd and Trigg, Maj. Harland, and my second son, were among the dead. We were afterwards informed that the Indians, on numbering their dead, finding that they had four more killed than we, four of our people they had taken were given up to their young warriors, to be put to death after their barbarous manner.

On our retreat we were met by Col. Logan, who was hastening to join us with a number of well-armed men. This powerful assistance we wanted on the day of battle. The enemy said one more fire from us would have made them give way.

I cannot reflect upon this dreadful scene without great sorrow. A zeal for the defence of their country led these heroes to the scene of action, though with a few men, to attack a powerful army of experienced warriors. When we gave way, they pursued us with the utmost eagerness, and in every quarter spread destruction. The river was difficult to cross, and many were killed in the flight, some just entering the river, some in the water, and others after crossing, in ascending the cliffs. Some escaped on horseback, a few on foot; and, being dispersed everywhere, in a few hours brought the melancholy news of this unfortunate battle to Lexington. Many widows were now made. The reader may guess what sorrow filled the hearts of the inhabitants, exceeding anything that I am able to describe. Being reinforced, we returned to bury the dead, and found their bodies strewed everywhere, cut and mangled in a dreadful manner. This mournful scene exhibited a horror almost unparalleled: some torn and eaten by wild beasts; those in the river eaten by fishes; all in such a putrid condition that no one could be distinguished from the other.

When Gen. Clark, at the falls of the Ohio, heard of our disaster, he ordered an expedition to pursue the savages. We overtook them within two miles of their town, and we should have obtained a great victory had not some of them met us, when about two hundred poles from their camp. The savages fled in the utmost disorder, and evacuated all their towns. We burned to ashes Old Chilicothe, Peccaway, New Chilicothe, and Wills Town, entirely destroyed their corn and other fruits, and spread desolation through their country. We took seven prisoners and fifteen

26

scalps, and lost only four men, two of whom were accidentally killed by ourselves. This campaign damped the enemy, yet they made secret incursions.

In October, a party attacked Crab Orchard, and one of them, being a good way before the others, boldly entered a house, in which were only a woman and her children, and a negro man. The savage used no violence, but attempted to carry off the negro, who, happily, proved too strong for him, and threw him on the ground, and in the struggle the woman cut off his head with an axe, whilst her little daughter shut the door. The savages instantly came up and applied their tomahawks to the door, when the mother putting an old rusty gun-barrel through the crevices, the savages immediately went off.

From that time, till the happy return of peace between the United States and Great Britain, the Indians did us no mischief. Soon after this, the Indians desired peace.

Two darling sons and a brother I have lost by savage hands, which have also taken from me forty valuable horses and abundance of cattle. Many dark and sleepless nights have I spent, separated from the cheerful society of men, scorched by the summer's sun and pinched by the winter's cold, an instrument ordained to settle the wilderness.

CHAP. XIV.

EXPEDITION OF GENERAL HARMER, AND HIS DEFEAT BY THE INDIANS.—DEFEAT OF GENERAL ST. CLAIR, NEAR THE MIAMI VILLAGE.

ALTHOUGH a peace was at length happily effected between the two contending parties, Great Britain and America, in 1785, yet the savages, who had been persuaded to take a part with the former, were unwilling to bury the bloody hatchet. They had not sufficiently bathed that destructive weapon in the blood of Americans. Without any pretext whatever, they continued to exercise towards them the most wanton acts of barbarity.

It appeared from respectable evidence, that from the year 1783, until the month of October, 1790, the time the United States commenced offensive operations against the Indians, that on the Ohio, and the frontiers on the south side, they killed, wounded, and took prisoners fifteen hundred men, women, and children, besides carrying off upwards of two thousand horses, and other property to the amount of fifty thousand dollars.

The particulars of many of the instances of barbarity exercised upon the prisoners, of different ages and sexes, although supported by indisputable evidence, are of too shocking a nature to be presented to the public. It is sufficient here to observe, that the scalping-knife and tomahawk were the mildest instruments of death; that in some cases torture by fire, and other execrable means, were used.

But the outrages which were committed upon the frontier inhabitants were not the only injuries that were sustained. Repeated attacks upon detachments of the troops of the United States were at different times made. The following, from its peculiar enormity, deserves recital. In April, 1790, Major Doughty, in the service of the United States, was ordered to the friendly Chickasaws, on public business. He performed his duty in a boat, having with him a party of fifteen men. While ascending the Tennessee river, he was met by a party of Indians, in four canoes, consisting principally of Shawanese and outcast Cherokees. They approached under a white flag, the well-known emblem of peace. They came on board the major's boat, received his presents, continued with him nearly an hour, and then departed in the most friendly manner. But they had scarcely cleared his oars, before they poured in a fire upon his crew, which was returned as soon as circumstances would permit; and a most unequal combat was sustained for several hours, when they abandoned their design, but not until they had killed and wounded eleven out of fifteen of the boat's crew.

All overtures of peace failing, and the depredations still continuing, an attempt at coercion became indispensable. Accordingly, on the 30th of September, 1790, the President, with the consent and advice of the Congress of the United States, despatched Gen. Harmer, with three hundred federal troops, and eleven hundred and thirty-three militia, under his command, to their principal villages.

The troops, after seventeen days' march from Miami, reached the Great Miami village, without any other molestation than that of having a number of their pack-horses stolen. On their arrival, they found the village deserted, and all the village buildings in flames, set on fire by the Indians. After a short tarry, they proceeded to the neighboring villages without molestation, and destroyed five of them, and a large quantity of corn, which they found buried in different places, and very large quantities of vegetables of every kind.

The first opposition that was met with, a party of about one hundred and fifty Kentucky militia, and eighty regular troops, all under the command of Col. Harding, of Kentucky, were detached from the main body, lying in the Great Miami village, to pursue the trail of a party of Indians, which had that day been discovered. After a pursuit of about six miles, they came up with and were attacked on surprise by a large body of Indians, who were concealed in the thickets on every side of a large plain; and on the first onset, the militia, without exchanging a single shot, made a most precipitate retreat, and left the regular troops to stand the whole charge of the Indians. The conflict was short and bloody. The troops were soon overpowered by numbers, and all fell except two or three officers and two or three privates, after defending themselves at their bayonet-points with the greatest possible obstinacy. Ensign Hartshorn was one of the officers who providentially escaped, and his escape appeared to depend more on a lucky circumstance of falling over a log in his retreat, and by that means screening himself from the eyes of his pursuers, than from any other circumstance. Capt. Armstrong, who commanded the party, likewise made his escape by plunging himself into a pond or swamp, up to his neck, within two hundred yards of the field of action, where he remained the whole night, a spectator to the horrid scenes of the war-dance, performed over the dead and wounded bodies of the poor soldiers that had fallen the preceding day, where their shrieks, mixed with the horrid yells of the savages, rendered his situation shocking.

After this, some few skirmishes succeeded, but nothing material, until the second capital action, which happened two days after the army left Miami village. At ten miles' distance from the town, the general ordered a halt, and detached from four to five hundred militia, and about sixty regular soldiers, under the command of Major Wileys and Col. Harding, who were ordered to march back to the town. On their first entrance, there appeared a small body of Indians, who immediately fled at the first onset, and by that means decoyed the whole body of the militia, by making their flight in different directions, and encouraging the militia to pursue. By this stratagem the few regular troops were left alone, and the Indians had effected their design, for the moment they found the small handful of regular troops detached from the main body of the militia, they commenced the attack with their whole force, executing the flying parties that had divided the militia; and, although they soon found some part of the militia returning, pursued their object of routing and destroying the troops, as the only sure plan of success, which, after a most bloody conflict, was effected.

Nothing could exceed the intrepidity of the savages

on this occasion. The militia they appeared to despise, and with all the undauntedness conceivable threw down their guns, and rushed upon the bayonets of the regular soldiers. A number of them fell, but being so far superior in numbers, the regulars were soon overpowered; for while the poor soldier had his bayonet in one Indian, two more would sink their tomahawks in his head. The defeat of the troops was complete. The dead and wounded were left on the field of action, in possession of the savages.

The regular troops, except nine, including two commissioned officers, were killed. Among the slain was Major Wileys, and a number of brave and valuable soldiers. The Indians, it appeared, from some cause, did not think it prudent to pursue their successes from the field of action, as most of the troops that were not killed or badly wounded made their escape, which they could not have effected had the enemy pursued with their usual fury. Whole number killed, one hundred and eighty-three; wounded, thirty-one.

In the fall of 1791, Gen. St. Clair took command of the western army, and marched against the Indians, who had assembled in great force on the Miami river. He met with a total defeat. The particulars of the fight, which was very sanguinary, will be given in his own words, which is taken from his letter to the secretary of war.

"Yesterday, the remains of the army under my command got back to this place, (Fort Washington;) and I have now the painful task to give an account of a warm and as unfortunate an action as almost any that has been fought, as every corps was engaged and worsted, except the first regiment; this had been detached upon a service that I had the honor to inform you of in my last despatch, and had not joined me.

"On the 3d inst., the army had reached a creek about twelve yards wide, running to the southward of west, which I believed to have been the river St. Mary, that empties into the Miami of the lake; arrived at the village about four o'clock in the afternoon, having marched near nine miles, and were immediately encamped upon a very commanding piece of ground, in two lines, having the above-mentioned creek in front. The right wing, composed of Butler, Clark, and Patterson's battalions, commanded by Major General Butler, formed the first line; and the left wing, consisting of Bedinger and Gaither's battalions, and the second regiment, commanded by Col. Drake, formed the second line, with an interval between them of about seventy yards, which was all the ground would allow.

"The right flank was pretty well secured by the creek, a steep bank, and Faulkener's corps. Some of the cavalry, and their piquets, covered the left flank. The militia were sent over the creek, and advanced about a quarter of a mile, and encamped in the same order.

"There were a few Indians who appeared on the opposite side of the creek, but fled with the utmost precipitation on the advance of the militia. At this place, which I judged to be about fifteen miles from the Miami village, I had determined to throw up a slight work, the plan of which was concerted that evening with Major Ferguson, wherein to have deposited the men's knapsacks, and everything else that was not of absolute necessity, and to have moved on to attack the enemy as soon as the first regiment came up; but they did not permit me to execute either, for on the 4th, about half an hour before sunrise, and when the men had just been dismissed from parade, (for it was a constant practice to have them all under arms a considerable time before daylight,) an attack was made upon the militia, who gave way in a very little time, and rushed into camp through Major Butler's battalion, which, together with part of Clark's, they threw into considerable disorder, and which, notwithstanding the exertions of both these officers, was never altogether remedied. The Indians followed close at their heels; the fire, however, of the front line checked them, but almost instantaneously a very heavy attack began upon that line, and in a few minutes it was extended to the second likewise. The great weight of it was directed against the centre of each, where the artillery was placed, and from which the men were repeatedly driven with great slaughter. Finding no great effect from the fire, and a confusion beginning to spread from the great number of men who were falling in all quarters, it became necessary to try what could be done with the bayonet.

"Lieut. Drake was accordingly ordered to charge with a part of the second line, and to turn the left flank of the enemy. This was executed with great spirit, and at first promised much success. The Indians instantly gave way, and were driven back three or four hundred yards, but for want of a sufficient number of riflemen to pursue this advantage, they soon returned, and the troops were obliged to give back in their turn. At this moment they had entered our camp by the left flank, having pursued the troops that were posted there.

"Another charge was made here by the second regiment, Butler and Clark's battalions, with equal effect, and it was repeated several times, and always with success; but in all of them many men were lost, and particularly the officers, which, among raw troops, was a loss altogether irremediable. In that I just spoke of, made by the second regiment and Butler's battalion, Major Butler was dangerously wounded, and every officer of the second regiment fell, except three, one of which, Capt. Greaton, was shot through the body. Our artillery being now silenced, and all the officers killed, except Capt. Ford, who was badly wounded, more than half of the army fallen, being cut off from the road, it became necessary to attempt the regaining it and to make a retreat if possible. To this purpose the remains of the army was formed, as well as circumstances would admit, towards the right of the encampment, from which, by the way of the second line, another charge was made upon the enemy, as if with the design to turn their right flank, but it was in fact to gain the road. This was effected, and as soon as it was open the militia entered it, followed by the troops; Maj. Clark with his battalion covering the rear.

"The retreat in these circumstances was, you may be sure, a precipitate one. It was, in fact, a flight. The camp and artillery were abandoned; but that was unavoidable, as not a horse was left alive to have drawn it off, had it otherwise been practicable. But the most disgraceful part of the business is, that the greatest part of the men threw away their arms and accoutrements, even after the pursuit, which continued about four miles, had ceased.

"I found the road strewed with them for many miles, but was not able to remedy it, for, having had all my horses killed, and being mounted upon one that could not be pricked out of a walk, I could not get forward myself; and the orders I sent forward, either to halt the front, or prevent the men from parting with their arms, were unattended to.

"The rout continued quite to fort Jefferson, twenty-nine miles, which was reached a little after sunset. The action began about half an hour before sunrise, and the retreat was attempted at half past nine o'clock.

"I have not yet been able to get the returns of the killed and wounded, but Major General Butler, Lieut. Colonel Oldham of the militia, Majors Ferguson, Hunt, and Clark, are among the former.

"I have now, sir, finished my melancholy tale; a tale that will be felt, sensibly felt, by every one that has sympathy for private distress, or for public misfortune. I have nothing, sir, to lay to the charge of the troops but their want of discipline, which, from the short time they had been in service, it was impossible they should have acquired, and which rendered it difficult, when they were thrown into confusion, to reduce them again to order, and is one reason why the loss has fallen so heavily upon the officers, who did everything in their power to effect it. Neither were my own exertions wanting; but worn down with illness, and suffering under a painful disease, unable either to mount or dismount a horse without assistance, they were not so great as they otherwise would, or perhaps ought to have been.

"We were overpowered by numbers; but it is no more than justice to observe, that, though composed of so many different species of troops, the utmost harmony prevailed through the whole army during the campaign.

"At fort Jefferson, I found the first regiment, which had returned from the service they had been sent upon, without either overtaking the deserters or meeting the convoy of provisions. I am not certain, sir, whether I ought to consider the absence of this regiment from the field of action as fortunate or otherwise. I incline to think it was fortunate; for I very much doubt whether, had it been in the action, the fortune of the day had been returned, and if it had not, the triumph of the enemy would have been more complete, and the country would have been destitute of means of defence.

"Taking a view of the situation of our broken troops at fort Jefferson, and that there was no provisions in the fort, I called on the field-officers for their advice what it was proper further to be done; and it was their unanimous opinion, that the addition of the first regiment, unbroken as it was, did not put the army on so respectable a footing as it was in the morning, because a great part of it was now unarmed; that it had been found unequal to the enemy, and should they come on, which was probable, would be found so again; that the troops could not be thrown into the fort, because it was too small, and there was no provision in it; that provisions were known to be upon the road, at the distance of one, or, at most, two marches; that therefore it would be proper to move, without loss of time, to meet the provisions, when the men might have the sooner an opportunity of some refreshment, and that a proper detachment might be sent back with it, to have it safely deposited in the fort.

"This advice was accepted, and the army was put in motion again at ten o'clock, and marched all night, and the succeeding day met with a quantity of flour. Part of it was distributed immediately, part taken back to supply the army on the march to fort Hamilton, and the remainder, about fifty horse-loads, sent forward to fort Jefferson."

The defeat of Gen. St. Clair took place within three miles of the Miami village. The loss on this occasion was about six hundred killed and wounded, (said to be nearly equal to Braddock's defeat,) with seven pieces of artillery and all the stores. General St. Clair had about eleven hundred men; had reason to expect an attack, and kept his men under arms all night, drawn up in a square. The attack commenced about dawn of day on all the lines, but principally on the rear line, which was composed of the militia. The Indians gave one fire and rushed on, tomahawk in hand. The militia gave way to the centre, and before the artillery could be brought into action, the matrosses were all killed and it fell into the hands of the enemy. It was retaken, but was useless for want of men to manage the pieces. The action was continued obstinately until nine o'clock, when the troops gave way. St. Clair rallied his men, and brought them off in tolerable order, with most of the wounded, to fort Jefferson, thirty miles in the rear of the action. The enemy pursued five miles.

Few officers of distinction escaped, except Gen. St. Clair, who had many narrow escapes. Eight balls passed through his clothes. The attack was conducted with astonishing intrepidity on the part of the Indians. In a few moments the general's tent was surrounded. However, he was rescued by a party of regular soldiers, who repelled the enemy with fixed bayonets. There was a party of the Chickasaw nation on their way to join Gen. St. Clair, but did not arrive in season. There was but one fellow only of that nation in the action, who killed and scalped eleven of the enemy with his own hands, and engaging with the twelfth, he fell, greatly lamented by the Americans.

Maj. Gen. Butler was wounded, and carried to a convenient place to have his wounds dressed; but an Indian, having discovered the place to which he was conveyed, broke through the troops who attended him, and tomahawked and scalped the general before he was killed by the soldiers.

Agreeably to the statement of the Indians, they killed six hundred and fifty of the American troops, and took seven pieces of cannon, two hundred oxen, and a great number of horses, but no prisoners, and their loss was only fifty-six warriors killed. They stated that they were four thousand strong, and were commanded by one of the Missassago Indians, who had been in the British service in the late war; that he planned and conducted the attack, which was even contrary to the opinion of a majority of the chiefs; and that after the Americans began to retreat, he told the Indians they had killed enough, and that it was proper to give over the pursuit, and return and enjoy the booty they had taken. He was six feet in height, about forty-five years of age, of a very sour and morose countenance, and apparently very crafty and subtle. His dress was the Indian hose and moccasons, a blue petticoat that came half way down his thighs, and European waistcoat and surtout. His head was bound with an Indian cap that came half way down his back, and almost entirely filled with plain silver broaches, to the number of more than two hundred. He had two ear-rings to each ear. The upper part of each was formed of three silver medals about the size of a dollar; the lower part was formed of quarters of dollars, and fell more than twelve inches from his ears; one from each ear over his breast, the others over his back. He had three very large nose jewels of silver that were curiously pointed.

The party of friendly Chickasaws, who were on their way to join the American troops, arrived at fort Jefferson two days after the bloody action. They were commanded by Piomingo, or the Mountain Leader. On their way they discovered that the troops had been defeated, and saw one of the enemy, who, mistaking Piomingo's party for some of his comrades, made up to them. He perceived his mistake, but too late to retreat. He was accosted by Piomingo with "Rascal, you have been killing white men!" He endeavored to excuse himself, but Piomingo ordered two of his warriors to expand his arms, and a third, an old man (for, says Piomingo, "none of my young men shall disgrace themselves so much as to kill a wretch like thee") to shoot him through the heart, which was accordingly executed. They afterwards took off his scalp.

During St. Clair's bloody engagement, Adjutant Bulgess received two wounds, the second of which proved mortal. After the receipt of the first, he continued to fight with distinguished gallantry; the second unfortunately stopped his progress. Faint with the loss of blood, he fell. A woman who attended him, and was particularly attached to him, raised him up, and while supporting him in her arms, received a ball in her breast, which put an immediate end to her existence!

Soon after Ensign Wilson (a much-lamented youth) fell, one of the savages attempted to take off his scalp, which Colonel Drake perceiving, he hastened to the spot, and with his sword stabbed the Indian through the body.

A few weeks after the defeat of the troops under Gen. St. Clair, Gen. Scott despatched from the men under his command two spies two reconnoitre the enemy, who, when they arrived at the distance of a few miles from the fatal spot where the bloody action was fought, discovered a large party of Indians, diverting and enjoying themselves with the plunder they had taken, riding the bullocks, &c., and appeared to be mostly drunk. The men returned and communicated the important information to Gen. Scott, who immediately divided his troops into three divisions, and advanced on the enemy by surprise. The contest was short, but victorious on the part of the American troops. Two hundred of the enemy were killed on the spot, all the cannon and stores in their possession retaken, and the remainder of the savage body put to flight. General Scott, losing but six men, returned to head quarters in triumph, with most of the cattle, stores, &c.

Gen. Scott gave the following affecting account of the appearance of the field on which the bloody action between the American troops under Gen. St. Clair and the savages was fought. "The place had a very melancholy appearance. Nearly in the space of three hundred and fifty yards lay three hundred skull-bones, which were buried by my men while on the ground; from thence, about five miles on, the road through the woods was strewed with skeletons, muskets, &c."

On the 29th of July, 1794, Maj. M'Mahon marched with eighty riflemen, under the command of Capt. Hartshorn, and fifty dragoons, under the command of Capt. Taylor, for fort Recovery, as an escort to three hundred pack-horses, loaded with flour for the garrison. On the morning following, after they had deposited their loading, and were preparing to set out on their return, they were attacked by an army of twelve hundred Indians. Capt. Hartshorn, who had advanced with the riflemen about a quarter of a mile into the woods, immediately took post on a very strong, commanding piece of ground near the garrison, and with unparalleled bravery maintained the unequal fight till Major M'Mahon, who had put himself at the head of the cavalry, was killed, as was Capt. Taylor and Cornet Terry, and many of the men wounded. The enemy now put their force against Capt. Hartshorn, and in the moment when they were pushing to cut off his communication with the garrison, Lieut. Drake and Ensign Dodd sallied out at the head of twenty brave fellows, who turned out voluntarily on the occasion, and joined him after beating the enemy at the point of the bayonet At this instant, the brave Captain Hartshorn received a shot, which broke his thigh. Lieut. Craig was killed, and Lieut. Marks taken prisoner. Lieut. Drake now ordered a retreat, and on endeavoring to hold the enemy in check so as to give the men time to save Capt. Hartshorn, he received a shot in the groin. The enemy now pressed so hard as to compel the men to leave their captain.

Great numbers of the Indians must have been killed, as they came forward in solid columns up to the very muzzles of the guns. Lieut. Mitchel, who was with Capt. Hartshorn, but whom he had detached with a few active men to the flank of the enemy, was now missing; and while their companions in the fort were deploring their fate, and had given them up as lost, they saw him and Lieut. Marks rushing through the thick of the enemy at opposite directions, and although numbers of guns were fired at them, they got in safely. Lieut. Mitchel lost every man of his party except three, and Lieut. Marks got off by knocking down the Indian who took him.

The Indians were observed to carry off great numbers of killed and wounded on pack-horses. The loss of the Americans was twenty-three killed, and about forty wounded. The party commanded by Capt. Hartshorn brought in ten scalps of the enemy.

CHAP. XV.

DEPREDATIONS OF THE INDIANS ON THE FRONTIERS DURING THE YEARS 1791, 1792, AND 1793.

On the 19th of December, 1791, as two men and three boys were fishing on Floyd's fork of Salt river, they were suddenly attacked by a party of Indians, who killed the two men and made prisoners of the boys. Soon after, they liberated one of the lads, first presenting him with a tomahawk, which they desired him to carry to his friends, and inform them what had become of his companions.

About the 20th, a party of Indians attacked the house of a Mr. Chenoweth, situated near the mouth of the Wabash. They killed and scalped two of his children, and tomahawked and scalped his wife, whom they left for dead. Mr. Chenoweth, who had his arm broken by the fire of the savages, with the remainder of the family, made their escape. A sick daughter, who was confined to her chamber, and who during the bloody affray had been forgotten by her father, remained ignorant of the horrid massacre until the succeeding day, when, no one of the family coming to her assistance, she succeeded in crawling down stairs, where she was inexpressibly shocked at the sight of a beloved parent stretched upon the floor almost lifeless, and at the side of whom lay the mangled bodies of her dear brothers. Fortunately, her unhappy father returned the succeeding day to the house, and conveyed the two surviving members of his family to the house of a friend, where they finally recovered.

On the 24th, a party of Indians attacked the dwelling-house of a Mr. John Merrill, in Nelson county, Kentucky. Mr. Merrill, who was first alarmed by the barking of his dog, hastened to the door to discover the cause, on opening which, he received the fire of the Indians, which broke his right leg and arm. The Indians now attempted to enter the house, but were prevented by the door being immediately closed and secured by Mrs. Merrill and her daughter. The Indians succeeded in hewing away a part of the door, through which passage one of them attempted to enter, but the heroic mother, in the midst of her screaming children and groaning husband, seized an axe and gave the ruffian a fatal blow, after which she hauled him through the passage into the house. The others, unconscious of the fate of their companion, supposing that they had now nearly succeeded in their object, rushed forward, four of whom Mrs. Merrill in like manner despatched before the others discovered their mistake. The remaining Indians, after retiring a few moments, returned and renewed their efforts to enter the house. Despairing of succeeding at the door, they got on the top of the house and attempted to descend the chimney; to prevent which Mr. Merrill directed his little son to empty upon the fire the contents of a feather bed, which had the desired effect, as the smoke and heat caused thereby soon brought down, rather unexpectedly, two of the enemy. Mr. Merrill, exerting every faculty at this critical moment, seized a billet of wood, with which he soon despatched the half-smothered Indians, while, in the mean time, his heroic wife was busily engaged in defending the door against the efforts of the only remaining one, whom she so severely wounded with an axe that he was soon glad to retire.

A prisoner who escaped from the enemy soon after the transaction, informed that the wounded savage above mentioned was the only one of the party that escaped, which consisted of eight; that on his return, being asked by the prisoner "What news?" he answered, "Bad news for poor Indian. Me lose a son, me lose a brother; the squaws have taken the breech clout, and fight worse than the 'long knives!'"

Copy of a letter from a gentleman residing at the westward, to a friend in New York, dated Marietta, Feb. 1, 1792.

"Our prospects are much changed. Instead of peace and friendship with our Indian neighbors, a horrid savage war stares us in the face. The Indians, instead of being humbled by the destruction of the Shawnee towns, and brought to beg for peace, appear to be determined on a general war, in which our settlements are already involved. On the evening of the 2d inst., they fell on a settlement about forty miles up the Muskingum, surprised a block-house, killed fourteen persons, and carried off three others. What num-

28

ber of Indians were concerned in this mischief, or from what tribe, we know not; except it be by those Indians who till lately used to visit our settlements every day, who have withdrawn themselves entirely from our sight ever since the expedition against the Shawanese; and there is little reason to doubt that the Delawares and Wyandots, as well as others, have had a hand in the business.

"It is impossible for me to give a just idea of the distress into which this event has thrown the inhabitants, especially those of the out settlements. For my own part, I have for some time been of opinion that the spring would open with a general attack on the frontiers, in which event I did not expect we should escape, unless government should timely send troops for our protection, which we were in hopes would be the case. But it seems the enemy are determined to take advantage of our defenceless situation. I consider this event as the forerunner of other attacks of a more serious nature, and which may involve us in complete ruin, unless prevented by the government immediately taking measures for our protection. To their protection I conceive we always had an indisputable claim, which claim, if possible, is increased by the circumstances that have brought us under the resentment of the Indians, and at least in some measure produced the mischief that we are fallen into."

Copy of a letter from a gentleman in Kentucky to his friend in Philadelphia, dated March 3, 1792.

"As to the Indians, they have been troublesome all winter. Since October last, sixty persons have been killed within the limits of this district, besides a number destroyed on the Ohio, among whom is our old acquaintance Mr. John May, late of Botetoute, whose exit deserves notice, because he was actuated by motives of humanity. The affair is thus related by a captive who has lately made his escape from the Indians, and who was a spectator and an unwilling instrument in the tragedy.

"Mr. May, in descending the Great Kenhawa and

Ohio, about the 20th of February last, discovered on the western shore of the latter, near the mouth of the Sciota, a white man, who with a plaintive voice was calling, "For God's sake, come and take a poor prisoner on board, who is endeavoring to escape from the savages." This had the desired effect. Mr. May ordered the boat towards the shore, but did not discover his mistake until the Indians rose up from their ambush, shot him dead, and wounded some others of the passengers on board, who immediately endeavored to make off, but being told in the English tongue they should have good quarters, surrendered without resistance. The Indians, however, on boarding the boat, massacred all without discrimination. Two days after, the same party attempted to decoy three large boats ashore, that were coming down from fort Pitt, but luckily they were discovered in time, and our people sheered off. The enemy, being prepared, manned their boats with about thirty warriors, and gave chase. The crew of two of the boats, fearing they might be overtaken, quitted them, and went on board the best sailer, where they threw overboard all their horses, and some heavy articles, and plied all their oars to effect their escape. The Indians also exerted themselves in the pursuit, keeping on a steady course for about twenty miles, notwithstanding twenty-four well-armed white men were on board the American boat, with one of our colonels of militia.

"Thus, for want of a little resolution and skill, a favorable opportunity was lost to destroy a number of the vile enemies of the human race. The Indians, on their return, took possession of the two boats that were abandoned, and found in them seventeen horses, five thousand dollars' worth of merchandise, and considerable property belonging to the emigrants.

"Fort M'Intosh, on the Ohio, was a short time since attacked by a party of the Indians. They secreted themselves near the fort, and succeeded in killing the sentinel on duty. They then rushed into the fort, and discharged their pieces at those within. One man only was wounded, who, in endeavoring to escape, was tomahawked by an Indian. One ball just grazed the temple of Capt. Forbes, who commanded the guard, and four others struck a log above his head, the splinters and bits of which cut his face. The garrison consisted of twenty men, and there were forty of the enemy.

"Thus we find that Indian treaties do not secure our country from the depredations of the savages. Our last hope now is, that the President of the United States will, ere long, adopt such measures as will prove the efficiency of the federal government to protect the citizens of the United States, however remotely situated from the seat of government."

Copy of a letter from a gentleman in South Carolina, to a friend in New York, dated Charleston, Aug. 6, 1792.

"An express arrived from Gen. Pickens and Col. Anderson, which brings advices to the governor, stating that a general Indian war on the western frontiers of the southern states seems inevitable; that, by intelligence from the country of the Creeks, all the tribes except the Custawas are determined for war, urged by Galphin, the successor of M'Gillivray, and that they have already commenced hostilities within the Carolina line, a party of them having killed and scalped a man on Tugaloo. We hear that the governor has ordered one third of the militia in the upper districts to be drafted, and held in readiness for immediate service, should the savages make further depredations on the frontiers.

"Yesterday evening, a gentleman arrived here from Augusta, who informed us that six of the Creek towns, with a number of the Cherokees, had declared war against the United States, and were actually marching, under the command of Bowls and Galphin, to attack the frontiers.

"On the 22d ult., the Indians, thirty-seven in number, came to the house of Mr. Richard Thresher, in Augusta, and fired upon and killed him, two children, and a negro woman. Mrs. Thresher, to avoid if possible the fate with which she was threatened, fled with an infant of about five or six weeks old in her arms, and leaped into the river. The Indians pursued, shot her through each thigh and right breast, stabbed her in the left breast with a knife, cut her left arm nearly off, and then scalped her. In this horrid situation she remained until the neighbors could assemble in sufficient numbers to cross the river and pursue the Indians. As the first canoe was crossing, she had strength enough to call for assistance. They went, found her hanging by a bush in water nearly up to her chin, her infant at the bottom of the river a few yards from her. She lived twenty-four hours, and when informed by her physician that it was impossible for her to survive much longer, she, with a fortitude that is rarely to be met with, called her friends around her, and in a calm but pathetic manner gave her hand to each one, wishing them a better fate than had befallen herself and family; and after her speech had failed, as neighbors were continually coming in, she continued to give her hand until about five minutes before she resigned her breath, which was without a groan.

" Mrs. Thresher was about twenty-five years of age, of a respectable family and elegant person, and possessed an uncommon education.

" On Thursday the 24th, two men were killed in Franklin, and forty horses carried off; and the people on the frontiers have retreated into forts, without arms or ammunition. At one meeting of near forty persons they could muster only five old muskets; and to heighten the horror of their condition, the Indians were momentarily expected.

" As similar murders were daily committed, it called up the spirit of nine hundred gallant fellows, who marched last week against the savages, determined to revenge the cruelties perpetrated on the infant, the mother, and the defenceless.

" To see the country all in forts, breaking up, leaving their farms, their corn, and their houses burnt up, is truly distressing. At this time, nearly half the country are in forts.

"Capt. Kenton, with about thirty-five men, who went up the Ohio, in order to intercept the Indians, who took Morgan's station, fell in with a trail of a party of Indians on the waters of Point Creek, coming in to the settlement. He followed them, and at night, observing he was near them, sent forward some spies to discover their fires. Unluckily the spies fell in with their camp, and before they discovered it the Indians were alarmed by a dog, which flew out at the spies, upon which the Indians fired on them. The spies returned the fire. Upon hearing the firing, the whole of the party came up, and the Indians retreated, leaving their baggage, among which was a quantity of powder, lead, and blankets. Kenton had one man killed. It is supposed two Indians were killed and carried off, from some discoveries that were made next morning."

Copy of a letter from fort Washington, dated April 20, 1792.

"On Tuesday morning, the 6th inst., Maj. Adair, with one hundred and twenty volunteers from Kentucky, having charge of a large number of pack-horses, laden with provisions, destined for the advanced posts, was most daringly attacked by nearly an equal party of Indians, although under cover of fort St. Clair; notwithstanding which, and that our people fought desperately, the Indians drove them into the fort, and carried off all their provisions and horses, both pack and cavalry, save about twenty killed and four wounded, and stripped the camp of everything, carrying the whole off with the most audacious insult and triumph. But as soon as the party were re-supplied with ammunition from the garrison, they sallied forth, but too late to recover the booty which the Indians had made. The courage and daring spirit of these savages were particularly conspicuous on this occasion, as they fought almost under the guns of the fort. Our loss was one captain and ten privates killed, and some wounded, besides horses and provisions, estimated at fifteen thousand dollars. Two of the enemy were found dead a short distance from the field of action. If these Indians had writers among them, what honorable testimony and eulogy might they not give of the noble spirit and heroic bravery of the native American character, rather than depreciate it as the Europeans do. Two of our men have lately made their escape from the Miami villages, and arrived here, who give an account of a mock fight, lately exhibited by the Indians assembled there, to divert the squaws and children. It was in ridicule of Gen. St. Clair's disposition of his troops on the 4th of November last, and of his flight before the Indians, who pursued him and his army, while others plundered his camp. They have given out that they mean to celebrate this event annually by a like sham fight, and a great dance, to be called Gen. St. Clair's fight and dance. It is to be hoped we yet shall have an opportunity to retaliate, and to teach our enemy to amuse themselves at our expense in a less ludicrous manner. It seems that Gen. St. Clair's field of action was on a branch of the Wabash, twenty-four leagues from the Miami towns, which are now inhabited by the hostile Indians.

"A letter from a correspondent, on whose veracity we can rely, in the territory of the United States, south of the river Ohio, dated the 17th ult., states that everything wears a gloomy aspect on the western frontiers; that about the last of December, the Cherokees sent in peace talkers to Gov. Blount, which were only intended to facilitate the commission of further depredations by them, when the guards from our outposts were withdrawn; that from the 16th to the 26th of January, the Indians killed and wounded nineteen persons in Cumberland, among whom was Edwin Shelby, brother to the governor of Kentucky; that four of the Chickamogga towns, and the Upper Creeks, have declared war; that the Creeks have killed a family in the county of Georgia, that the barbarity exercised by them in this massacre was enough to make human nature shudder at the bare recital;—they butchered them like so many dogs, caught their blood and bowels, exposed them to view, and then gave the whole to a tame bear to devour; that the Cherokees had killed two Creeks, wounded several, and taken two prisoners; that the Creeks threaten to retaliate, and cut them all off; that the inhabitants of the territory are waiting with impatience for the general government to afford them succor and protection; that treaties with the savages will avail nothing, as what promise they make to-day they will not hesitate to break to-morrow."

Copy of a letter from Mr. John Corbly, a Baptist minister, to his friend in Philadelphia, dated Muddy Creek, Penn., Sept. 1, 1792.

"The following are the particulars of the destruction of my unfortunate family by the savages. On the 10th of May last, being my appointment to preach at one of my meeting-houses, about a mile from my dwelling-house, I set out with my loving wife and five children for public worship. Not suspecting any danger, I walked behind a few rods, with my Bible in my hand, meditating. As I was thus employed, on a sudden I was greatly alarmed by the frightful shrieks of my dear family before me. I immediately ran to their relief with all possible speed, vainly hunting a club as I ran. When within a few yards of them, my poor wife, observing me, cried out to me to make my escape. At this instant, an Indian ran up to shoot me. I had to strip, and by so doing outran him. My wife had an infant in her arms, which the Indians killed and scalped; after which they struck my wife several times, but not bringing her to the ground, the Indian who attempted to shoot me approached her and shot her through the body; after which they scalped her! My little son, about six years old, they despatched by sinking their hatchets into his brains! My little daughter, four years old, they in like manner tomahawked and scalped! My eldest daughter attempted an escape by concealing herself in a hollow tree about six rods from the fatal scene of action. Observing the Indians retiring, as she supposed, she deliberately crept from the place of her concealment, when one of the Indians, who yet remained on the ground, espying her, ran up to her and with his tomahawk knocked her down and scalped her. But, blessed be God, she yet survives, as does her little sister, whom the savages in like manner tomahawked and scalped. They are mangled to a shocking degree, but the doctors think there are some hopes of their recovery.

"When I supposed the Indians gone, I returned to see what had become of my unfortunate family, whom, alas, I found in the situation above described. No one, my dear friend, can form a true conception of my feelings at this moment. A view of a scene so shocking to humanity quite overcame me; I fainted, and was unconsciously borne off by a friend, who at that moment arrived to my relief.

"Thus, dear sir, have I given you a faithful though a short narrative of the fatal catastrophe; amidst which my life is spared, but for what purpose the Great Jehovah best knows. Oh, may I spend it to the praise and glory of his grace, who worketh all things after the counsel of his own will. The government of the world and the church is in his hands. I conclude with wishing you every blessing, and subscribe myself your affectionate though afflicted friend and unworthy brother in the gospel ministry."

On the 27th September, 1792, as five gentlemen were on their way to Detroit, at a place called the Burdle, on lake Erie, they were suddenly attacked by four Mahagon or Delaware Indians, armed with muskets and tomahawks, who fired on them and killed Mr. Taller and Mr. Barclay. They then rushed on with their tomahawks. One attacked Mr. Arnold, who, after a smart struggle, in which he received several wounds in his head, disengaged himself, and having a musket at the instant presented him by Mr. Stewart, snapped at the Indian, who immediately thereupon,

29

with the three others, fled to the woods. As soon as they had disappeared, Mr. Arnold and his companions hastened to the shore of the lake, in which they launched their batteau, but when about thirty rods from the shore they were hailed by Mr. Van Alstyne, who during the bloody contest had secreted himself in the bushes. He begged of his companions to return and take him in. Mr. Van Alstyne, it was supposed, misunderstanding his friend, proceeded directly up the lake, to the very spot where the Indians were then assembled, who with their tomahawks instantly despatched him; after which they followed the two survivors, in an old canoe, two or three miles down the lake, but being unable to overtake them, discontinued the pursuit.

Copy of a letter from a gentleman in Marietta to his friend in Washington, dated March 4, 1793.

"About two weeks since two brothers by the name of Johnson, one twelve and the other nine years of age, were playing on the western bank of Short Creek, about twelve miles from this, skipping stones on the water. At a distance they discovered two men, who appeared to be settlers, being dressed with coats and hats. These men, to amuse and deceive the children, engaged in the same sport, advancing towards the boys, till by degrees they got so near that the children discovered them to be Indians; but it was then too late to make their escape. The Indians seized and carried them six miles into the woods, where they made a fire and took up their lodgings for the night. Their rifles and tomahawks they rested against a tree, and then laid down, each Indian with a boy on his arm. The children, as may be supposed, kept awake. The eldest began to move, and finding his Indian sound asleep, by degrees disengaged himself and went to the fire, which had then got low, and stirred it up; the Indian not waking, he whispered to his brother, who likewise crept away, and both of them went to the fire.

"The oldest boy then observed to his brother, 'I

think we can kill these Indians and get rid of them.' The youngest agreed to the proposal of attempting it. The oldest then took one of the rifles, and placing the muzzle, which he rested on a small stick that he found for the purpose, close to the head of one of the Indians, and committing the execution of this part of the business to his brother, ordered him to pull the trigger at the moment he saw him strike the other Indian with one of the tomahawks. The oldest gave the signal. The youngest pulled the trigger. The rifle shot away the lower part of the Indian's face, and left him senseless. He then told his brother to lay on, for he had done the deed for his; after which he snatched up the gun and ran. The boy with the tomahawk gave the stroke with the wrong end. The Indian started on his seat. The boy found the mistake, and turning the tomahawk in his hand, gave him another blow, which brought him to the ground. He repeated his strokes until he had despatched him, and then made the best of his way after his brother. When the boys had found the path which they recollected to have travelled the day before, the oldest fixed his hat on a bush as a directory to find the scene of action the next day. The tomahawked Indian was found near the place where the boys had left him. The other was not there, but was tracked by his blood, and although so weakened by his wounds that he could not raise his rifle to fire at the pursuers, they suffered him to escape, but it is supposed he must have died of his wounds. These two Indians were sent out to reconnoitre the best place for an attack, which was to have been made by a party of warriors waiting in the neighborhood."

Copy of a letter from Col. Robertson to Gen. Washington, dated Nashville, Feb. 1, 1793.

"Sir—By accounts received from the Chickasaw nation of Indians, we are informed that, at a grand council of their warriors, it was unanimously determined to commence active operations against the whites. The Cherokees they expect will join them. The white inhabitants in this quarter are drawing together, and are doing everything possible for their defence; but I fear without some timely assistance we shall all fall a sacrifice to the wanton barbarity of our savage foes, who we expect are now on their way to this place to the number of one thousand. Major Hall and his eldest son fell a sacrifice to their fury two days ago near Bedoloe's Lick. They have killed about twenty-four persons in the course of a few months in this settlement, besides a great number more who were near it.

"From Burke county we learn that on the 11th instant two men, a woman, and her infant daughter, were scalped at William's swamp, on the Ogechee river, by a party of Indians. The little girl, to deter them from their cruel design, held out a bottle of honey, telling them it was rum, begging them in the mean time to spare her life. They told her they did not want rum, but her hair! They knocked her down and scalped her, but we are happy to learn that she is in a fair way of recovery.

"By a letter from Kentucky I am informed that the Indians have done more mischief in that state the present year, than for at least four years past. Scarcely a boat can pass below Limestone but what is attacked by them. Six or seven have been captured, some with very valuable lading. By a prisoner who escaped from them a short time since, we are informed that the Indians have procured a boat, or rather a kind of floating battery, with the sides built high and rendered bullet proof. This boat is situated near the mouth of the Great Miami. They a few days since captured a boat in which were a Capt. Ashley and his family. A son of the captain having been very spirited in the opposition, the savages immediately put him to death, cut out his heart and broiled it, which they afterwards devoured in the presence of the unhappy father, who has since made his escape."

Copy of a letter from Gen. Clark to the governor of the state of Georgia, dated Long Creek, September 24th, 1793.

"Sir—I had certain information that a man was killed on the 14th, near Greensborough, by a party of six or seven Indians, and that, on the 16th, Col. Barber, with a small party, was waylaid by about fifty or sixty Indians, by whom three of his party were killed. This, together with a variety of other accounts equally alarming, determined me to raise what men I could in the course of twenty-four hours, and march with them to protect the frontiers; in which space of time I collected one hundred and sixty-four men, chiefly volunteers, and proceeded to the place where Col. Barber had been attacked, where I found the bodies of the three men mentioned above, mangled in a shocking manner, and after I had buried them, proceeded on the trail of the murderers as far as the south fork of the Oakmulgee, where, finding I had no chance of overtaking them, I left it and went up said river until I met with a fresh trail of Indians coming towards our frontier settlements. I immediately turned and followed this trail until the morning of the 21st, when I came up with them. They had just crossed a branch called Jack's Creek, through a thick cane-brake, and were encamped and cooking on an eminence. My force then consisted of one hundred and thirty men, thirty having been sent back on account of their horses having been tired and lost. I drew up my men in three divisions, the right commanded by Col. Freeman and Maj. Clark, who were ordered to surround and charge the Indians, which they did with such dexterity and spirit that they immediately drove them from their encampment back into the cane-brake, where, finding it impossible for them to escape, they obstinately returned our fire until half past four o'clock, when they ceased, except now and then a shot.

"During the latter part of the action, they seized every opportunity of escaping by small parties, leaving the rest to shift for themselves. About sunset, I thought it most advisable to draw off, as the men had suffered for want of provisions nearly two days, and for want of water during the action, but more particularly to take care of the wounded, which amounted to eleven; and six killed. From every circumstance, I am certain there were not less than twenty-five Indians killed, and probably double that number wounded. In short, they were totally defeated, with the loss of their provisions, clothing, &c., consisting of the following articles:—four muskets, thirty-two brass kettles, and one hundred large packs, containing blankets, match-coats, boots, moccasons, tomahawks, pipes, upwards of one hundred halters and bridles, &c., from all of which I judge their number was fully equal to ours. Col. Freeman and Maj. Clark distinguished themselves, and from the spirit and bravery with which the whole of my little party acted during the action, I do not believe that, had we met them in the open woods, we should have been more than five minutes in destroying them all.

"While I was on this excursion, two skirmishes happened near Greensborough, in one of which one man was wounded, and in the other six stands of arms were lost, being guarded by only two men, while the rest of the party were gathering fodder."

Copy of a letter from an officer in the service of the United States to his friend in New York, dated Buffalo Creek, Sept. 27, 1793.

"I left fort Franklin the 3d inst., and arrived here the 11th in the evening, at the house of Mr. Winney, who informed me that upwards of four thousand hostile Indians were now assembled at the Miami villages, and that their number was daily increasing. Capt. Powell, and several other gentlemen of the British army, dined with me yesterday, and from their conversation I am perfectly convinced that the Indians are supported by the British in the war against us. Indeed, Capt. Powell told me that all the intentions of the Indians were well known to them, and the Indians were their allies, and of course they must support them. He also informed me that ten scouts of the hostile Indians were then out to strike on the frontiers, and they would soon attack the Six Nations. Some of the chiefs of the hostile Indians passed here about five days ago, on their way to Canada, but what their business is I cannot learn."

CHAP. XVI.

DECISIVE BATTLE GAINED BY THE AMERICAN ARMY, UNDER THE COMMAND OF GENERAL WAYNE, OVER THE HOSTILE INDIANS ON THE RIVER MIAMIS.

After the defeat of two armies, and the great sufferings of the inhabitants, by the Indians, as related in the preceding chapter, our government came to the determination to adopt more effective measures for the protection of the western frontiers. Gen. Anthony Wayne was appointed to the command of the forces raised for that purpose, and ordered to proceed against the hostile Indians, who had assembled in great force on the river Miamis. He gained a decisive victory over them, which put an end to their depredations for several years. The particulars of the battle are related in the following official despatch from him to the secretary of war.

"It is with infinite pleasure that I announce to you the brilliant success of the federal army under my command, in a general action with the combined force of the hostile Indians, and a considerable number of the volunteers and militia of Detroit, on the 20th of August, 1794, on the banks of the Miamis, in the vicinity of the British post and garrison at the foot of the rapids.

"The army advanced to Roach de Bout on the 15th, and on the 19th we were employed in making a temporary post for the reception of our stores and baggage, and in reconnoitering the position of the enemy, who were encamped behind a thick bushy wood and the British fort.

"At eight o'clock on the morning of the 20th, the army again advanced in columns, agreeably to the standing order of the march: the legion on the right, its right flank covered by the Miamis; one brigade of mounted volunteers on the left, under Brig. Gen. Todd, and the other in the rear, under Brig. Gen. Barbee. A select battalion of mounted volunteers moved in front of the legion, commanded by Major Price, who was directed to keep sufficiently advanced, and to give timely notice for the troops to form in case of action, it being yet undetermined whether the Indians would decide for peace or war.

"After advancing about five miles, Major Price's corps received so severe a fire from the enemy, who were secreted in the woods and high grass, as to compel them to retreat.

"The legion was immediately formed in two lines, principally in a close, thick wood, which extended for miles on our left, and for a very considerable distance in front, the ground being covered with old fallen timber, probably occasioned by a tornado, which rendered it impracticable for the cavalry to act with effect, and afforded the enemy the most favorable covert for their mode of warfare. The savages were formed in three lines, within supporting distance of each other, and extending for near two miles at right angles with the river. I soon discovered, from the weight of the fire and extent of their lines, that the enemy were in full force in front, in possession of their favorite ground, and endeavoring to turn our left flank. I therefore gave orders for the second line to advance to support the first, and directed Major General Scott to gain and turn the right flank of the savages, with the whole of the mounted volunteers, by a circuitous route. At the same time I ordered the front line to advance and charge with trailed arms, and rouse the Indians from their covert at the point of the bayonet, and when up to deliver a close and well-directed fire on their backs, followed by a brisk charge, so as not to give them time to load again or to form their lines. I also ordered Capt. M. Campbell, who commanded the legionary cavalry, to turn the left flank of the enemy next the river, which afforded a favorable field for that corps to act in. All these orders were obeyed with spirit and promptitude; but such was the impetuosity of the charge by the first line of infantry, that the Indians and Canadian militia and volunteers were driven from all their coverts in so short a time, that, although every possible exertion was used by the officers of the second line of the legion, and by Gens. Scott, Wood, and Barbee of the mounted volunteers, to gain their proper positions, but part of each could get up in season to participate in the action, the enemy being driven in the course of one hour more than two miles through the thick woods already mentioned, by less than one half their number.

"From every account the enemy amounted to two thousand combatants. The troops actually engaged against them were short of nine hundred. This horde of savages, with their allies, abandoned themselves to flight and dispersed with terror and dismay, leaving our victorious army in full and quiet possession of the field of battle, which terminated under the influence of the guns of the British garrison.

"The bravery and conduct of every officer belonging to the army, from the generals down to the ensigns, merit my approbation.

"Lieut. Covington, upon whom the command of the cavalry devolved, (Capt. Campbell being killed,) cut down two savages with his own hand, and Lieut. Webb one in turning the enemy's left flank.

"The wounds received by Captains Slough, Prior, Van Renselaer, and Rawlins, and Lieuts. M'Kenny and Smith, bear honorable testimony of their bravery and conduct. In fact, every officer and soldier who had an opportunity to come into action, displayed that true bravery which always ensures success. And here permit me to declare that I never discovered more true spirit and anxiety for action than appeared to pervade the whole of the mounted volunteers, and I am well persuaded that had the enemy maintained their favorite ground for one half hour longer they would have felt most severly the prowess of that corps.

"But whilst I pay this just tribute to the living, I must not neglect the gallant dead, among whom we have to lament the early death of those worthy and brave officers, Capt. Campbell and Lieut. Towles, who fell in the first charge.

"The loss of the enemy was more than double to that of the federal army. The woods were strewed for a considerable distance with dead bodies of Indians and their white auxiliaries, the latter armed with British muskets and bayonets. We remained three days and nights on the banks of the Miamis in front of the field of battle, during which time all the houses and cornfields were consumed and destroyed for a considerable distance above and below the garrison, among which were the houses, stores, and property of Col. M'Kee, the British Indian agent, and principal stimulator of the war now existing between the United States and the savages.

"The army returned to head quarters on the 27th, by easy marches, laying waste the villages and cornfields for about fifty miles on each side of the Miamis. It is not improbable that the enemy may make one desperate action against the army, as it is said a reinforcement was hourly expected at fort Miamis from Niagara, as well as numerous tribes of Indians living on the margins and islands of the lakes. This is an event rather to be wished for than dreaded whilst the army remains in force; their numbers will only tend to confuse the savages, and the victory will be the more complete and decisive, and which may eventually ensure a permanent and happy peace. Total killed, thirty-eight; wounded, one hundred and one."

The following circumstances, which took place previous to and during Gen. Wayne's engagement, are worthy of record.

At the instant Capt. Campbell was attempting to turn the left flank of the enemy, three of them plunged into the river. Two friendly negroes being on the opposite side, and observing the Indians making for the shore, they placed themselves on the bank behind a log, and as soon as the Indians approached within shot, one of the negroes fired and killed one of the Indians; the other two got hold of him to drag him out, when the other negro fired and killed another; the remaining Indian got hold of both the dead to pull them ashore, when the negro who killed the first, having again reloaded, fired and killed the third, and they all floated down the river.

Another circumstance is also related, viz. A soldier, soon after the conclusion of the action, proceeding some distance from the camp, met an Indian; they attacked each other, the soldier with his bayonet, and the Indian with his tomahawk. Some of the soldiers passing by that way two days after, found them both dead, the soldier with his bayonet in the body of the Indian, and the Indian with his tomahawk in the soldier's head.

The following circumstances took place previous to the action. A Mr. Wells, who, when very young, was taken prisoner by the Indians, and had resided several years among them, had made his escape, and was employed by Gen. Wayne as a spy. The day before the action he was taken by the Indians, who determined to put him to death. Finding it impossible to escape, he informed them that Gen. Wayne had not five hundred men under his command, and did not expect an attack. On hearing this, the Indians attacked Gen. Wayne, with a confidence inspired by their supposed superiority of numbers, and were repulsed, as before mentioned. After the action, Major Campbell, in whose custody the Indians had left Wells, inquired his motives for deceiving them; he answered, "For the good of my country." For this heroic action he was unfeelingly delivered to the Indians, in whose hands it is supposed he experienced every torture that savage barbarity could invent or inflict. The circumstances respecting Mr. Wells were related to Gen. Wayne by a British drummer who deserted from the fort.

A council of Indians was held a few days after their defeat by Gen. Wayne, in which British agents endeavored to persuade them to risk another action; but this they refused to do, expressing a willingness to bury the bloody hatchet and return to their homes. Their loss they declared to be two hundred, and that their whole force at the commencement of the action amounted to fifteen hundred Indians and eighty Canadians. The body of the collector of Niagara was found among the slain.

CHAP. XVII.

EXPEDITION OF GEN. WILLIAM H. HARRISON AGAINST THE SAVAGES ON THE WABASH.—BATTLE OF TIPPECANOE.

We should have been extremely happy to have closed the list of savage barbarities with the last chapter; but, after a cessation of hostilities on their part of more than sixteen years, we find them once more collecting in a formidable body on our frontiers, and (instigated by a blood-thirsty savage of the Shawanee tribe, termed "the Prophet") commencing an unprovoked attack on the American troops stationed there.

The conduct of the Wabash Indians becoming suspicious to our government, in consequence of their many thievish excursions and hasty preparations for an offensive attack, Gen. Harrison, who was governor of the Northwestern Territory, with two thousand men, (three hundred and fifty regulars, and the remainder militia,) were ordered to proceed from the neighborhood of Vincennes to the line, and demand of the Prophet the object of his real intentions. The troops commenced their march on the 26th September, and nothing important occurred till their arrival on the line, where they remained near a month, and built a strong fort, which, in honor of the commander in chief, was called fort Harrison. The Indians, in a friendly manner, almost every day visited the camp, and held councils with the governor, but would not accede to his terms, which were, that their leader, the Prophet, should give up the property stolen from the Americans, and send all their warriors to their different tribes; the governor, therefore, determined on attacking him. On the 29th of October, 1811, the troops took up their line of march for the Prophet's town, where they arrived on the 6th November. When within about half a mile of the town, the troops formed the line of battle, which the Indians perceiving, they sent three of their chiefs with a flag of truce, begging that their lives might be spared, pledging themselves that they would not take up the tomahawk against the troops, and that, if they would encamp near the town, in the morning they would come to such terms as the governor should propose. This lulled the troops into security, and they encamped about half a mile back of the town.Ffteen minutes before five o'clock the next morning, the savages commenced a furious attack on the left flank of the troops, but not a single gun was fired by the sentinels or the guard in that direction, nor did they make the least resistance, but abandoned their post and fled into camp, and the first notice which the troops of that flank had of the danger was from the yells of the savages within a short distance of the line; but even under those circumstances, the men were not wanting to themselves or the occasion. Such of them as were awake, or were easily awakened, seized their arms and took their stations; others, who were more tardy, had to contend with the enemy in the very doors of their tents. The storm first fell upon Capt. Barton's company of the 4th U. S. regiment and Capt. Geiger's company of mounted riflemen, which formed the left angle of the rear line. The fire upon these was excessively severe, and they suffered severely before relief could be brought to them. Some few Indians passed into the encampment near the angle, and one or two penetrated to some distance before they were killed.

Under all these discouraging circumstances, the troops, nineteen twentieths of whom had never been in action before, behaved in a manner that can never be too much applauded. They took their places without noise, and with less confusion than could have been expected from veterans placed in a similar situation. As soon as Gen. Harrison could mount his horse, he rode to the angle that was attacked. He found that Barton's company had suffered severely, and the left of Geiger's entirely broken. He immediately ordered Cook's company and the late Capt. Wentworth's, under Lieut. Peters, to be brought up from the centre of the rear line, where the ground was much more defensible, and formed across the angle in support of Barton's and Geiger's. His attention was there engaged by a heavy firing upon the left of the front line, where were stationed the small company of the U. S. riflemen, (then, however, armed with muskets,) and the companies of Baen, Snelling, and Prescott, of the 4th regiment. He found Maj. Daviess forming the dragoons in the rear of those companies, and, understanding that the heaviest part of the enemy's fire proceeded from some trees about fifteen or twenty paces in front of those companies, he directed the major to dislodge them with a part of his dragoons. Unfortunately, the major's gallantry determined him to execute the order with a smaller force than was sufficient, which enabled the enemy to avoid him in front, and attack his flanks. He was mortally wounded, and his party driven back. The Indians were, however, immediately and gallantly dislodged from their advantageous position by Capt. Snelling, at the head of his company. In the course of a few minutes after the commencement of the attack, the fire extended along the left flank and part of the rear line. Upon Spencer's mounted riflemen, and the right of Warwick's company, which was posted on the right of the rear line, it was excessively severe. Capt. Spencer and his first and second lieutenants were killed, and Capt. Warwick was mortally wounded. These companies, however, still bravely maintained their posts; but Spencer's had suffered so severely, and having originally too much ground to occupy, the commander reinforced him with Robb's company of riflemen, which had been driven, or, by mistake, ordered from their position on the left flank towards the centre of the camp, and filled the vacancy that had been occupied by Robb with Prescott's company of the 4th U. S. regiment. His great object was to keep the lines entire, to prevent the enemy from breaking into the camp until daylight, which would enable them to make a general and effectual charge. With this view, he had reinforced every part of the line that had suffered much, and as soon as the approach of morning discovered itself, he withdrew from the front line Snelling's, Poesy's, (under Lieut. Albright,) and Scott's companies, and from the rear line Wilson's and Norris' companies, and drew them upon the left flank; at the same time ordered Cook's and Baen's companies, the former from the rear and the latter from the front line, to reinforce the right flank, foreseeing that at these points the enemy would make their last efforts. Maj. Wells, who commanded on the left flank, not knowing his intentions precisely, had taken the command of these companies, and had charged the enemy before he had formed the body of dragoons, with which he meant to support the infantry. A small detachment of these were ready, and proved amply sufficient for the purpose; the Indians were thrown into confusion, and driven by the infantry at the point of the bayonet, and the dragoons pursued and forced them into a marsh, where they could not be followed. Capt. Cook and Lieut. Larrabee had marched their companies to the right flank, formed them under the fire of the enemy, and, being then joined by the riflemen of that flank, they charged the Indians, killed a number, and put the rest to a precipitate flight.

The action was maintained with the greatest obstinacy and perseverance by both parties. The Indians manifested a ferocity quite uncommon even with them. To their savage fury our troops opposed that cool and deliberate valor which is characteristic of the christian soldier.

Capt. Spencer was wounded in the head. He exhorted his men to fight valiantly. He was shot through the thighs, and fell, still continuing to encourage them. He was raised up, and received a ball through his body, which put an immediate end to his existence. Capt. Warwick was shot immediately through the body. Being taken to the surgery to be dressed, as soon as it was over, (being a man of great bodily vigor, and still able to walk,) he insisted upon going back to head his company, although it was evident he had but a few hours to live.

There were one hundred and eighty-eight of the troops killed and wounded. It is supposed the enemy were about seven hundred strong, and that they had lost about four hundred in the engagement. The day succeeding the action, the troops set fire to the town, and destroyed everything valuable, and the morning ensuing struck their tents and commenced their march for Vincennes, where they arrived in safety, after a most fatiguing campaign of fifty-five days, and marching the distance of three hundred and twenty miles.

The victory gained by Gen. Harrison at Tippecanoe was justly deemed of the greatest importance to the country. President Madison, in his message to Congress soon after, says :—

"Congress will see with satisfaction the dauntless spirit and fortitude victoriously displayed by every description of the troops engaged, as well as the collected firmness which distinguished their commander, on an occasion requiring the utmost exertion of valor and discipline. It may reasonably be expected that the good effects of a critical defeat and dispersion of a combination of savages, which appears to have been spreading to a greater extent, will be experienced, not only in the cessation of the murders and depredations committed on our frontier, but in the prevention of any hostile incursions otherwise to have been apprehended."

Copy of a letter from Gen. Harrison to the secretary of war, dated Vincennes, Dec. 14, 1811.

"Sir—I have the honor to inform you that two principal chiefs of the Kickapoos of the prairie arrived here, bearing a flag, on the evening before last. They informed that they came in consequence of a message from the chief of that part of the Kickapoos which had joined the Prophet, requiring them to do so, and that the said chief is to be here in a day or two. The account which they gave of the late confederacy under the Prophet is as follows:—

"The Prophet, with his Shawanees, is at a small Huron village, about twelve miles from his former residence, on this side the Wabash, where also are twelve or fifteen Hurons. The Kickapoos are encamped near the Tippecanoe. The Powtawsiomies have scattered and gone to different villages of that tribe. The Winnebagoes had all set out on their return to their own country, excepting one chief and nine men, who remained at their former village. The latter had attended Tecumseh in his tour to the southward, and had only returned to the Prophet's town the day before the action. The Prophet had sent a message to the Kickapoos of the prairie, to request that he might be permitted to retire to their town. This was positively refused, and a warning sent to him not to come there. He then sent to request that four of his men might attend the Kickapoo chief here. This was also refused.

"These chiefs say, on the whole, that all the tribes who lost warriors in the late action attribute their misfortunes to the Prophet alone; that they constantly reproach him with their misfortunes, and threaten him with death; that they are all desirous of making their peace with the United States; that the Prophet's followers were fully impressed with a belief that they could defeat us with ease; that it was their intention to have attacked us at fort Harrison if we had gone higher; that the attack made on our sentinels at fort Harrison was intended to shut the door against the accommodation; that the Winnebagoes had forty warriors killed in the action, and the Kickapoos eleven, and ten wounded; that they have never heard how many Pottawatomies and other tribes were killed; that the Pottawatomie chief left by me on the battle-ground is since dead of his wounds, but that he faithfully delivered my speech to the different tribes, and warmly urged them to abandon the Prophet, and submit to my terms.

"I cannot say how much of the above may be depended on. I believe, however, that the statement made by the chief is generally correct, particularly with regard to the present disposition of the Indians. It is certain that our frontiers have never enjoyed more profound tranquillity than at this time. Before the expedition, not a fortnight passed over without some vexatious depredation being committed. The Kickapoo chiefs certainly tell an untruth when they say that there were but eleven of this tribe killed and ten wounded. It is impossible to believe that fewer were wounded than killed. They acknowledge, however, that the Indians have never sustained so severe a defeat since their acquaintance with the white people."

CHAP. XVIII.

GEN. HARRISON'S ENGAGEMENTS WITH THE INDIANS DURING THE LATE WAR WITH GREAT BRITAIN.—GALLANT DEFENCE OF FORT MEIGS.—ATTACK ON FORT STEPHENSON.—BATTLE OF THE THAMES.—DEATH OF TECUMSEH.

In the course of the late war which prevailed between America and Great Britain, the latter having engaged many of the savages in her cause, Gen. Harrison (who was appointed to the command of the volunteers and drafted militia of Ohio, &c.) held a council with a number of Indian chiefs who had professed neutral sentiments, to whom he made three propositions: "to take up arms in behalf of the United States—to remove within the lines and remain neutral—or, to go to the enemy and seek their protection." After a short consultation, many of them accepted the first, and made preparations to accompany him in the invasion of Canada.

After the surrender of Detroit to the British forces under Gen. Brock, the whole northwestern frontier became exposed to the inroads of the enemy. Gen Brock having been killed at the battle of Queenston, the command of the British army devolved upon Gen. Proctor, who had under him a large body of regular troops, with all the savages friendly to the English, who had joined him in great numbers, and were commanded by the famous Tecumseh. Their head quarters were established at Malden; and frequent attacks were made by them upon the settlements on the frontiers of Ohio and Indiana.

Our government at this time adopted the most efficient measures in their power, not only to defend the frontier inhabitants from their savage enemies, but to recover what had been lost, by carrying the war into the enemy's country. Large bodies of volunteers were raised by the western states, who were ordered, with the drafted militia, immediately to join the western army, which was placed under the command of Gen. Wm. H. Harrison.

The first of September, 1812, a considerable body of British and Indians proceeded from fort Malden to lay waste the frontiers of Ohio. A principal object appears to have been the capture of fort Wayne. They burnt several valuable buildings, and killed many of the inhabitants; among whom was a brother of Gov. Meigs.

On the 8th of November, a detachment of seven hundred men, commanded by Col. Campbell, left Franklinton, on an expedition against the Miami Indians, residing at the head of the Wabash. On the 17th December, they reached one of their villages, killed eight warriors, and took thirty-six prisoners. They set fire to the village, and encamped a few miles therefrom. A little before the break of day, they were attacked by the exasperated savages in their camp, shouting and yelling horribly.

The Americans sustained the attack until daylight, when the Indians were charged and dispersed, with the loss of thirty-five killed. The loss of the American troops was eight killed and twenty-nine wounded.

On the 14th of January, 1813, Col. Lewis was despatched to attack a large body of Indians encamped near the river Raisin. On the 18th the attack commenced. On the first onset the savages raised their accustomed yell, but the noise was drowned in the returning shouts of their dauntless assailants. They advanced boldly to the charge and drove them in all directions. On the first fire sixteen of the Indians fell. About forty were killed. Col. Lewis' party lost twelve killed and fifty-two wounded.

On the 18th, Gen. Winchester proceeded with a reinforcement of eight hundred men to the village of Frenchtown. On the 22d, they were attacked by a combined force of the enemy under the command of Tecumseh and Proctor. The American troops were in a moment ready for the reception of the enemy. The right wing sustained the attack for about thirty minutes, when, overpowered by numbers, they retreated over the river, and were met by a large body of Indians. The troops, finding their retreat cut off, resolved to sell their lives as dear as possible, and fought with desperation; but few of these brave fellows, however, escaped the tomahawk. The left wing with equal bravery maintained their ground within their pickets. The Indians and regulars made three different charges upon them, but the troops, with the most determined bravery and presence of mind, reserved their fire until the enemy advanced within point blank shot; they then opened a most galling fire upon them, and mowed down their ranks until they were compelled to retreat in confusion. The Americans lost nearly four hundred men, in killed, wounded, and missing. The courage of brave men was never more severely tested. The party that sought a retreat at the commencement of the action were closely pursued, surrounded, and literally cut to pieces by the savages. Not one escaped the scalping-knife!

On the 30th of January, Gen. Harrison despatched Capt. Lamor, Doctor M'Keenhan, and a Frenchman with a flag of truce to Malden. They encamped the first night near the rapids, and hoisted the white flag; but this was not respected. The Indians fired upon them while asleep, killed Lamor, wounded Doctor M'Keenhan, and took him and the Frenchman prisoners.

Gen. Harrison, receiving information that a large body of Indians were collected on Presque Isle, near the Miami, on the 9th of February proceeded with a detachment to attack them. The enemy fled on the approach of the troops, who pursued them almost to the river Raisin, but without being able to overtake them. Such was their desire to come up with the foe that they marched sixty miles in twenty-four hours.

The hostile Indians continued to make inroads into

the settlements, and committed many murders. An event took place, however, that served in some measure to check the audacity of the Indians. As Col. Ball, with a small squadron, was descending the Sandusky, the foremost of his party were fired upon by a band of eighteen or twenty Indians, who had placed themselves in ambush for the purpose of intercepting the mail-carrier. The colonel instantly charged upon them, and drove them from their hiding-place. The ground was favorable for cavalry, and the savages, finding neither mercy nor the possibility of escape, whooped and shouted horribly, and fought desperately, till they were all, to a man, cut to pieces. Col. Ball was twice dismounted, and opposed in personal contest to an Indian of gigantic stature. It was a desperate and doubtful struggle; life was at stake; both exerted to the utmost. An officer rode up and rescued the colonel, by shooting the Indian through the head. Not an Indian after this ventured to cross the Sandusky in quest of plunder.

If the massacre of the river Raisin filled the West with sorrow, it also awakened there a sense of indignation and outrage, of which the effects were afterwards seen. Its immediate influence was prejudicial to the objects of the campaign. Winchester's own movement had been not only without the knowledge or consent of Harrison, but contrary to his views and plans for the conduct of the campaign. When he heard that the movement had been made, he and those about him felt that it was to the last degree imprudent, and looked for nothing less from it than the certain and inevitable destruction of the left wing of the army, which had thus thrown itself into the very jaws of the enemy, and away from the possibility of succor. On the evening of the 16th, being at Upper Sandusky, he received from Col. Perkins, at Lower Sandusky, intelligence, for the first time, that Winchester, having arrived at the Rapids, meditated some unknown movement against the enemy. Alarmed at this, and ignorant what it implied, Gen. Harrison gave orders for the advance of troops and artillery, and hastened to Lower Sandusky himself. Here he was met by information from the Rapids of the march of Col. Lewis to Frenchtown. Fresh troops were immediately put in motion, by forced marches, for the Rapids; to which point he himself pushed with the utmost speed. All the disposable troops at the Rapids, and others as they came in, were ordered on with anxious expedition; but they were met on the road by the fugitives from the field of battle, and nothing remained but to protect them and the houseless people of Frenchtown. In short, all possible efforts were made to protect Winchester from the apprehended consequences of his own ill-advised acts.

After this, in expectation of an attack on the position at the Rapids, the army fell back to the portage, to admit of an expected reinforcement under Gen. Leftwich; on the arrival of which, the position at the Rapids, on the east bank of the Miami, was resumed, and strongly fortified, as the winter quarters of the army. It was called Camp Meigs, in honor of the governor of Ohio.

This position, being attacked by the British, became the scene of a brilliant triumph to the arms of the United States. So soon as it became known that the attack was contemplated, Gen. Harrison, having made arrangements for strong reinforcements to follow him, repaired to Camp Meigs, to conduct the defence of it in person. The enemy made his appearance on the 26th of April; consisting of a numerous force, British and Indians, commanded by Gen. Proctor; who, having ascended on the north side of the Miami in boats, landed at old fort Miami, and proceeded to construct three powerful batteries directly opposite the American camp. Meanwhile, our troops had thrown up a breastwork of earth, twelve feet in height, traversing the camp in rear of the tents, so that when the batteries of the enemy were completed and mounted, and his fire opened, the tents of the Americans, being struck and removed to the rear of the traverse, were completely sheltered and protected. A severe fire was now kept up on both sides until the 4th of May, when intelligence reached the camp of the approach of the expected reinforcements, composed of a brigade of Kentucky militia under Gen. Green Clay.

Gen. Harrison immediately determined to make a bold effort, by a sortie from the camp, combined with an attack of the enemy's lines by Gen. Clay, to raise the siege. Orders accordingly were despatched to Gen. Clay, requiring him that, instead of forming an immediate junction with the garrison, he should detach eight hundred of his men on the opposite side of the river, where two of the British batteries were, turn and take the batteries, spike the cannon, destroy the gun-carriages, and then regain the boats as speedily as possible; while the remainder of the brigade should land and fight their way into the camp, so as to favor a sortie to be made by the garrison against the third and only remaining British battery. This plan was ably conceived, and promised the best results. Gen. Clay, after detaching Col. Dudley to land on the west side of the Miami, fought his way safely into the camp. A part of the garrison also, under Col. (now Gen.) Miller, consisting in part of regular troops and the residue militia and Kentucky volunteers, gallantly assaulted and carried the battery on the eastern bank, made a number of prisoners, and drove the British and Indians from their lines.

Meanwhile, Dudley had landed his men, and charged and carried the two batteries, without the loss of a man. Unhappily, these gallant citizens were not sufficiently aware of their exposed situation, and of the necessity of retreating to their boats, in punctual observance of their orders, so soon as they should have destroyed the enemy's artillery. Instead of this, they were, without due consideration, drawn into a fight with some straggling Indians, and so detained until Proctor had time to interpose a strong force between them and the means of retreat. The result was the destruction rather than defeat of the detachment, for three fourths of it were made captives or slain. The British arms were again dishonored by giving up the prisoners to be massacred by the Indians. Dudley and many of his companions were tomahawked at once. Others of the prisoners were put into fort Miami, for the Indians to stand on the ramparts and fire into the disarmed crowd. Those Indians who chose selected their victims, led them to the gateway, and there, *under the eye of Gen. Proctor, and in the presence of the whole British army, murdered and scalped them.* Not until Tecumseh came up from the batteries did the slaughter cease. "For shame! it is a disgrace to kill defenceless prisoners!" he exclaimed, thus displaying more of humanity than Proctor himself.

Unfortunate as this incident was, the events of the day satisfied Proctor that he could not continue the siege with any hope of success. He resolved to retreat, to cover which he sent in a flag of truce, requiring the immediate surrender of the American post and army, as "the only means left for saving the latter from the tomahawks and scalping-knives of the savages." Considering this base and insolent message unworthy of any serious notice, Gen. Harrison simply admonished Proctor not to repeat it; with which manly and decided answer, Proctor, being perforce content, hastily broke up his camp, and retreated in disgrace and confusion towards Malden.

In May following, however, Proctor, thinking to surprise fort Meigs, made a second attack upon it with a large force of British regulars and Canadians, and several thousand Indians under Tecumseh, but was again obliged to retreat in disgrace.

On the first day of August Gen. Proctor appeared with five hundred regulars, and about eight hundred Indians of the most ferocious kind, before fort Stephenson, twenty miles above the mouth of the river Sandusky. There were not more than one hundred and thirty-three effective men in the garrison, and the works covered one acre of ground; it was a mere outpost of little importance; and Gen. Harrison, acting

32

with the unanimous advice of his council of war, had sent orders to Major Croghan, who commanded the garrison, to evacuate the fort, and make good his retreat to head quarters, provided the enemy should approach the place with artillery, and a retreat be practicable. But the first step taken by Proctor was to isolate the fort by a cordon of Indians, thus leaving to Major Croghan no choice but between resistance and submission. A messenger was sent to demand the surrender of the fort. He was met by Ensign Shipp, to whom the messenger observed that Gen. Proctor had a considerable body of regular troops, and a great many Indians, whom it was impossible to control, and if the fort was taken by force, he must expect that the mildest instruments made use of would be the tomahawk and scalping-knife! Shipp replied, that it was the commander's intention to defend the garrison or be buried in it, and that they might do their worst. The messenger, startled at the reply of Shipp, again addressed him: "You are a fine young man. I pity your situation. For God's sake surrender, and prevent the dreadful slaughter which must inevitably follow resistance!" The gallant Shipp turned from him with indignation, and was immediately seized by a frightful-looking savage, who attempted to wrest his sword from him, but the ensign was fortunately too quick for him, and buried the blade to the hilt in his body, and succeeded in reaching the fort in safety. The attack now commenced. About four P. M. all the enemy's guns were concentrated against the northwestern angle of the fort, for the purpose of making a breach. To counteract the effect of their fire, the commander caused that point to be strengthened by means of bags of flour, sand, and other materials, in such a manner that the balls of the enemy did but little injury. But the enemy, supposing that their fire had sufficiently shattered the pickets, advanced to the number of six hundred to storm the place, the Indians shouting in their usual manner. As soon as the ditch was pretty well filled with the copper-colored assailants, the commander of the fort ordered a six-pounder, which had been masked in the block-house, to be discharged. It had been loaded with a double charge of musket-balls and slugs. The piece completely raked the ditch from end to end. The yell of the savages was at this instant horrible. The first fire levelled the one half in death; the second and third either killed or wounded all except eleven, who were covered by the dead bodies. The Americans had but one killed, and seven slightly wounded. Early the ensuing morning the few regulars and Indians that survived retreated down the river, abandoning all their baggage.

The time was now at hand when Gen. Harrison and his army were to reach the full completion of all the contemplated objects of the expedition.

Among the earliest recommendations of Gen. Harrison to the government the year before, and immediately after he commenced operations, had been that of constructing and equipping a naval armament on the lakes. In one letter he says, "Admitting that Malden and Detroit are both taken, Mackinaw and St. Joseph will both remain in the hands of the enemy until we can create a force capable of contending with the vessels which the British have in lake Michigan," &c. And again, in another letter,—"Should any offensive operation be suspended until spring, it is my decided opinion that the cheapest and most effectual plan will be to obtain command of lake Erie. This being once effected, every difficulty will be removed. An army of four thousand men, landed on the north side of the lake, below Malden, will reduce that place, retake Detroit, and, with the aid of the fleet, proceed down the lake to co-operate with the army from Niagara." These sagacious instructions, being repeatedly and strenuously urged by him, and reinforced also from other quarters, were adopted and acted upon by the government. Commodore Perry was commissioned to build, equip, and command the contemplated fleet; and, on the 10th of September, with an inferior force, he met the enemy, and gained the brilliant victory of Lake Erie.

Meanwhile, Col. Richard M. Johnson, then a member of Congress from Kentucky, had devised the organization of two regiments of mounted militia, which he was authorized by the government to raise, as well for service against the Indians, as to co-operate with Harrison. Col. Johnson crossed the country of Lower Sandusky, where he received orders from the war department to proceed to Kaskaskia, to operate in that quarter; but, by the interference of Har rison, and at the urgent request of Col. Johnson,—who said, for himself and his men, that the first object of their hearts was to accompany Harrison to Detroit and Canada, and to partake in the danger and honor of that expedition, under an officer in whom they had confidence, and who had approved himself "to be wise, prudent, and brave,"—the orders of the department were countermanded, and Col. Johnson attained his wish.

Gen. Harrison now prepared to strike the great blow. Aided by the energetic efforts of Gov. Meigs, of Ohio, and Gov. Shelby, of Kentucky, he had ready on the southern shore of lake Erie, by the middle of September, a competent force, destined for the immediate invasion of Canada. Between the 16th and the 24th of September, the artillery, military stores, provisions, and troops, were gradually embarked, and on the 27th the whole army proceeded to the Canada shore. "Remember the river Raisin," said Gen. Harrison, in his address to the troops, "but remember it only whilst victory is suspended. The revenge of a soldier cannot be gratified on a fallen enemy." The army landed in high spirits; but the enemy had abandoned his strong-hold, and retreated to Sandwich, after dismantling Malden, burning the barracks and navy-yard, and stripping the adjacent country of horses and cattle. Gen. Harrison encamped that night on the ruins of Malden.

On the 2d of October, arrangements were made for

pursuing the retreating enemy up the Thames. The army was put in motion on the morning of the 4th. Gen. Harrison accompanied Col. Johnson, and was followed by Gov. Shelby with the infantry. Having passed the ground where the enemy had encamped the night before, the general directed the advance of Col. Johnson's regiment to accelerate their march, for the purpose of ascertaining the distance of the enemy.

The troops had now advanced within three miles of the Moravian town, and within one mile of the enemy. Across a narrow strip of land, near an Indian village, the enemy were drawn up in a line of battle, to prevent the advance of the American troops. The British troops amounted to six hundred, the Indians to more than twelve hundred. About one hundred and fifty regulars, under Col. Ball, were ordered to advance and amuse the enemy, and, should a favorable opportunity present, to seize his cannon. A small party of friendly Indians were directed to move under the bank. The regiment of Col. Johnson was drawn up in close column, with its right a few yards distant from the road. Gen. Desha's division covered the left of Johnson's regiment. Gen. Cass and Commodore Perry volunteered as aids to Gen. Harrison.

On the 5th, the enemy was discovered in a position skilfully chosen, in relation as well to local circumstances as to the character of his troops. A narrow strip of dry land, flanked by the river Thames on the left and by a swamp on the right, was occupied by his regular infantry and artillery, while on the right flank lay Tecumseh and his followers, on the eastern margin of the swamp. But, notwithstanding the judicious choice of the ground, Proctor had committed the error of forming his infantry in open order. Availing himself of this fact, and aware that troops so disposed could not resist a charge of mounted men, he directed Col. Johnson to dash through the enemy's line in column. The movement was made with brilliant success. The mounted men charged with promptitude and vigor, broke through the line of the enemy, formed in the rear, and assailed the broken line with a success seldom equalled, for nearly the whole of the British regular force was either killed, wounded, or taken.

On the left the contest was much more serious. Col. Johnson's regiment, being there stationed, received a galling fire from the Indians, who seemed not disposed to give ground. The colonel gallantly led his men into the midst of them, and was personally attacked by a chief, whom he despatched with his cutlass at the moment the former was aiming a blow at him with his tomahawk. The savages, finding the fire of the troops too warm for them, fled across the hills and attempted to seek shelter in a piece of woods on the left, where they were closely pursued by the cavalry. At the margin of the wood Tecumseh stationed himself, armed with a spear, tomahawk, &c., endeavoring to rally and persuade his men to return to the attack. At this point a considerable body of Indians had collected; but this brave savage saw that the fortune of the day was against him, and the battle was lost. Proctor had cowardly fled from the field, and left him and his warriors alone to sustain themselves against a far superior force; and he knew that there was no chance of contending with any hope of success. He therefore stood, like a true hero, disdaining to fly, and was, with many of his bravest warriors around him, shot down by the Kentucky riflemen. It has been published to the world, and by many believed, that this distinguished warrior was killed by a pistol-shot from Col. Johnson; but this is undoubtedly a mistake, which probably originated from the circumstance of the colonel's having killed a chief by whom he was attacked, as has before been related. That he fell by a rifle-shot, there can be no doubt; but by whom fired, it was not certainly known, or probably never can be satisfactorily proved. No less than six of the riflemen and twenty-two Indians fell within twenty-five yards of the spot where Tecumseh was killed.

The Indians continued a brisk fire from the margin

of the wood until a fresh regiment was called into action to oppose them. A company of cavalry having crossed the hills and gained the rear of the savages, the rout became general. They fought bravely, and sustained a heavy loss in killed and wounded. The death of their leader, Tecumseh, was an irreparable loss to them.

Tecumseh was the most extraordinary Indian that has ever appeared in history. He was by birth a Shawanese, and would have been a great man in any age or nation. Independent of the most consummate courage and skill as a warrior, and all the characteristic acuteness of his race, he was endowed by nature with the attributes of mind necessary for great political combinations. His acute understanding, very early in life, informed him that his countrymen had lost their importance; that they were gradually yielding to the whites, who were acquiring an imposing influence over them. Instigated by these considerations, and, perhaps, by his natural ferocity and attachment to war, he became a decided enemy to the whites, and imbibed an invincible determination (he surrendered it with his life) to regain for his country the proud independence he supposed she had lost. For a number of years he was foremost in every act of hostility committed against those he conceived the oppressors of his countrymen, and was equally remarkable for intrepidity as skill, in many combats that took place under his banner. Aware, at length, of the extent, number, and power of the United States, he became fully convinced of the futility of any single nation of red men attempting to cope with them. He formed, therefore, the grand scheme of uniting all the tribes east of the Mississippi into hostility against the United States. This was a field worthy of his great and enterprising genius. He commenced in the year 1809; and in the execution of his project he displayed an unequalled adroitness, eloquence, and courage. He insinuated himself into every tribe from Michilimackinack to Georgia, and was invariably successful in his attempts to bring them over to his views. He played upon all their feelings, but principally upon their superstition, and sometimes assumed the character of a prophet, and carried with him a red stick, to which he attached certain mystical properties, and the acceptance of which was considered as the joining of his party; hence the name of Red Sticks applied to all Indians hostile to the United States. Unfortunately for Tecumseh, but happily for the United States, was it, that, before his plan had become matured, before his arrangements for general hostility were perfected, before, in fact, he had brought into the field any of his forces, his brother made a premature attack upon the forces of the United States under the command of Gen. Harrison, in the summer of 1811, at Tippecanoe, in which he suffered a signal defeat.

This disaster marred the prospects of the gallant Tecumseh. His own soul was unshaken; but it damped the ardor of his associates; and although many continued firm in their warlike attitude, nor shrunk from a contest that had commenced with defeat, all the efforts of Tecumseh were unavailing to supply the links thus broken in his chain of operations. The war against England, declared soon after this event by the United States, opened new views to the talents of Tecumseh. His merits were duly appreciated by the British government, and they made him a brigadier general in their service. At the head of his formidable warriors, he more than once turned the scale of victory against the Americans, and laid down his life for the cause he had espoused.

Tecumseh had fought during the first year of the war under Gen. Brock, to whom he gave great praise, not only for his bravery, but for his kindness and gentlemanly treatment to him and the warriors under his command. They had been remarkably successful in all their operations during the campaigns in which they fought together. But in Gen. Proctor he had no confidence, and they never agreed in the plans that were adopted in prosecuting the war. A few days before the last battle, in a talk he had with him at a council, he expressed in the strongest manner his entire disapprobation of all his measures. Being in company with some British officers, he was asked his opinion of Gen. Brock, in comparison with the merits of their present general. He answered—"Gen. Brock very brave man, great general. He say, Tecumseh, come, *we* go. Gen. Proctor say, Tecumseh, *you* go. Proctor no Brock."

The day after the battle, the American troops took possession of the Moravian towns, where they found great quantities of such provisions as were very acceptable to the troops. Among the trophies of the day, captured from the British, were six brass field-pieces that had been surrendered by Hull, on two of which was the motto—"Surrendered by Burgoyne at Saratoga." The town was found deserted, and so panic-struck were some of the squaws in their flight, that they are said to have thrown their papooses into the river, to prevent their being butchered by the Americans! The Indians who inhabited this town had been very active in committing depredations upon the frontiers, massacring the inhabitants, &c., for which reason the town was destroyed by the troops previous to their leaving it.

Soon after the return of Gen. Harrison to Detroit, the Ottawas, Chippewas, Pottawatomies, Miamis, and Kickapoos, proposed a suspension of hostilities, and agreed to "take hold of the same tomahawk with the Americans, and to strike all who were or might be enemies of the United States." They offered their women and children as hostages. Walk-in-the-water, a distinguished chief who had taken an active part in the late engagement, waited upon the general in person to implore peace. The white flag which he bore in his hand attracted a great crowd, who were struck with admiration at the firmness with which this distinguished warrior passed through the ranks of the American troops, whom he so gallantly opposed but a few days before; yet his adverse fortune was calcu-

33

lated to depress his spirits and produce humility. Almost all the other chiefs had been killed, or had surrendered themselves prisoners, and he was without the means of living or resisting.

CHAP. XIX.

WAR WITH THE CREEK NATION.—MASSACRE AT FORT MIMS.—BATTLES OF TALLUSHATCHES, TALLEDAGA, ANTOSSE.—ATTACK UPON CAMP DEFIANCE, AND BRILLIANT VICTORY AT THE BEND OF THE TALLAPOOSA.

THE enemy, apparently disposed to enlist the savages in the war at its commencement, despatched messengers to several of the Indian tribes in the Mississippi Territory, distinguished by the names of Creeks, Choctaws, and Chickasaws, to persuade them to take a part with them in their contest with the United States. The most friendly relations had subsisted between these tribes and the United States for many years; and the latter, dictated by a generous policy, had been successful in their endeavors to introduce among them the improvements of civilized society. But so ardent is the propensity of the Indian character for war, that many were induced to commit the most wanton and unprovoked acts of barbarity upon the Americans.

The most experienced and well-disposed chiefs, aware of the evils a war with the United States must produce upon the tribes, made use of their best endeavors to suppress their acts of cruelty; but those determined on war were not disposed to listen to the dictates of discretion or wisdom, and commenced open hostilities against the United States by one of the most bloody massacres recorded in Indian history. The particulars of the bloody transaction are copied from a letter of Judge Toulman, dated September 7th, 1813.

"The dreadful catastrophe which we have been some time anticipating has at length taken place. The Indians have broken in upon us, in numbers and fury unexampled. Our settlement is overrun, and our country, I fear, is on the eve of being depopulated. The accounts which we received led us to expect an attack about the full moon of August; and it was known at Pensacola, when the ammunition was given to the Indians, who were to be the leaders of the respective parties destined to attack the different parts of our settlement. The attempt made to deprive them of their ammunition, issued by the Spaniards on the recommendation of a British general, on their way from Pensacola, and in which it was said the Indians lost more than twenty men, although only one third of our people stood their ground, it is highly probable, in some measure, retarded their operations; and the steady succession of rain contributed to produce the same effect. Had their attempt been conducted with more judgment and supported with more vigor, there would have been an end, for a time, of Indian warfare. In consequence of the delay, our citizens began to grow careless and confident; and several families who had removed from Tensaw to fort Stoddert, returned again, and fell a sacrifice to the merciless savages.

"A few days before the attack, some negroes of Mr. M'Girt, who lived in that part of the Creek territory which is inhabited by half-breeds, had been sent up the Alabama to his plantation for corn; three of them were taken by a party of Indians. One escaped and brought down news of the approach of the Indians. The officer gave but little credit to him; but they made some further preparation to receive the enemy. On the next day Mr. James Cornels, a half-breed, and some white men, who had been out on the late battle-ground, and discovered the trail of a considerable body of Indians going towards Mr. M'Girt's, came to the fort and informed the commanding officer of the discovery.

Though their report did not appear to receive full credit, it occasioned great exertions; and on Saturday and Sunday considerable work was done to put the fort in a state of defence. On Sunday morning three negroes were sent out to attend the cattle, who soon returned with an account that they had seen twenty Indians. Scouts were sent out to ascertain the truth of the report. They returned and declared they could see no signs of Indians. One of the negroes belonging to Mr. Randon was whipped for bringing what they deemed a false report. He was sent out again on Monday, and saw a body of Indians approaching; but, afraid of being whipped, he did not return to Mims but to Pierce's fort; but before his story could be communicated, the attack was made. The commanding officer called upon Mr. Fletcher, who owned another of the negroes, to whip him also. He believed the boy, and resisted two or three applications; but at length they had him actually brought out for the purpose, when the Indians appeared in view of the fort. The gate was open. The Indians had to come through an open field one hundred and fifty yards wide before they could reach the fort, and yet they were within thirty steps of the fort, at eleven o'clock in the morning, before they were noticed. The sentry then gave the cry of 'Indians!' and they immediately set up a most terrible war-whoop, and rushed into the gate with inconceivable rapidity, and got within it before the people of the fort had an opportunity of shutting it. This decided their fate. Major Beasely was shot through the body near the gate. He called to the men to take care of the ammunition and retreat to the house. He went himself to a kitchen, where it is supposed he must have been burnt.

"There was a large body of Indians, though they probably did not exceed four hundred. Our people seemed to sustain the attack with undaunted spirit. They took possession of the port-holes in the other lines of the fort, and fired on the Indians who remained in the field. Some of the Indians got on the block-house, at one of the corners; but, after much firing upon the people, they were dislodged. They succeeded, however, in setting fire to a house near the pickets, from which it communicated to the kitchen, and from thence to the main dwelling-house. They attempted to do it by burning arrows, but failed. When the people in the fort saw the Indians retained full possession of the outer court, and the gate continued open, that their men fell very fast, and that their houses were in flames, they began to despond. Some determined to cut their way through the pickets and escape. Of the whole number of white men and half-breeds in the fort, it is supposed that not more than twenty-five or thirty escaped, and of these many were wounded. The rest, and almost all the women and children, fell a sacrifice either to the shot of the Indians or the flames. The battle terminated about an hour before sunset.

"The women and children took refuge in an upper story of the dwelling-house; and it is said that the Indians, when the buildings were in flames, danced around them with savage delight. The helpless victims perished in the flames. It is also reported that, when the buildings were burning, and the few who remained were exposed to the fire of the enemy, they collected many of the guns of the deceased and threw both them and the remaining stock of ammunition into the flames, to prevent their becoming subservient, in the hands of the Indians, to the destruction of their fellow-citizens. Surely this was an instance of determined resolution and benevolent foresight, of which there are not many examples.

"But notwithstanding the bravery of our fellow-citizens, the Indians carried all before them, and murdered the armed and the helpless without discrimination. Our loss is seven commissioned officers, and about one hundred non-commissioned officers and privates, of the first regiment of the Mississippi territory volunteers. There were about twenty-four families of men, women, and children in the fort, of whom almost all have perished, amounting to one hundred and sixty souls. I reckon, however, among them about six families of half-breeds and seven Indians. There were also about one hundred negroes, of whom a large proportion were killed. The half-breeds have uniformly done themselves honor, and those who survive will afford great assistance in the prosecution of the war."

On the first of November, Gen. Jackson, receiving information that a considerable number of hostile Creeks were embodied at Tallushatches, detached Gen. John Coffee with a number of men to attack and destroy the place, which he completely effected.

The following is an extract from Gen. Coffee's official report to Gen. Jackson of the expedition.

"Pursuant to your order of the 2d, I detached from my brigade of cavalry and mounted riflemen nine hundred men and officers, and proceeded directly to the Tallushatches towns, crossing Coosey river at the Fish-dam ford, three or four miles above this place. I arrived within one and a half miles of the town on the morning of the 3d, at which place I divided my detachment into two columns: the right, composed of the cavalry, commanded by Col. Allcorn, to cross over a large creek that lay between us and the towns; the left column was of the mounted riflemen, under the command of Col. Cannon, with whom I marched myself. Col. Allcorn was ordered to march up on the right and encircle one half of the towns, and at the same time the left would form half a circle on the left, and unite the head of the columns in front of the town; all of which was performed as I could wish. When I arrived within half a mile of the town, the drums of the enemy began to beat, mingled with their savage yells, preparing for action. It was an hour after sunrise when the action was brought on by Capt. Hammond and Lieut. Patterson's companies, who had gone on within the circle of alignment for the purpose of drawing out the enemy from their buildings, which had the most happy effect. As soon as Capt.

Hammond exhibited his front in view of the town (which stood in wood-land) and gave a few scattering shot, the enemy formed and made a violent charge on him; he gave way as they advanced, until they met our right column, which gave them a general fire and then charged. This changed the direction of the charge completely. The enemy retreated, firing until they got around and in their buildings, where they made all the resistance that an overpowered soldiery possibly could do; they fought as long as one existed. But their destruction was very soon completed; our men rushed up to the doors of the houses, and in a few minutes killed the last warrior of them. The enemy fought with savage fury, and met death with all its horrors without shrinking or complaining; not one asked to be spared, but fought as long as they could stand or sit. In consequence of their flying to their houses and mixing with the families, our men, in killing the males, without intention killed and wounded a few of the squaws and children, which was regretted by every officer and soldier of the detachment, but it could not be avoided.

"The number of the enemy killed was one hundred and eighty-six that were counted, and a number of others that were killed in the woods and not found. I think the calculation a reasonable one to say two hundred of them were killed, and eighty-four prisoners of women and children were taken. Not one of the warriors escaped to carry the news, a circumstance hitherto unknown.

"I lost five men killed and forty wounded, none mortally, the greater part slightly, a number with arrows; two of the men killed was with arrows. This appears to form a very principal part of the enemy's arms for warfare; every man having a bow with a bundle of arrows, which is used after the first fire with the gun, until a leisure time for loading offers."

Gen. Jackson, receiving information on the seventh of November that a party of friendly Creeks at the fort at Tallegada were threatened with an attack from a considerable body of hostile Creeks, marched to their relief in the evening. At four o'clock in the morning of the 9th, he fell in with the enemy within a quarter of a mile of the fort, and after a short action succeeded in dispersing them with great slaughter.

The following is an extract from the general's official letter, giving the particulars of the battle.

"At sunrise we came within half a mile of them, and having formed my men, I moved on in battle order. The infantry were in three lines; the militia on the left, and the volunteers on the right. The cavalry formed the extreme wings; and were ordered to advancé in a curve, keeping their rear çonnected with the advance of their infantry lines, and enclose the enemy in a circle. The advanced guard, whom I sent forward to bring on the engagement, met the attack of the enemy with great intrepidity; and having poured upon them four or five very gallant rounds, fell back, as they had been previously ordered, to the main army. The enemy pursued, and the front line was now ordered to advance and meet them; but, owing to some misunderstanding, a few companies of militia, who composed a part of it, commenced a retreat. At this moment a corps of cavalry commanded by Lieut. Dyer, which I had kept as a reserve, was ordered to dismount and fill up the vacancy occasioned by the retreat. This order was executed with a great deal of promptitude and effect.

"The militia, seeing this, speedily rallied, and the fire became general along the first line, and on that part of the wings which was contiguous. The enemy, unable to stand it, began to retreat, but were met at every turn and pursued in every direction. The right wing chased them with the most destructive fire to the mountains, a distance of about three miles; and had I not been compelled by the faux pas of the militia in the onset of the battle to dismount my reserve, I believe not a man of them would have escaped. The victory, however, was very decisive; two hundred and ninety of the enemy were left dead, and there can be no doubt but many more were killed who were not found.

Wherever they ran they left behind traces of blood; and I believe that very few will return to their villages in as sound a condition as they left them. I was compelled to return to this place to protect the sick and wounded, and get my baggage. In the engagement we lost fifteen killed and fifteen wounded, two of whom have since died."

On the 11th of November a detachment of the Tennessee militia, under Gen. White, was sent against the Hillibee towns, for the purpose of punishing the hostile Creeks in that quarter. Extract from Gen. White's official letter to Major Gen. Cocke, giving an account of the expedition.

"Under your order of the 11th November, I immediately marched with the mounted infantry under the command of Major Porter, and a few of the Cherokee Indians under Col. Morgan, with very short rations only. We continued our march to Little Oakfuskie, when we fell in with and captured five hostile Creek warriors, supposed to be spies. Finding no other Indians at that place, we burned the town, which consisted of thirty houses. We then proceeded to a town called Genalga, and burned the same, consisting of ninety-three houses. Thence we proceeded to Nitty Chapota, consisting of about twenty-five houses, which I considered it most prudent not to destroy, as it might possibly be of use at some future period. Thence we marched to the Hillibee town, consisting of about twenty houses, adjoining which was Grayston's farm. Previous to our arrival at that place, I was advised that a part of the hostile Creeks were assembled there. Having marched within six or seven miles of it on the 17th, I dismounted a part of the force under my command, and sent them, under the command of Col. Burch, with the Cherokees under the command of Col. Morgan, in advance, to surround the town in the night, and make the attack at daylight on the 18th. Owing to the darkness of the night, the town was not reached until after daylight; but so complete was the surprise, that we succeeded in surrounding the town, and killing

34

and capturing almost, if not entirely, the whole of the hostile Creeks assembled there, consisting of about three hundred and ten; of which number about sixty warriors were killed on the spot, and the remainder made prisoners. Before the close of the engagement my whole force was up and ready for action, had it become necessary; but, owing to the want of knowledge on the part of the Indians of our approach, they were entirely killed and taken before they could prepare for any effectual defence. We lost not one drop of blood in accomplishing this enterprise."

The Georgia militia under Gen. Floyd, on the 29th November, succeeded in defeating a large body of hostile Creeks at Antosse. The following is from his letter to Gen. Pinckney, detailing the particulars of the battle.

"Having received information that numbers of the hostile Indians were assembled at Antosse, a town on the northern bank of the Tallapoosa, about eighteen miles from the hickory ground, and twenty above the iunction of that river with the Coosa, I proceeded to it with nine hundred and fifty of the Georgia militia, accompanied by between three and four hundred friendly Indians. Having encamped within nine or ten miles of the point of destination the preceding evening, we resumed the march a few minutes before one, on the morning of the 29th, and at half past six were formed for action in front of the town.

"Booth's battalion composed the right column, and marched from its centre. Watson's battalion composed the left, and marched from its right. Adams' rifle company, and Merriwether's, under Lieut. Hendon, were on the flanks. Capt. Thomas' artillery marched in front of the right column in the road.

"It was my intention to have completely surrounded the enemy, by applying the right wing of my force on Canlabee creek, at the mouth of which I was informed the town stood, and resting the left on the bank below the town; but to our surprise, as day dawned, we perceived a second town, about five hundred yards below that which we had first viewed and were preparing to attack. The plan was immediately changed; three companies of infantry on the left were wheeled to the left, into echelon, and were advanced to the low town, accompanied by Merriwether's rifle company, and two troops of light dragoons under the command of Captains Irwin and Steel.

"The residue of the force approached the upper town, and the battle soon became general. The Indians presented themselves at every point, and fought with the desperate bravery of real fanatics. The well-directed fire, however, of the artillery, added to the charge of the bayonet, soon forced them to take refuge in the out-houses, thickets, and copses in the rear of the town; many, it is believed, concealed themselves in caves, previously formed, for the purpose of secure retreat, in the high bluff of the river, which was thickly covered with reed and brush-wood. The Indians of the friendly party who accompanied us on the expedition, were divided into four companies, and placed under the command of leaders of their own selection. Some time after the action commenced, our red friends thronged in disorder in the rear of our lines. The Cowetas under M'Intosh, and the Tookabatchians under Mad-Dog's-Son, fell into our flanks, and fought with an intrepidity worthy of any troops.

"At nine o'clock the enemy were completely driven from the plain, and the houses of both towns wrapped in flames. As we were then sixty miles from any depot of provisions, and our five days' rations pretty much reduced, in the heart of the enemy's country, which in a few months could have poured from its numerous towns hosts of its fiercest warriors; as soon as the dead and wounded were disposed of, I ordered the place to be abandoned, and the troops to commence their march to Chatahouche."

Gen. Floyd was attacked by a large body of hostile Creeks in his encampment, forty-eight miles west of Colahoochie, on the 27th January; but succeeded in repelling them after a very bloody conflict. The particulars are contained in a letter of the general to Maj. Gen. Pinckney, dated on the day of the engagement.

"This morning, at twenty minutes past five o'clock, a very large body of hostile Indians made a desperate attack upon the army under my command. They stole upon our sentinels, fired on them, and with great ferocity rushed upon our line. In twenty minutes the action became general, and our front, right, and left flanks were closely pressed; but the brave and gallant conduct of the field and line officers, and the firmness of our men, repelled them at every point.

"The steady firmness and incessant fire of Capt. Thomas' artillery, and Capt. Adams' riflemen, preserved our front lines. Both of these companies suffered greatly. The enemy rushed within thirty yards of the artillery, and Capt. Broadnax, who commanded one of the piquet guards, maintained his post with great bravery, until the enemy gained his rear, and then cut his way through them to the army. On this occasion, Timpoche Barnard, a half-breed, at the head of the Uchies, distinguished himself, and contributed to the retreat of the piquet guard; the other friendly Indians took refuge within our lines, and remained inactive, with the exception of a few who joined our ranks. As soon as it became light enough to distinguish objects, I ordered Majors Watson and Freeman's battalions to wheel at right angles with Majors Booth and Cleveland's battalions, which formed the right wing, to prepare for the charge. Capt. Duke Hamilton's cavalry, which had reached me but the day before, was ordered to form the rear of the right wing, to act as circumstances should dictate. The order for the charge was promptly obeyed, and the enemy fled in every direction before the bayonet. The signal was given for the charge of the cavalry, who pursued and sabred fifteen of the enemy, and left thirty-seven dead on the field. From the effusion of blood, and the number of head-dresses and war-clubs found in various directions, their loss must have been considerable, independent of their wounded.

"I directed the friendly Indians, with Merriwether and Ford's rifle companies, accompanied by Capt. Hamilton's troops, to pursue them through Canlebec swamp, where they were trailed by their blood, but they succeeded in overtaking but one of the wounded."

On the 14th January, Gen. Jackson, having been reinforced by about eight hundred volunteers, commenced his march in quest of the enemy upon the Tallapoosa river. The objects and particulars of the expedition are disclosed in the following extract of a letter from him to Maj. Gen. Pinckney, dated Fort Strother, Jan. 29.

"I had the honor of informing you in a letter of the 31st ult., forwarded by Mr. M'Candles, of an excursion I contemplated making still further into the enemy's country, with the new raised volunteers from Tennessee. I had ordered those troops to form a junction with me on the 10th instant; but they did not arrive until the 14th. Their number, including officers, was about eight hundred.

"The motives which influenced me to penetrate still farther into the enemy's country with this force, were many and urgent. The term of service of the new raised volunteers was short, and a considerable part of it was expired; they were expensive to the government, and were full of ardor to meet the enemy. The ill effects of keeping soldiers of this description long stationary and idle, I had been made to feel but too sensibly already. Other causes concurred to make such a movement not only justifiable, but absolutely necessary.

"I took up the line of march on the 17th inst., and on the night of the 18th encamped at Tallegada fort, where I was joined by between two and three hundred friendly Indians, sixty-five of whom were Cherokees, the balance Creeks. I was informed that an attack was intended soon to be made by nine hundred of the enemy. I resolved to lose no time in meeting this force, which was understood to have been collected from New Yorkcau, Oakfuskie, and Ufauley towns, and were concentrated in the bend of the Tallapoosa, near the mouth of the creek called Emuckfau, on an island below New Yorkcau.

"On the morning of the 21st, I marched from Enotachopee, as direct as I could for the bend of the Tallapoosa, and about two o'clock P. M. my spies, having discovered two of the enemy, endeavored to catch them, but failed. In the evening, I fell in upon a large trail, which led to a new road, much beaten and lately travelled. Knowing that I must have arrived within the neighborhood of a strong force, and it being late in the day, I determined to encamp, and reconnoitre the country in the night. I chose the best site the country would admit, encamped in a hollow square, sent out my spies and pickets, doubled my sentinels, and made the necessary arrangements before dark for a night attack. At about ten o'clock at night, one of the pickets fired at three of the enemy, and killed one, but he was not found until the next day. At eleven o'clock, the spies whom I had sent out returned with the information that there was a large encampment of Indians at the distance of about three miles, who, from their whooping and dancing, seemed to be apprized of our approach. One of these spies, an Indian in whom I had great confidence, assured me that they were carrying off their women and children, and that the warriors would either make their escape, or attack me before day. Being prepared at all points, nothing remained to be done but await their approach, if they meditated an attack, or to be in readiness, if they did not, to pursue and attack them at daylight. While we were in this state of readiness, the enemy, about six o'clock in the morning, commenced a vigorous attack on my left flank, which was vigorously met. The action continued to rage on my left flank, and on the left of my rear, for about half an hour. The brave Gen. Coffee, with Col. Sittler, the adjutant general, and Col. Carroll, the inspector general, at the moment the firing commenced, mounted their horses, and repaired to the line, encouraging and animating the men to the performance of their duty. As soon as it became light enough to pursue, the left wing, having sustained the heat of action, and being somewhat weakened, was reinforced by Capt. Ferrill's company of infantry, and was ordered and led on to the charge by Gen. Coffee, who was well supported by Col. Higgins and the inspector general, and by all the officers and privates who composed that line. The enemy was completely routed at every point, and the friendly Indians joining in the pursuit, they were chased about two miles with great slaughter.

"The chase being over, I immediately detached Gen. Coffee, with four hundred men and all the Indian force, to burn their encampment; but it was said by some to be fortified. I ordered him, in that event, not to attack it, until the artillery could be sent forward to reduce it. On viewing the encampment and its strength, the general thought it most prudent to return to my encampment, and guard the artillery thither. The wisdom of this step was soon discovered. In half an hour after his return to camp, a considerable force of the enemy made its appearance on my right flank, and commenced a brisk fire on a party of men who had been on a picket guard the night before, and were then in search of the Indians they had fired upon, some of whom they believed had been killed. Gen. Coffee immediately requested me to let him take two hundred men and turn their left flank, which I accordingly ordered; but, through some mistake which I did not then observe, not more than fifty-four followed him, among whom were the old volunteer officers. With these, however, he immediately commenced an attack on the left flank of the enemy; at which time I ordered two hundred of the friendly Indians to fall in upon the right flank of the enemy, and co-operate with the general. This order was promptly obeyed, and at the moment of the execution what I expected was realized. The enemy had intended to attack on the right, as a feint, and expecting me to direct all my attention thither, meant to attack me again with their main force on the left flank, which they hoped to find weakened and in disorder; but they were disappointed. I had ordered the left flank to remain firm to its place, and the moment the alarm gun was heard in that quarter, I repaired thither, and ordered Capt. Ferrill, with part of my reserve, to support it. The whole line met the approach of the enemy with astonishing intrepidity, and having given a few fires, they forthwith charged with great vigor. The effect was immediate and inevitable. The enemy fled with precipitation, and were pursued to a considerable distance by the left flank and the friendly Indians, with a galling and destructive fire. Col. Carroll, who ordered the charge, led on the pursuit, and Col. Higgins and his regiment again distinguished themselves.

"In the mean time, Gen. Coffee was contending with a superior force of the enemy. The Indians whom I had ordered to his support, and who had set out for the purpose, hearing the firing on the left, had returned to that quarter, and when the enemy were routed there, entered into the chase. That being now over, I forthwith ordered Jim Fife, who was one of the principal commanders of the friendly Creeks, with one hundred of his warriors, to execute my first order. As soon as he reached Gen. Coffee, the charge was made and the enemy routed. They were pursued about three miles, and forty-five of them slain, who were found. Gen. Coffee was wounded in the body, and his aid-de-camp, A. Donaldson, killed, together with three others.

"I had indeed hoped to have met the enemy there, but having met and beat them a little sooner, I did not think it necessary or prudent to proceed any further. I commenced my return march at half past ten on the twenty-third, and was fortunate enough to reach Enotachopco before night, having passed without interruption a dangerous defile, occasioned by a hurricane. I again fortified my camp, and having another defile to pass in the morning, across a deep creek and between two hills, which I had viewed with attention as I passed on, and where I expected I might be attacked, I determined to pass it at another point, and gave directions to my guide and fatigue men accordingly. My expectation of an attack in the morning was increased by the signs of the night, and with it my caution. Before I removed the wounded from the interior of my camp, I had my front and rear guards formed, as well as my right and left columns, and moved off my centre in regular order, leading down a handsome ridge to Enotachopco creek, at a point where it was clear of reed, except immediately on its margin.

"The front guard had passed with part of the flank columns, the wounded were over, and the artillery in the act of entering the creek, when an alarm gun was heard in the rear. I heard it without surprise, and even with pleasure, calculating with the utmost confidence on the firmness of my troops, from the manner in which I had seen them act on the twenty-second. I had placed Col. Carroll at the head of the centre column of the rear guard; its right column was commanded by Col. Stump. Having chosen the ground, I expected there to have entirely cut off the enemy, by wheeling the right and left columns on their pivots, recrossing the creek above and below, and falling in upon their flanks and rear. But, to my astonishment and mortification, when the word was given by Col. Carroll to halt and form, and a few guns had been fired, I beheld the right and left columns of the rear guard precipitately give way. This shameful retreat was disastrous in the extreme; it drew along with it the greater part of the centre column, leaving not more than twenty-five men, who, being formed by Col. Carroll, maintained their ground as long as it was possible to maintain it; and it brought consternation and confusion into the centre of the army, a consternation which was not easily removed, and a confusion which could not soon be

35

restored to order. There was then left to repulse the enemy the few who remained of the rear guard, the artillery company, and Capt. Russell's company of spies. They, however, realized and exceeded my highest expectations. Lieut. Armstrong, who commanded the artillery company, ordered them to form and advance to the top of the hill, while he and a few others dragged up the six-pounder. Never was more bravery displayed than on this occasion. Amid the most galling fire from the enemy, more than ten times their number, they ascended the hill, and maintained their position until their piece was hauled up, when, having levelled it, they poured upon the enemy a fire of grape, reloaded and fired again, charged, and repulsed them.

"The enemy were pursued for more than two miles, who fled in consternation, throwing away their packs, and leaving twenty-six of their warriors dead on the field. This last defeat was decisive, and we were no more disturbed by their yells.

"In these several engagements, our loss was twenty killed and seventy-five wounded, four of whom have since died. The loss of the enemy cannot be accurately ascertained; one hundred and eighty of their warriors were found dead; but this must fall considerably short of the number really killed. Their wounded can only be guessed at."

Gen. Jackson, determined on the extermination of the Creeks for their atrocious conduct, on the 10th of March, 1814, penetrated as far as the bend of the Tallapoosa, where a most decisive victory was obtained, and the destruction of the nation nearly accomplished. The following is an extract from Gen. Jackson's account of the brilliant achievement, in a letter to Gov. Blount, dated Fort Williams, March 31, 1814.

"I took up the line of march from this place on the morning of the 21st instant, and having opened a passage of fifty-two and a half miles over the ridges which divide the waters of the two rivers, I reached the bend of the Tallapoosa, three miles beyond where I had the engagement of the 22d of January, and at the southern extremity of New Yorkcau, on the morning of the 27th.

"Early on the morning of the 27th, having encamped the preceding night at the distance of five miles from them, I detailed Gen. Coffee, with the mounted men and nearly the whole of the Indian force, to cross the river at a ford about three miles below their encampment, and to surround the bend in such a manner that none of them should escape by attempting to cross the river. With the musketry and rifles I kept up a galling fire wherever the enemy showed themselves behind their works, or ventured to approach them. This was continued with occasional intermissions for about two hours, when a detachment under Col. Morgan crossed over to the peninsula in canoes, and set fire to a few of their buildings there situated.

"Having maintained for a few minutes a very obstinate contest, musket to musket, through the port-holes, in which many of the balls were wedded to the bayonets of the muskets, our troops succeeded in gaining possession of the opposite side of the works. The event could no longer be doubtful. The enemy, although many of them fought to the last with that kind of bravery which desperation inspires, were at length entirely routed and cut to pieces.

"Both officers and men, who had the best opportunities of judging, believe the loss of the enemy in killed not far short of eight hundred. Among the dead was found their famous prophet Monahell. Two other prophets were also killed; leaving no others, as I can learn, on the Tallapoosa. I lament that two or three women and children were killed by accident. I do not know the exact number of prisoners taken, but it must exceed three hundred; all women and children except three.

"The battle may be said to have continued with severity for about five hours; but the firing and slaughter continued until it was suspended by the darkness of the night. The next morning it was resumed, and sixteen of the enemy slain, who had concealed themselves under the banks. Our loss was twenty-six white men killed, and one hundred and seven wounded; Cherokees, eighteen killed and thirty-six wounded; friendly Creeks, five killed and eleven wounded."

The brilliant and decisive victories obtained by Gen. Jackson and his brave men over the Creeks, induced many of those who survived to surrender and sue for peace. A few of them, however, otherwised disposed, fled towards Pensacola, before the arrival of the general at Tallapoosa. Many of the runaway negroes, who were captured at fort Mims, were restored to their masters, and an unfortunate white female captive, Polly Jones, who, with her two children, had been taken prisoners by the Indians, were released and restored to their friends. The Tallapoosa and Tostahatchee kings were taken prisoners, as was Peter M'Quin, a distinguished chief, but he unfortunately afterwards made his escape. Hillinhagee, their great prophet, fled with the fugitives towards Pensacola. Weatherford, their speaker, and who through the war had been one of the most active and enterprising chiefs, conceiving it in vain any longer to resist, and being informed that Gen. Jackson intended, if he could take him, to put him to death, was advised by his friends, as his warriors were almost all slain, as his country was ruined, and his escape almost impracticable, to surrender himself to the general; that it was useless to attempt further resistance; and this was the only means by which his life could be saved. Weatherford determined so to do, and presented himself to Gen. Jackson at his quarters, by whom it was demanded of him who he was and how he came there. He replied, "My name is Weatherford, one of the chiefs of the Red Sticks. I have fought you till my warriors are all slain. If I had warriors I would fight you still; but I have none. My country is overrun, and my soldiers are fallen. Here I am, in your power; do with me as you please; only recollect that I am a soldier!" The patriotic speech of this distinguished chief had its desired effect.

Gen. Jackson declined to consider him even as a prisoner of war. Weatherford, although as bold and intrepid as a lion, had been many times defeated by his enemies.

Gen. Jackson, after having made known to the surviving Creeks the terms upon which he was authorized to make peace, in the latter part of April withdrew his forces from the Creek country. The terms offered them were—That the United States were to retain as much of the conquered territory as would indemnify them for the expenses of the war, and as a retribution for the injuries sustained by their citizens, and such of the Creeks as had remained on friendly terms with them during the war. The United States were to establish whatever military posts and trading-houses they should think proper, and to have the free navigation of the rivers and water-courses throughout the Creek country. The Creeks were to surrender their prophets, and other chiefs who remained, or who should thereafter prove hostile to the interest and welfare of the States. The Tallisee king, of whom we have made frequent mention, and who was supposed to have been killed in one of Gen. Floyd's engagements with the Creeks, surrendered himself a prisoner to the Americans. He was upwards of a hundred years of age, with a head as white as snow, and had been regarded by the enemy as a very great prophet. The friendly Creeks viewed him as their most inveterate enemy, and although nearly bent double with age, they were anxious to put him to death, and would have done so had it not been for the interposition of the American officers.

CHAP. XX.

SEMINOLE WAR.—INDIAN DEPREDATIONS.—CAPTURE OF FORT ST. MARKS.—EXECUTION OF ARBUTHNOT AHD AMBRISTER.—PENSACOLA TAKEN BY GEN. JACKSON.

The Creek war happily terminating in the spring of 1814, and a treaty of peace having been mutually concluded upon between the surviving chiefs of that nation and commissioners appointed on the part of the United States, but little opposition was then apprehended from the fugitives who had fled towards Pensacola, and who remained hostile to the interest of the Americans. But, contrary to the expectations of our government, it was soon after discovered that these Indians had sought refuge among the different savage tribes living within and on the borders of the Floridas, denominated Seminole Indians, who, it was suspected, cherished feelings of hostility to the United States. This fact having been ascertained, the executive department of the government deemed it necessary, for the security of the frontier, to establish a line of forts near the southern boundary of the United States, and to occupy these fortifications with portions of the regular forces; and by this means peace was maintained with the Indians until the spring or summer of 1817, when the regular forces were withdrawn from the posts on the Georgia frontier, and concentrated at fort Montgomery, on the Alabama river, a considerable distance west of the Georgia line. But it seems that about this time a border warfare was commenced between the Seminole Indians and the frontier inhabitants of Georgia. Many horrid barbarities are said to have been perpetrated by the former; some of which it may not be improper here to mention. The house of a Mr. Garret, residing near the boundary of Wayne county, was attacked by a party of Indians during his absence. They shot

MILLY FRANCIS entreating her Father to spare the life of an American Captive.

Mrs. Garrett in two places, and then despatched her by stabbing and scalping. Her two children, one about three years and the other two months old, were also murdered, and the eldest scalped. The house was then plundered of every article of value, and set on fire! A boat soon after ascending the Alabama river, containing thirty men, seven women, and four small children, was captured by the Indians. Six of the men escaped, one woman was taken captive, and the remainder inhumanly butchered. The children were taken by the leg and their brains dashed out against the boat!

Duncan M'Krimmon, (a resident of Milledgeville, a Georgia militia man, stationed at fort Gadsden,) being out one morning on a fishing excursion, in attempting to return, missed his way, and was several days lost in the surrounding wilderness. After wandering about in various directions, he was espied and captured by a party of hostile Indians, headed by the well-known prophet Francis. The Indians having obtained the satisfaction they wanted respecting the determination of government, the position of the American army, &c., they began to prepare for the intended sacrifice. M'Krimmon was bound to a stake, and the ruthless savages, having shaved his head and reduced his body to a state of nudity, formed themselves into a circle and danced round him some hours, yelling most horribly. The youngest daughter of the prophet, about fifteen years of age, remained sad and silent the whole time. She participated not in the general joy, but was evidently, even to the affrighted prisoner, much pained at the savage scene she was compelled to witness. When the burning torches were about to be applied to the fagots which encompassed the prisoner, and the fatal tomahawk was raised to terminate forever his mortal existence, Milly Francis, (for that was her name,) like an angel of mercy, placed herself between it and death, resolutely bidding the astonished executioner, if he thirsted for human blood, to shed hers; being determined, she said, not to survive the prisoner's death.

A momentary pause was produced by this unexpected occurrence, and she took advantage of the circumstance to implore upon her knees the pity of the ferocious father, who finally yielded to her wishes; with the intention, however, it is suspected, of murdering them both, if he could not sell M'Krimmon to the Spaniards, which was luckily effected a few days after at St. Marks, for seven gallons and a half of rum. As long as M'Krimmon remained a prisoner, his benefactress continued to show him acts of kindness. The fortune of war has since placed her, as we shall hereafter have occasion to notice, in the power of the white people, being compelled, with a number of others of her tribe who were in a starving condition, to surrender themselves prisoners. As soon as this fact was known to M'Krimmon, in manifestation of a due sense of the obligation which he owed to the woman who saved his life at the hazard of her own, he sought her to alleviate her misfortune, and to offer her marriage; but Milly would not consent to become his wife as a consideration of having saved his life, declaring that she did no more than her duty, and that her intercessions were the same as they would ever have been on similar occasions.

In the frequent outrages committed upon the frontiers, it was somewhat difficult to determine who were the first aggressors, or on whom the greatest injuries were inflicted. Gen. Gaines, however, demanded a surrender of the Indians who had committed depredations on the frontier of Georgia. With this demand they refused to comply, alleging that the first and the greatest aggressions had been made by the white men.

In consequence of this refusal, Gen. Gaines was authorized by the secretary of war, at his discretion, to remove the Indians still remaining on the lands ceded to the United States by the treaty made with the Creeks. In so doing, he was told that it might be proper to retain some of them as hostages, until reparation was made for depredations committed by the

Indians. In pursuance of this discretionary authority, Gen. Gaines ordered a detachment of near three hundred men, under the command of Major Twiggs, to surround and take an Indian village called Fowl Town, about fourteen miles from fort Scott, and near the Florida line. This was partially carried into effect.

From this time the war became more serious. The Indians in considerable numbers were embodied, and an open attack was made on fort Scott. Gen. Gaines, with about six hundred regular soldiers, was confined to the garrison. In this state of things, information having been communicated to the war department, Gen. Jackson was ordered to take the field. He was put in command of the regular and military force, amounting to eighteen hundred men, provided for that service; and directed, if he should consider the force provided insufficient to beat the enemy, (whose force was estimated by Gen. Gaines at two thousand eight hundred strong,) to call on the governors of the adjoining states for such portions of the militia as he might think requisite. On the receipt of this order, Gen. Jackson, instead of observing the orders of the department of war, by calling on the governor of Tennessee, then in Nashville, near the place of his residence, chose to appeal (to use his own expression) to the patriotism of the West Tennesseans, who had served under him in the last war. One thousand mounted gunmen, and two companies of what were called life-guards, with the utmost alacrity, volunteered their services from the states of Tennessee and Kentucky, and repaired to his standard. Officers were appointed to command this corps by the general himself, or by other persons acting under his authority. Thus organized, they were mustered into the service of the United States.

About the time Gen. Jackson was organizing this detachment of volunteers in the state of Tennessee, or previous thereto, Gen. Gaines was likewise employed in raising forces among the Creek Indians. There was this difference in the two cases—Gen. Jackson raised his army in disregard to positive orders; Gen. Gaines, without orders, took upon himself the authority of raising an army of at least sixteen hundred Creek Indians, appointing their officers, with a brigadier general at their head, and likewise mustering this force into the service of the United States.

It appears that Gen. Jackson advanced into Florida, with a force of eighteen hundred men, composed of regulars, volunteers, and the Georgia militia; and afterwards, on the 1st day of April, was joined by Gen. M'Intosh and his brigade of sixteen hundred Indians, who had been previously organized by Gen. Gaines. Opposed to whom, it appears, from the report of Capt. Young, topographical engineer, and other evidence, the whole forces of the fugitive Seminole Indians and runaway negroes, had they all been embodied, could not have exceeded nine hundred or one thousand men, and at no time did half that number present themselves to oppose his march. Of course, little or no resistance was made.

The Miskasmusky towns were first taken and destroyed. The army marched upon St. Marks, a feeble Spanish garrison, which surrendered without firing a gun, and was then occupied as an American post, the Spanish commandant having first by humble entreaties, and then by a timid protest, endeavored to avert the measure. Here Alexander Arbuthnot was found, taken prisoner, and put in confinement, for the purpose, as it was stated by Gen. Jackson, "of collecting evidence to establish his guilt;" and here also were taken two Indian chiefs, one of whom pretended to possess the spirit of prophecy; they were hung without trial and without ceremony. Francis, who, by the entreaties of his daughter, was persuaded to spare the life of M'Krimmon, a captive, was the prophet above alluded to.

This being done, and St. Marks garrisoned with American troops, the army pursued their march eastward to Suwaney river, on which they found a large

Indian village, which was consumed, and the Indians and negroes were dispersed; after which the army returned to St. Marks, bringing with them Robert C. Ambrister, who had been taken prisoner on their march to Suwaney.

During the halt of the army for a few days at St. Marks, a general court martial was called, Arbuthnot was arraigned, found guilty, sentenced to suffer death, and hung.

Ambrister was tried in like manner, found guilty, and sentenced to whipping and confinement. Gen. Jackson annulled the sentence, and ordered him to be shot, and this order was executed.

It is stated that Arbuthnot, who was publicly executed as a spy, by order of Gen. Jackson, had been a captain in the British service, was about forty years of age, of genteel appearance, and met his fate like a soldier. When the executioner was fixing the rope around his neck, he desired not to be handled so roughly; observed he was a gentleman, and spoke of his death being avenged. His property he requested should be given to his son. Ambrister (who was charged with a similar offence, and suffered with Arbuthnot) was a young man, not exceeding twenty-five years. At first he appeared undaunted and quite indifferent as to his fate; but as death began to look him in the face, he lost his composure, and died more like a woman than a man.

The prophet Francis, who was executed a little before, had in his pocket a commission of brigadier general, from the British government, supposed to have been presented him during his late visit to England, whence he had not long returned. His arrival in that country was thus announced in one of the English prints: "The double sound of a trumpet announced the approach of the patriot Francis, who fought so gloriously in our cause of America. He was dressed in a most splendid suit of red and gold, and by his side he wore a tomahawk, mounted in gold!" This warrior is said to have been the prime mover of the unprovoked and infernal massacre of the garrison, with the women, &c., of fort Mims; and him also who slaughtered Lieut. Scott and his party. An officer in Gen. Jackson's army, in writing to his friend, relative to the surrender of a number of the enemy as prisoners at St. Marks, thus speaks of the family of Francis: "The wife and the family of the prophet Francis are among the prisoners. Two of his daughters are very interesting young ladies, and speak very good English, as in fact the whole family do except the mother. The eldest, when her father was decoyed on board the American schooner, shortly after followed, supposing her to be a British vessel; before she got alongside, however, she discovered the deception, pushed off, and made her escape. The youngest and most beautiful is caressed by all the officers, for having saved the life of the Georgia militia man."

In a communication from the war department to Gen. Gaines, dated Oct. 30, 1817, he was directed, that, should the hostile Indians persevere in their refusal to make reparation for their depredations, it was the wish of the President that he should not, on that account, pass the line, and make an attack upon them within the limits of Florida. In a later communication, he says: "The state of our negotiation with Spain, and temper manifested by the principal European powers, make it impolitic, in the opinion of the President, to move a force at this time into the Spanish possessions, for the mere purpose of chastising the Seminoles for depredations which have heretofore been committed by them."

Subsequently, the following order was received by Gen. Gaines from the war department: "On the receipt of this letter, should the Seminole Indians still refuse to make reparations for their outrages and depredations on the citizens of the United States, it is the wish of the President that you consider yourself at liberty to march across the Florida line, and to attack them within its limits, should it be found necessary, unless they should shelter themselves under a Spanish fort. In the last event, you will immediately notify this department."

On the 1st of December, 1817, Gen. Gaines informed the secretary of war, in a letter from fort Scott, which was then the head quarters, that there was no ground to calculate upon the future security of the frontier settlements, and says,—"It is now my painful duty to report an affair of a more serious nature than has heretofore occurred, and which leaves no doubt of the necessity of an immediate application of force, and active measures on our part. A large party of Seminole Indians, on the 30th ult., formed an ambuscade upon the Appalachicola river, a mile below the junction of the Flint and Chatahoochie, attacked one of our boats ascending near the shore, and killed, wounded, and took the greater part of the detachment, consisting of forty men, commanded by Lieut. R. W. Scott, of the 7th infantry. There were also on board, killed or taken, seven women, the wives of soldiers. Six men of the detachment only escaped, four of whom were wounded. They report that the strength of the current at that point of attack had obliged the lieutenant to keep his boat near the shore; that the Indians had formed along the bank of the river, and were not discovered until their fire had commenced; in the first volley of which, Lieut. Scott and most of his valuable men fell."

In December, 1817, Gen. Jackson received orders from the secretary of war to take command of the southern army, and to proceed against the hostile Indians, with all the forces that had been raised for that purpose, and to bring the war to as speedy a termination as possible. He proceeded to fort Scott and made preparations for prosecuting the war with all the energy in his power. On the 10th of March, 1818, he commenced his march, and soon after passed the line in pursuit of the enemy, who had fled into Florida. He met with very little opposition from them; they divided themselves into small parties, and defended themselves with a desperate courage and boldness seldom before known, even in Indian warfare. A few prisoners were taken, principally women and children; many Indian villages were burned, and a large quantity of corn and other property destroyed.

On the 25th of April the Americans took possession of fort St. Marks without opposition, in which was placed a garrison. Gen. Jackson, in a letter to the secretary of war, gives his reasons for the measure as follows: "It could not be maintained by the Spanish force garrisoning it. The Indians and negroes viewed it as an asylum if driven from the towns, and were preparing to occupy it in this event. It was necessary to anticipate their movements, independent of the position, being deemed essential as a depot on which the success of my future operations measurably depended. In the spirit of friendship, I, therefore, demanded its surrender to the army of the United States, until the close of the Seminole war. The Spanish commandant required time to reflect; it was granted, and a negotiation ensued, and an effort was made to protract it to an unwarrantable length. In the conversation between my aid-de-camp, Lieut. Gadsden, and the Spanish commandant, circumstances transpired convincing him of a disposition to favor the Indians, and having taken an active part in aiding and abetting them in this war. I hesitated, therefore, no longer; and, as I could not be received in friendship, I entered the fort by violence."

The American army soon after moved on in pursuit of the enemy, who were able to make very little resistance, destroying their settlements, and taking a few stragglers prisoners, until they arrived before Pensacola, which was surrendered, and taken possession of by the American troops. The following extract of a letter from Gen. Jackson to the secretary of war, dated Fort Montgomery, June 2d, will acquaint the reader with his reasons, as therein stated, for having penetrated so far, and taken forcible possession of Pensacola.

"On the 10th of May my army crossed the river at the Ochessee village, and after a fatiguing, tedious, and circuitous march of twelve days, misled by the ignorance of our pilots, and exposed to the severest privations, we finally reached and effected a passage over the Escandria. On my march on the 23d of May, a protest from the governor of Pensacola was delivered to me by a Spanish officer, remonstrating in warm terms against my proceedings, and ordering me and my force instantly to quit the territory of his Catholic Majesty, with a threat to apply force in the event of a non-compliance. This was so open an indication of a hostile feeling on his part, after having been early and well advised of the objects of my operations, that I hesitated no longer on the measures to be adopted. I marched for and entered Pensacola with only the show of resistance, on the 24th of May. The governor had previously fled to the Carlos de Barrancas, where it is said he resolved upon a most desperate resistance. The peaceable surrender of the fort at the Barrancas was denied. I marched for and invested it on the evening of the 25th of May, and on the same night pushed reconnoitering parties under its very guns. On the morning of the 26th a military reconnoisance was taken, and on the same night a lodgment was made, under a fire from the Spanish garrison, by Capt. Gadsden of the engineers, aided by Captains Call and Young, on a commanding position within three hundred and eighty-five yards of the Spanish works, and a nine-pounder mounted. A howitzer battery was simultaneously established on the capitol, and within seven hundred and fifty yards of the fort. At daylight on the 27th, the Spanish garrison opened their artillery on our batteries; a parley was sounded, a flag sent in, and the surrender of fort Carlos de Barrancas again demanded; the favorable positions obtained were pointed out, and the inutility of resistance urged. Anxious to avoid an open contest, and to save the effusion of blood, the same terms previously offered were again tendered. These were rejected, and offensive operations recommenced. A spirited and well-directed fire was kept up the greater part of the morning, and at intervals during the afternoon. In the evening a flag was sent from the Spanish commandant, offering to capitulate, and a suspension of hostilities was granted until eight o'clock the next day, when articles of capitulation were signed and agreed to. The terms are more favorable than a conquered enemy would have merited; but, under the peculiar circumstances of the case, my object obtained, there was no motive for wounding the feelings of those whose military pride or honor had prompted to the resistance made. The articles, with but one condition, amount to the complete cession to the United States of that portion of the Floridas hitherto under the government of Don Jose Masot.

"The Seminole war may now be considered at a close, tranquillity again restored to the southern frontier of the United States, and as long as a cordon of military posts is maintained along the gulf of Mexico, America has nothing to apprehend from either foreign or Indian hostilities. Indeed, sir, to attempt to fortify or protect an imaginary line, or to suppose that a frontier on the thirty-first degree of latitude, in a wilderness, can be secured by a corridor of military posts, whilst the Spanish authorities were not maintained in the Floridas, that the country lay open to the use and excitement of an enemy, is visionary in the extreme. On the immutable principle, therefore, of self-defence, authorized by the law of nature and of nations, have I bottomed all my operations. On the fact that the Spanish officers had aided and abetted the Indians, and thereby become a party in hostility against us, do I justify my occupying the Spanish fortresses. Spain has disregarded the treaties existing with the American government, or had not power to enforce them. The Indian tribes within her territory, and which she was bound to keep at peace, visited our citizens with all the horrors of savage war. Negro brigades were establishing themselves when and where they pleased, and foreign agents were openly and knowingly practising their intrigues in this neutral territory. The immuta-

BLACK HAWK.

ble principles of self-defence justified, therefore, the occupancy of the Floridas, and the same principles will warrant the American government in holding it until such time as Spain can guarantee, by an adequate military force, the maintaining her authority within the colony."

CHAP. XXI.

HOSTILITIES WITH THE INDIAN TRIBES ON THE NORTHWESTERN FRONTIERS, CALLED BLACK HAWK'S WAR.

The Winnebagoes, Menominies, Pottowatamies, and Sacs and Foxes, were engaged in this border war with Black Hawk. In order to understand the causes of this war, it will be necessary for us to recount some circumstances which occurred in 1823.

This year the United States agent held a treaty, at Prairie du Chien, with the Sacs, Foxes, Winnebagoes, Chippeways, Sioux, &c., principally to effect a peace between the Sacs and the other tribes. The better to effect this object, bounds were set to each tribe.

The Galena lead mines about the same time attracted considerable attention, and the avarice of those concerned in them drove several thousand miners into the country of the Winnebagoes, beyond the limits of the United States. It is supposed this great encroachment was the cause of the murder of a family, living near Prairie du Chien, by a party of Winnebagoes, two of whom were afterwards imprisoned in the jail of Crawford county.

An article in the above-mentioned treaty provided that any of the five nations concerned in this treaty,

37

visiting in the United States, should be protected from all insults by the garrison.' Notwithstanding this, in the summer of 1827, a party of twenty-four Chippeways, on a visit to fort Snelling, were fallen upon by a band of Sioux, who killed and wounded eight of them. The commandant of the fort captured four of the Sioux, and delivered them into the hands of the Chippeways, who immediately shot them.

Red Bird, the Sioux chief, repaired to Prairie du Chien with three companions, desperate as himself, about the first of July, and there killed two persons, wounded a third, and, without taking plunder, retired to Bad-axe river. Here, soon after, he waylaid two keel boats that had been conveying some missionaries to fort Snelling, in one of which two persons were killed; the others escaped with little injury.

Not long after, Gen. Atkinson marched into the Winnebago country, and captured some hostile Winnebagoes and Red Bird, who died soon after in prison.

The Indians who were imprisoned for the murder at Prairie du Chien, were discharged, and Black Hawk and two others, who had been imprisoned for the attack on the boats, before mentioned, were also discharged.

Very little pains were taken to satisfy the Indians, or to make the settlers do justice to them. As the latter in many cases have very little to lose, and much to gain, if an Indian war be successful, we need not be surprised that they take so little pains to be first on conciliating to their red brethren. The gain which the settlers are sure of in a successful Indian war, arises from the Indians being obliged to give up their lands, in which case they are removed from them by settlers, and they are no longer a frontier, but a thoroughfare to one; and the consequent flocking in of new settlers raises the value of produce as well as of land, by creating a demand for them. Thus, it is not difficult to see the avaricious on the frontiers have every inducement to bring about an Indian war.

The foregoing account shows that Black Hawk was imprisoned on suspicion, perhaps justly; but this was not his sole cause of complaint. His friend Red Bird had died in prison, Indians were executed for murdering whites, but it did not follow whites were treated in like manner for murdering Indians. These causes had long been producing a feeling of disaffection among the northern and western tribes. Hence, it is not singular that the whites of the frontier of Illinois believed the Indians, from Canada to Mexico, more hostile than at any period since the war of 1812.

The Sacs, who had served Great Britain against the Americans, were the most conspicuous in their enmity. This band of Sacs rendezvoused at their chief village on the Mississippi, where they had collected such of their neighbors as wished to engage in the war.

Gen. Gaines marched to and possessed himself of this village on the 26th of June. This he did without opposition, for when the Indians discovered the army, they fled across the river, and displayed a flag for parley. Meantime, their associates had abandoned them, and the Sacs were left to manage affairs in the best manner they could. They, therefore, made peace with all due submission, and Gen. Gaines was of opinion they were as completely humbled as if they had been chastised in battle, and were less disposed to disturb the frontier than if that event had taken place. Previous to this, he had declared his belief that, whatever might be their hostile feelings, they would abstain from the use of tomahawks and fire-arms, except in self-defence.

About the same time, a difficulty seems to have arisen between the Sacs and Menominies, in which twenty-eight of the latter had been murdered. Agreeably to an article of the treaty before mentioned, the United States obliged themselves to interpose between these and other western tribes in cases of trouble. But these murders were not all the Sacs had done.

They had recrossed the Mississippi, and occupied the country on its east bank, which they had the year before ceded to the United States.

Black Hawk was the alleged leader in both cases. Therefore, Gen. Atkinson set out in an expedition, hoping to make prisoner of Black Hawk, who was said to be sole fomentor of all these disturbances. It was also alleged he had little respect for treaties, and that he had in former negotiations so far overreached our commissioners as to make peace on his own terms. This is the first acknowledgment of this chief's talents in matters of diplomacy.

Gen. Atkinson was at a place on Rock river, called Dixon's Ferry, May 15th, when he received news that a force which had marched to Sycamore Creek, thirty miles in advance of him, had met with a total defeat. This force had marched to Sycamore Creek on account of the great number of murders which had been committed there. Among the sufferers in that neighborhood were the family of a Mr. Hall, whose fate had created much sympathy. His two daughters, one eighteen and the other sixteen, had been carried into captivity, after having seen their mother tomahawked and scalped, and twenty others murdered in the same way at Indian Creek. These young women were humanely treated during their captivity, and afterwards restored to their friends.

The force that marched to Sycamore Creek was about two hundred and seventy-five strong, under the command of Maj. Stillman. When the news of this massacre at Indian Creek arrived, they obtained leave of Gen. Whitesides to march to the scene of murder. On Monday, the 14th of May, they came upon a few Indians, whether enemies or not it is not probable they inquired, for theirs was the march of death, therefore two of them were shot, and two more captured. The same day, at evening, when the army had arrived at a convenient place to encamp, and were making some preparations for that purpose, a small band of Indians was discovered bearing a white flag. One company of men went out to meet them, but soon discovered they were only a decoy. How they ascertained this fact, we are not informed. This company of discoverers therefore fell back upon the main body, which by this time had remounted, and, as strange as it is true, this misguided band rushed forward, regardless of all order, for several miles, till they crossed Sycamore creek, and were completely in the Indians' power. What follows equals a similar affair at Pawtucket. The Americans had crossed the creek man by man, as they came to it, and all the Indians had to do was to wait till a goodly number had come within their grasp. It was moonlight when the fight began, and after a few struggles, the whites fled in greater disorder, if possible, than they came. The Indians, after making the onset with their guns, fell on them with knives and tomahawks, and had not the night and situation of the country favored their flight, nearly all the army must have been cut off.

The Indians were supposed to be nearly two thousand strong, and it was said twelve of them were killed. Of the whites, only thirteen are reported killed. Their flight equalled that of Gen. St. Clair's army. Fourteen hundred men, immediately after, marched to the scene of the action to bury the dead, and their account of the barbarities committed on the bodies of the slain quite equals anything before recounted. One soldier only escaped disfiguration, which is not easily accounted for, unless he secreted himself until all the Indians but one had left the scene of action; for he was found side by side with an Indian, each grasping the other, and both in the arms of death. The soldier's head was nearly cut off, and the Indian shot through the body. Here it was supposed the two had exchanged their deadly shafts at the same moment; and, from the situation of the Indian, it was evident he had died in the very act of dealing the fatal blow upon his adversary.

An idea of the rapidity with which the Indians convey intelligence of important events, may be had from the fact, that a runner from Black Hawk and his allies, bearing the news of this victory to the Missouri Indians, arrived at Des Moines Rapids twenty-four hours before the express sent by Gov. Reynolds.

The cholera, the following July, raged among the troops opposed to the Indians so severely, that several companies were entirely broken up, and many among them perished, in a manner too revolting to be described. Of one corps of two hundred and eight men, but nine were left alive.

Gen. Dodge surprised a party of twelve Indians at Galena, and cut them off to a man; the whites scalped the slain, that they might not be outdone in these, or any other barbarities, by their foes.

Black Hawk assembled his forces, at a point between Rock and Ouisconsin rivers, where he expected to meet the whites in a general battle. His warriors amounted to a thousand or more. Gen. Atkinson had nearly double that number of men, and resolved to meet him as soon as possible. Great hopes were entertained that, in such an event, a finishing blow would be put to the war. But Black Hawk was too wary to thus expose himself to utter and irretrievable ruin, and accordingly made good his retreat into an interminable wilderness.

Gen. Atkinson made his way to Cashkonong, through woods, swamps, and defiles, almost impassable, and constantly exposed to the danger of an ambuscade. On his arrival at this place, he was, apparently, no nearer his enemy than at the commencement of this perilous march. Indeed, fair, open battle seemed to be a most unlikely thing to invite Black Hawk, as his numbers were greatly inferior to the Americans. Therefore no hope of bringing him to terms seemed left, unless effected by stratagem.

While Gen. Atkinson was making this fruitless march, Gen. Dodge was about forty miles from fort Winnebago, following the trail of Indians, who proved to be a flying and nearly starved band, capable of offering little or no resistance. But, as they were attacked in the evening after, sixteen were butchered; the rest escaped. To form some idea of the situation of these poor Indians, we have only to read the accounts of the American commander to the war department, in which he states, that they found many dead, as they marched along, very much emaciated, and having died, evidently, of starvation.

It became a matter of question to the two commanders, where they should seek their enemy. From the supposition that they might have descended the Ouisconsin, and so escaped across the Mississippi that way, Gen. Dodge recommended that a cannon should be placed on the river to cut them off; and Gen. Atkinson marched for the Blue Mounds, with an army, consisting of regular troops and mounted men, to the number of sixteen hundred.

Meanwhile Black Hawk, seeing the necessity of escape, and that it could not be effected with his whole company, crossed the country, and came to the Mississippi, some way above the mouth of the Ouisconsin. Here, the better to ensure the escape of his warriors, he allowed the women and children to descend the river in boats, many of whom were captured by the whites. Some of the boats, however, were upset, and the poor creatures drowned. Those who lived to arrive at Prairie du Chien were in a most pitiable condition, many of the children being so nearly famished it was almost impossible to revive them. And the report goes on to say, "they were *generally* received and treated humanely."

The steamboat Warrior was soon after sent up the Mississippi, with a small force on board, in hopes they might somewhere discover the savages. Upon the arrival of the boat at Prairie du Chien, the last of July, she was despatched to Wapashaws village, one hundred and twenty miles higher on the river, to inform the inhabitants of the approach of the Sacs, and to order all the friendly Indians down to Prairie du Chien. On the return of the steamboat, they met one of the

Sioux bands, who told them their enemies were encamped on Bad-axe river, to the number of four hundred. The Warrior here stopped to take in some wood and prepare for action. They discovered the enemy about four o'clock on the afternoon of August 1st, who, as they approached, raised a white flag, which being looked upon as a decoy, no attention was paid to it. They declined sending a boat on-board when ordered.

After giving them a few minutes to remove their women and children, (a piece of courtesy somewhat rare in our border wars,) the boat fired a six-pounder, loaded with canister, and followed by a severe fire of musketry. The battle continued for about an hour, when she weighed anchor and proceeded to Prairie du Chien. Twenty-three Indians were killed, and many wounded. The Americans lost none. Before the steamboat could return to the battle-field next morning, Gen. Atkinson and his army had engaged the Indians. The Warrior joined the contest. The Americans this day lost eight or nine killed, and seventeen wounded, whom the Warrior took to Prairie du Chien at night, and also captives to the number of thirty-six, women and children. The spot where this battle took place was about forty miles above Prairie du Chien, on the north side of the Mississippi, opposite the mouth of the Iowa. It was very fortunate for the whites that they were able to co-operate on land and water at the same time.

Gen. Atkinson having formed a junction with Gen. Dodge, the army crossed the Ouisconsin on the 28th of July, and soon after discovered the route of the Indians, who were flying from the scene of action.

The country through which the army had to march, was a continual series of mountains, covered entirely with a thick growth of heavy timber, and much underwood. The valleys were so deep as to make them almost as difficult to cross; but nothing could damp the ardor of the Americans, as they pressed on to overtake Black Hawk, before he should be able to escape across the Mississippi.

The place where the Indians were overtaken was very favorable for them, as may be judged by their being able to maintain a battle of more than three hours, in the wretched and nearly famished condition they were in, and when their whole force only amounted to three hundred warriors. They were discovered in a deep ravine, at the foot of a precipice, over which the army had to pass. Notwithstanding the misery of their condition, nothing but the bayonet's point routed them. Old logs, high grass, and large trees, covered them until the charge was made; and as they were driven from one covert, they readily found another, and thus protracted the contest. At length, Gen. Atkinson disposed his force so as to come upon them from above, below, and in the centre. No chance now remained to the Indians, but to swim the Mississippi, or elude the vigilance of their enemy by land, who had nearly encompassed them. Many therefore adventured to cross the river; but as the slaughter was greatest there, few escaped. However, a considerable number succeeded in escaping by land. One hundred and fifty of them were supposed to have been killed in this battle.

Black Hawk was among those who escaped, but in such haste as to leave even his papers behind him, one of which was a certificate from British officers, that he had served faithfully, and fought valiantly for them, in the late war against the United States. The prisoners taken at this battle stated that at the one which occurred at Ouisconsin, between their army and Gen. Dodge's, they lost sixty-eight, besides many wounded.

It was now believed the Sacs would be glad to make peace on any terms. Accordingly, Gen. Atkinson determined to order Keokuk to demand a surrender of the remaining principal men of the hostile party.

From the battle-ground, the commanders went down the river to Prairie du Chien, (fort Crawford,) in the

Warrior, and the army followed by land. On their way they killed and captured a few Sacs.

The desperate fortunes of the hostile Indians induced many of their countrymen to volunteer to hunt them down. One hundred Sioux obtained permission to seek them, and were followed by a small band of the same nation; they overtook the enemy, and killed about one hundred and twenty. About this time, Keokuk, the friendly Sac chief, above mentioned, found a nephew of his had been accused of the murder of a man named Martin; he gave him up to be dealt with according to the proof brought of his crime, which took place in Warren county, Illinois.

Among those who fought under Black Hawk, were the several chiefs of the different tribes, who acted as his counsellors and subalterns. At the last great battle of that chief on the Mississippi, Neopop, Black Hawk's second in command, was captured.

Gen. Scott questioned him about the murders which had been recently committed, of which, and his own history, he gave the following account: "I always belonged to Black Hawk's band. Last summer, I went to Malden; when I came back, I found, by the treaty with Gen. Gaines, the Sacs had moved across the Mississippi. I remained during the winter with the Prophet, on Rock river, thirty-five miles from its mouth. During the winter, the Prophet sent me across the river to Black Hawk with a message, to tell him and his band to cross back to his old village and make corn; that if the Americans came and told them to move again, they should shake hands with them. If the Americans had come and told us to move, we should have shaken hands and moved peaceably. We encamped on Syracuse creek. We met some Pottowatamies, and I made a feast for them. At that time, I heard there were some Americans (the force under Major Stilman) near us. I prepared a white flag to go and see them, and sent two or three young men on a hill, to see what they were doing. Before the feast was finished, I heard my young men were killed. This was at sunset. Some of my young men ran out, two were killed, and the Americans were seen rushing on to our camp. My young men fired a few guns and the Americans ran off, and my young men chased them about six miles."

Neopop farther said his guests, the Pottowatamies of the village, immediately left them, and no Kickapoos joined them, but those who were originally with Black Hawk; but the Winnebagoes joined with them, and frequently brought in scalps; that at last, when they found Black Hawk would be beaten, they joined the Americans.

It was also stated by some of the warriors, who were examined at the same time, that Black Hawk said, when the steamboat Warrior approached them, that he pitied the women and children, and began to make preparations to surrender, and for that purpose sent out a white flag to meet the boat, which immediately fired upon them; then said he, "I fired too." The truth of this will not be questioned, inasmuch as the facts agree entirely with the account given by the captain of the Warrior. But for a spirit of revenge, it is clear much blood might have been saved.

It is much to be lamented, in most of our border wars, precipitancy and hot-headedness on the part of the whites should go unpunished. Until such offenders are properly dealt with for their conduct, much blood will be unnecessarily shed, and a sense of injustice always felt by our red brethren, whose whole history goes to show they *never were* dealt with as we should feel obliged to deal with a more powerful and enlightened foe. But the instances where our army on the frontier have acted without coolness and judgment, are comparatively but a small item in the grievances the Indians have to complain of. The conduct of the white inhabitants on our frontier, almost without exception, towards these original owners of the soil, has been outrageous. They have reduced them to a state of beastly intoxication, as a preparatory measure, when they wished to make bargains with them, and then overreached and cheated them in every possible way. Nor is this all. The more desperate class of adventurers, who hang upon the outskirts of civilization, like a garment of pestilence, have not scrupled, for the slightest cause, or no cause at all, to shoot an Indian; and both they and the administrators of the laws in those districts seem to look upon it as little of a crime as it would be to shoot a partridge or a hare.

It has been mentioned as a matter of much astonishment on the frontier, that several of the peltry merchants will not make use of spirits in bartering with the Indians! May their example be followed.

To return to our account of Black Hawk;—hunted like the wild deer of the forest, the old chief, after many wanderings and much suffering, was at last captured, and delivered up to Gen. Street at Prairie du Chien. His companion in his flight and captivity was the Prophet before alluded to. They showed a proper sense of self-respect by appearing before the commander in full dress, which consisted of tanned white deer-skin. One of the Winnebagoes who captured them delivered a speech on the occasion to Gen. Street, desiring the fulfilment of the promises made to those who should capture and bring alive these men into the hands of the whites.

To this speech the general replied, he wished the captors and the prisoners to go to Rock Island, where the President had desired Gen. Scott and the governor of Illinois to hold a council. Both the Indians who had taken these prisoners seemed desirous that rewards for the deed should be to their tribe, rather than to them personally.

Eleven chiefs of the Sacs and Foxes, besides Black Hawk and the Prophet, were sent to Jefferson barracks, and there put in irons.

In September, a treaty was made by the United States with the Winnebagoes, and also with the Sacs and Foxes. The Winnebagoes ceded all their lands south of the Ouisconsin and east of the Mississippi, amounting to one million six hundred thousand acres of valuable land. The treaty with the Sacs and Foxes gave to the government six hundred thousand acres more, of a quality not inferior to any between the same parallels of latitude, and abounding with lead ore.

For these lands, the United States agreed to the following conditions: to pay an annuity of twenty thousand dollars for thirty years, to support a gunsmith and blacksmith, besides some already employed, to pay the debts of the tribes, and to supply provisions. As a reward for the fidelity of Keokuk and the friendly band, to allow a reservation to be made for them, of forty square miles on the Iowa river, to include Keokuk's principal village.

By this same treaty, Black Hawk, his two sons, the Prophet, Neopop, and five other principal warriors of the hostile band, were to remain in the hands of the whites, as hostages, during the President's pleasure.

A visiter at Jefferson barracks thus speaks of the captive Indians there: "We were struck with admiration at the gigantic and symmetrical figures of most of the warriors, who seemed, as they reclined in native ease and gracefulness, with their half naked bodies exposed to view, more like statues from some master hand, than like beings of a race whom we had characterized as degenerate and debased. They were clad in leggins and moccasins of buckskin, and wore blankets, which were disposed around them much like the Roman toga, so as to leave their right arms bare."

Black Hawk and his son were carried to Washington to visit the President. At different places on his route, he received many valuable presents, and was looked upon with great curiosity and interest. They returned by way of Detroit, and arrived at fort Armstrong in August, 1833.

The Indians were at first taciturn and gloomy on entering their own forests, and on arriving at Rock Island were much disappointed in not finding some of their friends, from whom they might obtain intelligence of their families. A band of Foxes, however, arrived the next day, who gave the desired intelligence.

Fort Armstrong, Rock Island, in Illinois, was selected as the most appropriate place for the liberation of Black Hawk and his party. It being the most central point from the surrounding villages, a great number of Indians could be assembled at short notice.

With most of the party it was delightful to return to old habits and pleasures. But to Black Hawk it was painful. He was bereft of his greatness, an isolated man, dependent on the kindness and hospitality of those whom he once commanded, and to be ranked as a Sac only, with Keokuk as his chieftain.

The latter was absent on a buffalo-hunt when Black Hawk arrived, but about noon the following day the din and shouting of the Indians announced his approach. He was seated on one of two large canoes lashed side by side, and followed by a train of twenty more, each carrying eight of his companions, who made the woods re-echo their wild songs. They proceeded up the river, and encamped on the opposite side from Black Hawk's camp.

After arranging their toilets, they again commenced their songs while crossing the river. Keokuk, highly decorated, was the first to land, and proceeded to Black Hawk and his party. The old chief was leaning upon his cane, apparently lost in reflection. They shook hands, and Keokuk welcomed his fallen chief with cordiality. Their pipes seemed to make the interchange of good feeling general. After smoking, Keokuk retired, saying he should be at the council of the next day.

Accordingly, the next morning Keokuk arrived at the room in the garrison appointed for the council, followed by his train. Here he was to be invested with the power of the brave old chief with whom he had been for many years struggling for supremacy. Black Hawk and his son felt all the humiliation thus publicly heaped upon them; however, they came into the council and took their seats. Maj. Garland then told them that he wished all present to understand that the President looked upon Keokuk as the chief of their nation, and wished Black Hawk to *listen* and *conform* to his discourse. Black Hawk became completely infuriated at this. He rose to speak, but could hardly articulate.

He said, "I am an old man; I will not conform to the counsel of any one. I will act for myself; no one shall govern me. I am old, my hair is gray. I once gave counsels to my young men—am I to conform to others? I shall soon go to the Great Spirit, where I shall rest. What I said to our great father in Washington, I say again; I will always listen to him. I am done." It was the last effort of expiring independence. It was explained to him that the President *requested* him to listen to Keokuk. He made no reply, but sat completely absorbed in his own feelings, when Keokuk, in a suppressed tone, said to him, "Why do you speak so before the white men? You trembled, you did not mean it." He consented, and Keokuk apologized for him, saying he was old, "and they would not remember what he had said." After some of the officers had addressed the chiefs, the council broke up.

In the evening, Major Garland invited the principal chiefs, with Black Hawk, to his quarters, to ascertain more particularly their feelings towards their fallen foe.

After the other chiefs had made speeches, Black Hawk said, in a very calm and dejected manner,—"I feel that I am an old man; once I could speak, but now I have little to say. To-day we met many of our brothers; we were glad to see them. I have listened to what my brothers have said; their hearts are good; the have been like Sacs since I left them; they have taken care of my wife and children, who had no wigwam. I thank them for it, the Great Spirit knows I thank them. Before the sun gets behind the hills tomorrow, I shall see them; I want to see them; when I left them I expected soon to return. I told our great father, when in Washington, I would listen to his counsels; I say so to you. I will listen to the counsel of Keokuk. I shall soon be far away; I shall have no village, no band; I shall live alone. What I said in council to any, I wish forgotten. If it has been put upon paper, I wish a mark to be drawn over it. I did not mean it. Now we are alone, let us say we will forget it. Say to our great father and Gov. Cass, that I will listen to them. Many years ago I met Gov. Cass in councils, far across the prairies to the rising sun. His counsels were good. My ears were closed. I listened to the great father across the great waters. My father listened to him whose band was large. My band was once large, now I have no band. I and my son, and all our party, thank our great father for what he has done. He is old, I am old, we shall soon go to the Great Spirit, where we shall rest. He sent us through his great villages. We saw many of white men, who treated us with kindness. We thank them, we say to them we thank them. We thank you and Mr. Sprague for coming with us. Your road was long and crooked. We never saw so many white men before. When you were with us we felt as though we had some friends among them. We felt safe. You knew them all. When you come upon the Mississippi again, you shall come to my wigwam. I have none now. On your road home you pass where my village once was. No one lives there now; all are gone. I give you my hand; we may never meet again. I shall long remember you. The Great Spirit will be with you, and your wives and children. Before the sun rises I shall go to my family. My son will be here to see you before you go. I will shake hands with my brothers now, then I am done." The party here separated in a cordial and friendly manner.

OSCEOLA.

CHAP. XXII.

REMARKS ON THE WAR WITH THE FLORIDA INDIANS, OR SEMINOLES, WITH ITS CAUSES.—PROGRESS OF THE WAR.—OSCEOLA'S TREACHEROUS CAPTURE.—HIS IMPRISONMENT AND DEATH..

The capture of Pensacola by Gen. Jackson put an end to the Seminole war for the time. The Indian warriors had retired to their various settlements, and were pursuing their occupations of hunting and cultivating their lands without molestation. They continued in this situation for several years, till a change of their political relations with the United States gave rise to new difficulties, which led to a renewal of hostilities; and a bloody and exterminating war has been carried on against these sons of the forest, with little success, to the present time. Every artifice and stratagem has been made use of to subdue them or to drive them from the country, in order that a set of unprincipled and greedy speculators might get possession of their lands. The resistance of these people has been the wonder of the world. That a few hundred Indian warriors could make a successful resistance to as many thousand regular and well-armed troops, commanded by some of our best generals, is the most astonishing event that has ever occurred in all our Indian warfare.

The Florida war has been the cause of the expenditure of over twenty millions of dollars, (much more than the whole territory is worth,) besides the loss of a vast numer of the lives of our citizen soldiers; and still there appears little prospect of bringing the war to a successful termination. In fact, there appears to be no other way to effect it but by exterminating the whole Indian race by fire and sword. That this will eventually be the end, there can be little doubt; but how long it will take to effect this object, and what sacrifices of life and money will have to be made, time only can disclose.

East and West Florida were ceded to the United States by the Spanish government, in 1823, as a set-off for a claim we had against them for spoliations committed on our commerce, for five hundred thousand dollars. Soon after this took place, a plan was laid to get rid of the Indians, in order to gain possession of the lands they owned and occupied. To effect this, it was necessary to gain the point either by negotiation and purchase, or by the sword. In September following, a council was held with their chiefs, and a treaty entered into by them, which was signed on the 18th by several of their principal chiefs. In this treaty it was agreed, on the part of the Indians, that they would remove to the westward after twenty years from that date. By the same treaty the American government secured to the Indians a tract of land in Florida, containing five millions of acres, for their subsistence during the time they remained in the territory; and agreed to pay them certain annuities, for surrendering all title to the rest of the Florida country; and the Indians engaged to confine themselves to the limits of the territory allotted to them. One article of the treaty runs as follows—"The United States will take the Florida Indians under their care and patronage, and will afford them protection against all persons whatsoever."

It was doing a great wrong, to say the least of it, for our government to bind itself to conditions that it was probable they never intended to fulfil, or that they could not carry into effect if they were ever so much disposed to do it. The consequence was, that the Indians were most shamefully robbed and plundered by a set of miscreants, who were probably sent among them, and hovered around their settlement for that purpose. Every kind of fraud was practised to cheat them out of their property. Their negroes and cattle were stolen, carried off, and sold by a set of land pirates, in defiance to all law and justice. When appeals were made to the authorities, they could get no redress, and the villains were allowed to escape. One of the chiefs had twenty slaves stolen from him, worth fifteen thousand dollars, who were carried to New Orleans and sold. An Indian woman employed a white man to recover some negroes that had been taken from her; but, instead of giving him a power of attorney, as she supposed, for the purpose, he got her signature to a bill of sale of all her negroes. They were robbed of large sums of money by the government agents, who got their signatures to receipts, under pretence that it was necessary to send them to Washington to get the money due them, and afterwards refused payment. In some cases, when their cattle were stolen, they pursued and brought them back; when they were punished for stealing them, although they showed their own marks on the cattle. But as the Indian's evidence could not be received in a court of justice, the white man's oath would condemn him to the most cruel punishment.

Numerous other such cases might be given from American writers; but enough has been stated, we should think, to satisfy any reasonable person that these Indians were justified in defending themselves from such outrages. Could it be expected that a people would quietly submit to suffer so much oppression and injustice without retaliating? Can it be thought strange that they should lose all confidence in the white people, and look upon them as their enemies? Whether the government suffered all this spoliation to take place, without even an attempt to prevent it, with a view to disgust the Indians and incline them to remove to the westward, is not for us to say; but after events will enable the reader the better to judge for himself.

The Florida people were now subjected to retaliation on the part of the Indians, who, finding that they could obtain no redress, naturally took the law into their own hands, and loss of life on both sides was the consequence. Petitions from the Florida white population were sent to the government, requesting that the Indians might be moved west prior to the time stipulated by treaty. Col. Gadsden was appointed commissioner to treat with the Indians, and had a meeting with Micanopah and a few other chiefs, April 8th, 1832. The chiefs appeared unwilling to agree to the removal, but were willing to abide by the former treaty. After many consultations and a delay of a month, their consent was obtained to comply with the wishes of the government, and a treaty was made for that purpose.

By this treaty the Indians agreed to remove west upon being paid a certain sum for the reserved land, an annuity for a certain number of years, and other advantages therein stated. The treaty was signed by Micanopah and fourteen others; but it was assented to upon one condition, that the Seminoles were satisfied with the lands apportioned to them west of the Mississippi. To ascertain this, seven chiefs were selected to explore the country, and if they were satisfied that it was equal to what was represented, the treaty was to be ratified, otherwise they were not to be bound by it. These chiefs reported unfavorably; and the government having delayed making any appropriation of land for the Indians for more than two years, they became dissatisfied, and the treaty was pronounced to be "a white man's treaty," which they did not any longer consider to be binding.

There was another difficulty which caused strong objections to their removal to the westward. The Seminole Indians owned a large number of negroes and many cattle, which they had good reason to believe would all be taken from them by their new neighbors, the Creeks and Pawanees, who were too powerful for them to resist. Therefore, as the first would take from them all their slaves and the latter all their cattle, they considered that utter destitution would be the consequence. An American writer, treating upon this subject, says: "It was then suggested to them that by a sale of these negroes before they left Florida, they would augment their resources, and could go into their new country without the dread of exciting the cupidity of the Creeks. But these Indians have always evinced great reluctance to parting with their slaves; indeed, the Indian loves his negro as much as one of his own children, and the sternest necessity alone would drive him to the parting. This recommendation was, therefore, viewed with evident alarm, and as the right of retaining possession of them was guaranteed by the commissioner, strong doubts were raised of the sincerity of the pledge.

"The Seminole Indians are poor agriculturists and husbandmen, and withal too indolent to till the ground, and, without their negroes, would literally starve; besides, should they dispose of them, they could not be replenished in a new country. Again; the opposition of the slaves themselves to being sold to the whites, would excite all their energies to prevent emigration, for they dread the idea of being transferred to sugar and cotton plantations, where they must be subject to the surveilance of the overseer. The life of a slave among the Indians, compared with that of negroes under overseers, is one of luxury and ease; the demands upon him are very trifling, scarcely ever exceeding eight or ten bushels from the crop, the remainder being applied to his own profit. They live separate, and often remote from their owners, and enjoy an equal share of liberty. The negro is also much more provident and ambitious than his master, and the peculiar localities of the country eminently facilitate him in furnishing the Indian with rum and tobacco, which gives him a controlling influence over the latter, and at the same time affords him an immense profit; so that it can be easily imagined that the negroes would in no manner be benefited by a change."

In October, 1834, a council of Indians was again summoned by the agent, when a long talk was held with them, in which many of the chiefs expressed themselves in the strongest manner against the removal, and gave their reasons. The agent made several proposals to them, to which he demanded an immediate answer. The chiefs retired and held a private council. It is said that Osceola, (the rising sun,) a distinguished chief of the Micosukee tribe, urged them strongly to resist going, and declared that he should consider as his enemy any one who agreed to go. Osceola had not signed the treaty, and had from the beginning showed a determined opposition to any agreement to sell their lands, or to give up any of their natural rights.

The next day the council was resumed, and the chiefs made their replies to the agent, in which they declared their determination not to go to the west till the expiration of twenty years, and that they should be paid their annuity agreeably to the first treaty in 1823. The agent made a long talk to them, in which he said, "I have told you that you must stand to your bargain. My talk is still the same. Your father, the President, who is your friend, will compel you to go. Therefore be not deluded by any hope or expectation that you will be permitted to remain here." The council and parties separated without coming to any agreement. The Indians, finding they had nothing to expect but oppression, laid up large stores of powder and lead, and prepared themselves for resistance. Six months elapsed, when they were informed that they were to hear the last talk of their father, the President, on this side of the Mississippi. On the 22d of April, the Indians assembled, and had the following communication from President Jackson:

"My Children—I am sorry to have heard that you have been listening to bad counsel. You know me, and you know that I would not deceive, nor advise you to do anything that was unjust or injurious. Open your ears and attend now to what I am going to say to you. They are the words of a friend, and the words of truth.

"The white people are settling around you. The game has disappeared from your country. Your people are poor and hungry. All this you have perceived for some time. And nearly three years ago you made an agreement with your friend Col. Gadsden, acting on the part of the United States, by which you agreed to cede your lands in Florida, and to remove and join your brothers, the Creeks, in the country west of the Mississippi. You annexed a condition to this agreement, that certain chiefs named therein, in whom you placed confidence, should proceed to the western country, and examine whether it was suitable to your wants and habits, and whether the Creeks residing there were willing to permit you to unite with them as one people; and if the persons thus sent were satisfied on these heads, then the arrangement with Col. Gadsden was to be in full force.

"In conformity with these provisions, the chiefs named by you proceeded to that country, and having examined it, and having become satisfied respecting its character and the favorable disposition of the Creeks, they entered into an agreement with commissioners on the part of the United States, by which they signified their satisfaction on these subjects, and finally ratified the treaty made with Col. Gadsden.

"I now learn that you refuse to carry into effect the solemn promises thus made by you, and that you have stated to the officers of the United States, sent among you, that you will not remove to the western country.

"My Children, I have never deceived, nor will I ever deceive any of the red people. I tell you that you must go, and that you will go. Even if you had a right to stay, how could you live where you now are? You have sold all your country. You have not a piece as large as a blanket to sit down upon. What is to support yourselves, your women, and children? The tract you have ceded will soon be surveyed and sold, and immediately afterwards will be occupied by a white population. You will soon be in a state of starvation. You will commit depredations upon the property of our citizens. You will be resisted, punished, perhaps killed. Now is it not better peaceably to remove to a fine, fertile country, occupied by your own kindred, and where you can raise all the necessaries of life, and where game is yet abundant? The annuities payable to you, and the other stipulations made in your favor, will make your situation comfortable, and will enable you to increase and improve. If, therefore, you had a right to stay where you now are, still every true friend would advise you to remove; but you have no right to stay, and you must go. I am very desirous that you should go peaceably and voluntarily. You shall be comfortably taken care of, and kindly treated on the road, and when you arrive in your new country, provisions will be issued to you for a year, so that you can have ample time to provide for your future support.

"But lest some of your rash young men should forcibly oppose your arrangements for removal, I have ordered a large military force to be sent among you. I have directed the commanding officer, and likewise the agent, your friend Gen. Thompson, that every reasonable indulgence be held out to you. But I have also directed that one third of your people, as provided for in the treaty, be removed during the present season. If you listen to the voice of friendship and truth, you will go quietly and voluntarily. But should you listen to the bad birds that are always flying about you, and refuse to remove, I have then directed the commanding officer to remove you by force. This will be done. I pray the Great Spirit, therefore, to incline you to do what is right."

The Seminoles became divided among themselves. Some of the sub-chiefs agreed to remove; but the principal chiefs not only refused to go, but considered all who agreed to submit as their enemies. One of the chiefs who had made arrangements to remove was shot by Osceola, and most of his warriors joined the hostile party. The agent undertook to deprive the opposing chiefs of their rank, and declared that Micanopah was no longer chief of the Seminoles; his name, with the other chiefs who joined with him, were struck out of the council of the nation. This caused great irritation; and the conduct of the agent was disapproved of by the secretary of war; but the government took no measures to remove the difficulty, or to do justice to the injured party.

In June, 1836, Osceola, the chief of the Micosukees, came in to complain of the treatment his people had received from some white men, one having been wounded. He received no redress, and, saying something offensive to the agent, was thrown into prison.

To obtain his liberty, it is said he signed the treaty; but this must be considered only as an Indian stratagem. He had been imprisoned without cause, and it may be presumed that he thought himself justified in escaping by a corresponding fraud on his part. In a month after this occurrence, some of his tribe murdered a government mail-carrier. This, with the killing of the friendly chief by Osceola, was the signal for the commencement of hostilities. The Indians immediately abandoned all the towns, and concealing their trails, removed their families to a place of safety, which has ever since baffled all conjecture, and been a subject of the greatest astonishment.

The white population of Florida was never very numerous, and is composed of various descriptions of people, from all nations. In 1830, there were eighteen thousand whites, and sixteen thousand slaves, exclusive of the Indians. The various bands or tribes of Indians in Florida have been called Seminoles; but there never was a tribe or nation of that name; it is a term for runaways or wanderers; being a compound of the old Florida Indians, two varieties of Creeks, who quitted the tribe previous to their removal west of the Mississippi, and negroes who are slaves to the Indians. The whole number of their warriors at the commencement of the war, was as follows:—The Micosukee Indians, of which Osceola was principal chief, four hundred; Creek and Spanish Indians, eight hundred and fifty; negroes, six to seven hundred; in all about nineteen hundred.

It is supposed that the hostile Indians retreated to some portion of the vast swamps which surrounded the Ouithlacoochee river. Marauding parties now commenced on the part of the Indians, who took summary vengeance on those who had robbed and maltreated them. The whole country was under conflagration, and the whites were compelled to abandon everything, and seek protection under the forts. Gen. Clinch, who commanded at fort Brooke, having been reinforced, no time was lost in preparing two companies to march

40

against the enemy. On the 24th of December, 1835, a force of one hundred men and eight officers, with a field-piece, under the command of Maj. Dade, commenced their march.

On the morning of the 28th, when it had proceeded four miles from the encampment of the previous night, this force was attacked by the Indians, whose first volley was very destructive, Maj. Dade, with almost every man of the advanced guard, falling dead. The Indians were repelled by the troops under Capt. Gardner, upon whom the command then devolved, and the Americans proceeded to throw up breastworks; but before they could raise them high enough for efficient protection, the Indians attacked them again. The Americans brought their field-piece into play, but the breastworks not being high enough, the Indians shot down every man who attempted to work the gun. All the officers and more than two thirds of the American troops had fallen, when the survivors found that all their ammunition was expended. The Indians, perceiving this, rushed in, and, with the exception of two men, who, although severely wounded, contrived to conceal themselves, and ultimately to make their escape, not one of the whole detachment was spared.

The force of the Indians is supposed to have amounted to from three hundred and fifty to four hundred. The contest lasted six hours; and it must be admitted that nothing could be more gallant than the defence which was made by the troops against such a superior force.

On the afternoon of the same day, the Americans had to lament the loss of Gen. Thompson, the Indian agent at fort King. Imprudently strolling out about three hundred yards from the fort, he was attacked by the Indians, who laid in ambush for him, and, with Lieut. Smith and three other people belonging to the fort, was shot dead. This party of Indians was headed by Osceolà, who warned Gen. Thompson that the white men should suffer for their treatment of him. His peculiar and shrill war-yell was given as the Indian party retreated, to let the whites know to whom they were indebted for the massacre.

Gen. Clinch having been reinforced at fort Brooke, where he had two hundred regular troops, with five hundred volunteers under the command of Gen. Call, now moved with the whole force of seven hundred men.

On the 30th of December, as they were passing the Ouithlacoochee river, the Indians watched their opportunity, and when a portion only of the troops had gained the opposite side, commenced an attack, which was vigorously and successfully resisted; the Indians, in little more than an hour, were beaten off. The battle was however severe, and the Americans sustained a loss of sixty-three killed and wounded. The Indian force is supposed to have amounted to seven hundred men.

But independent of these conflicts with the militia and regulars, the ravages of the Indians over the whole country are stated to have been most fearful. Women and children were murdered, and the hearth made desolate in every portion of the country. In the more settled parts, near St. Augustine, the sugar-cane plantations, with the expensive works attached to them, were destroyed, and in many cases the slaves who were on the plantations were either carried off, or, voluntarily joining the Indians, increased the strength of the enemy. More than a hundred estates were thus laid waste, the average loss upon each estate being computed, independent of the loss of the negroes, at fifty thousand dollars.

On the 13th February, 1836, Gen. Gaines, having arrived at fort Brooke, reviewed the force, which amounted to between eleven and twelve hundred men, and commenced his march to relieve fort King, at which post he arrived on the 2d February, without falling in with any of the Indians. The general then made a detour in pursuit of the Indians. On the 27th, when the force was crossing the Ouithlacoochee river, it was assailed by the Indians, who retired after a skirmish of three quarters of an hour, the Americans' loss being very trifling. On the 28th, when again fording the river, the Indians made another attack, which was continued for nearly four hours, and the Americans had to lament the loss of Maj. Izard, who was killed, and two other officers were also wounded. On the 20th, the Indians again attacked, with a force of at least a thousand men, with a view of forcing the American troops from the breastwork which they had thrown up. The Indians, after about two hours' fighting, set fire to the high grass; but, unfortunately for them, the wind suddenly changed, and, instead of burning out the American troops, all their own concealed positions were burnt up and exposed, and they were compelled to retire. The loss on the Indian side was not known, but supposed to be heavy; that on the part of the Americans amounted to thirty-two killed and wounded.

On the evening of the 5th of March, the Indian interpreter came in from the Seminoles, stating that they wished to hold a council, and did not want any more fighting. On the 6th, a truce was held, when Osceola and other chiefs made their appearance, saying that if the Americans would not cross the river, they would remain on their own side of it, and not commit any more ravages. This was in fact nothing but the original proposal of the Indians, that they should remain upon the land which had been assigned to them by the treaty of Camp Moultrie. The reply of Gen. Gaines was, that he was not authorized to make a treaty with them; their arms must be given up, and they must remain on the other side of the river, until the American government sent them away west of the Mississippi.

Gen. Gaines, who had heard that Gen. Scott had been appointed to the command in Florida, now resigned that authority to Gen. Clarke, and on the 11th the troops arrived at fort Drane. It hardly need be observed that the treating with the Indians ended in nothing. Gen. Scott, having assumed the command, arrived at fort Drane on the 13th March, 1836. He had previously to contend with heavy rains and almost impracticable roads, and was encumbered with a heavy baggage train. His whole force amounted to nearly five thousand men. This he divided into a centre and two wings, so as to scour the whole country, and force the Indians from their retreat; but in vain. The Indians being on the flanks of each division, occasional skirmishes took place; but when the troops arrived to where the Indians were supposed to be, not a man was to be seen, nor could they discover the retreat of their families. Occasionally the Indians attacked the outposts with great vigor, and were bravely repulsed; but the whole army of five thousand men did not kill and capture more than twenty Indians. The swamps extended over a great surface of ground, here and there was an island on which the Indians could remain, while to attack them the troops would have to wade up to their necks for miles, and as soon as they arrived the Indians were gone.

The whole of the contest with the Florida Indians has been nothing more than a sort of petty partisan warfare, a detail of the particulars of which would be of little interest to the reader. Frequent skirmishes took place between the hostile parties, without gaining much advantage on either side, or doing anything which tended in the least to bring the war to a close. Gen. Scott resigned the command, and was succeeded by Gen. Jessup, of whom much was expected by a vigorous prosecution of the war; but he met with as little success as his predecessors. Finding there was nothing to be gained but disgrace by open and honorable warfare, a plan was adopted to effect the purposes of the government by a new system; which was to get into their power the principal chiefs of the Seminoles by strata gem. These chiefs had always shown a readiness to meet their opponents and agree to bury the hatchet, provided they should be suffered to remain unmolested on the lands reserved to them by treaty, and be protected in their rights, as had been agreed upon by the government.

Osceola was known to be a brave and sagacious warrior, and was at this time the principal chief. He was viewed as the great master spirit and director of all the hostile bands of Seminole warriors. It was deemed, therefore, a great achievement by the American general to get him into his power. Gen. Jessup found means to communicate to the Indians that it was his wish to have the chiefs come in and hold a talk, in order to come to some agreement. White flags were displayed on the fort. On the 20th of October, 1837, Osceola, accompanied by other chiefs and a few warriors, came in agreeably to the invitation; he, carrying a white flag in his hand, and relying on the honor of the commanding general, put himself in his power; but instead of being received as was expected, they were immediately surrounded by bayonets, made prisoners, and confined in the fort. Whether Gen. Jessup was alone accountable for this act of treachery, or whether he acted under orders from the President, is not known; but the government having afterwards approved of the measure, it became their own act.

Osceola was kept there a prisoner for some time, when he was, by order of the government, conveyed, under a strong guard, to Sullivan island, in the harbor of Charleston, S. C., and confined in the fort. His proud, independent spirit could not bear the confinement, and he gradually pined away and died in prison. Thus fell another brave Indian chieftain, though not in fair fight, but in a manner that will ever be a stigma upon our national honor.

Other chiefs were kidnapped in the same treacherous manner; but, severe as the loss must have been to the Indians, it did not appear to discourage them. The war was still carried on by those who were left, and indeed is still continued; for the ranks of the Indians are said to be filled up by runaway slaves, and some of the Creek Indians who had not yet quitted Georgia. On the 24th of December, 1837, a severe battle was fought between the Indians and the American troops, at a spot between Pease creek and the Big Cyprus swamps. On this occasion the Americans lost Cols. Thompson and Gunty, with twenty-eight killed, and one hundred and eleven wounded.

In all ages and with all nations, civilized or uncivilized, the flag of truce has always been regarded as an emblem of peace, and a violation of it ought to be held in detestation by every friend of humanity. It often has the effect of staying the hand of slaughter, and preventing the shedding of much blood, by giving time for the passions to cool and for reason to assert its empire. The Indians in their most savage state have had their tokens, by which it has always been understood that hostilities were to cease for the time, that negotiation might commence. When the pipe of peace has been held out it has always been respected. Even the wild Arab never violates his pledge of friendship, when he eats the bread and salt with the stranger, though he should be his enemy. The white flag has been adopted by all christian nations as an emblem of peace, and the Indians have been taught that it must be held sacred as such, and never to be violated; and it is to be lamented that a nation who profess to be Christians should be the first to set the example of departing from a usage of so much importance, for the purpose of effecting by deception what they were unable to do by open and honorable warfare.

It has been thought that every invention that ingenuity could contrive had been used for the purpose of destroying the poor Indians; but it seems that a new plan has been adopted, which puts humanity to the blush, and leaves all other means heretofore adopted far in the back-ground. Agents have been sent to Havana, to purchase a large number of blood-hounds; these have been brought over at a great expense, and trained to track and hunt down the Indians. Fortunately, however, for the cause of humanity, the experiment has proved to be an entire failure. The Spaniards made use of these animals in their conquests of the Indians in South America; and it is said that they are now employed by them in their West India islands to hunt for runaway slaves, who secrete themselves in the mountains.

The war in Florida having been continued for so great a length of time, and been conducted with such a variety of defeats and successes, with the many negotiations that have taken place, and agreements entered into, which were declared to have put an end to all further difficulties, that the subject has created very little interest in the public mind, but has been treated rather as a matter for ridicule than as requiring any serious consideration. For the last two years, occasional accounts have been published in the papers of Indian murders, with now and then a skirmish, in which two or three Indians have been killed, and a few squaws and papooses taken prisoners; but nothing has been done that in the least has changed the situation of affairs. The war has been put an end to so many times, that the phrase, "Florida war ended," has become a standing joke. Yet it is a matter of the most serious nature, and our government is bound in honor, and for the cause of humanity, to take some decisive steps to do justice to the Indians, and bring about a speedy and honorable termination of all difficulties.

The following extract from the writings of the Genevese Traveller, on the Florida war, will be the conclusion of our work.

"The war was unrighteous in its commencement, and has been continued for years under circumstances the most profligate. There has not been a single campaign in which the army has not reaped a plentiful harvest of mortification and disgrace. When brought into action, both officers and men fought valiantly; but the character of the country, its deep morasses and swamps, and the ignorance of the troops of Indian war fare, have uniformly tended to produce the most disastrous defeats.

"There is not to be found on the page of history, in any country, an instance of a scattered remnant of a tribe, so few in number, defending themselves against the assaults of a disciplined and numerous army, with the same heroism and triumphant results, with those of the Seminoles in resisting the American troops. In every campaign the invaders have been at least ten to one against the invaded. At no period have the Indians been able to muster more than six or eight hundred warriors, and it is doubtful whether they have ever had more than half that number, while the American army, when in the field, has uniformly amounted to from six to ten thousand men."